The Eighteenth-Century Literature Handbook

Literature and Culture Handbooks

General Editors: Philip Tew and Steven Barfield

Literature and Culture Handbooks are an innovative series of guides to major periods, topics and authors in British and American literature and culture. Designed to provide a comprehensive, one-stop resource for literature students, each handbook provides the essential information and guidance needed from the beginning of a course through to developing more advanced knowledge and skills.

The Medieval British Literature Handbook
Edited by Daniel T. Kline

The Modernism Handbook
Edited by Philip Tew and Alex Murray

The Post-war British Literature Handbook
Edited by Katharine Cockin and Jago Morrison

The Renaissance Literature Handbook
Edited by Susan Bruce and Rebecca Steinberger

The Seventeenth-Century Literature Handbook
Edited by Robert C. Evans and Eric J. Sterling

The Shakespeare Handbook
Edited by Andrew Hiscock and Stephen Longstaffe

The Victorian Literature Handbook
Edited by Alexandra Warwick and Martin Willis

The Eighteenth-Century Literature Handbook

Edited by

Gary Day

and

Bridget Keegan

BLOOMSBURY

NEW DELHI • LONDON • OXFORD • NEW YORK • SYDNEY

First published in India 2017
First published by Continuum in 2009

This edition is published with permission from
Bloomsbury Publishing Plc, 50 Bedford Square, London WC1B3DP

British Library Cataloguing-in-Publication Data
A catalogue record for this book is available from the British Library.

ISBN 978 93 86349 62 0
10 9 8 7 6 5 4 3 2 1
For sale in the Indian subcontinent only

Bloomsbury Publishing India
Second Floor, LSC Building No. 4
Pocket C – 6 & 7, Vasant Kunj
New Delhi 110070
www.bloomsbury.com

Exclusively distributed in the Indian subcontinent by
Manohar Publishers & Distributors
4753/23, Ansari Road
Darya Ganj, New Delhi 110002
Tel.: 23284848, 23289100
Email: sales@manoharbooks.com, manoharbooks@gmail.com

Typeset byRefineCatch Limited, Bungay, Suffolk
Printed and bound in India

Dedication

For Charlotte, who keeps telling me the eighteenth century is over.
Gary Day

For Lillian Liyuwork, who doesn't yet know there is an eighteenth century.
Bridget Keegan

Contents

Detailed Table of Contents

Acknowledgements

The editors would like to thank Anna Fleming, Associate Publisher, and Colleen Coalter, Editorial Assistant, both of Continuum, for their professionalism and their patience. We would also like to thank series editor Philip Tew for his encouragement and advice.

Bridget Keegan is grateful for the support of the Dean of the Graduate School at Creighton University, Dr. Gail Jensen, who provided additional funding for graduate research assistants at different stages of the project. Bridget also wishes to thank her partner, Jeffrey L. Day.

Finally, the editors wish to acknowledge the assistance of Kathryn Montgomery, a second year Masters student at Creighton. We are grateful for her good work in helping to compile the index.

General Editors' Introduction

The Continuum *Literature and Culture Handbooks* series aims to support both students new to an area of study and those at a more advanced stage, offering guidance with regard to the major periods, topics and authors relevant to the study of various aspects of British and American literature and culture. The series is designed with an international audience in mind, based on research into today's students in a global educational setting. Each volume is concerned with either a particular historical phase or an even more specific context, such as a major author study. All of the chosen areas represent established subject matter for literary study in schools, colleges and universities, all are both widely taught and the subject of ongoing research and scholarship. Each handbook provides a comprehensive, one-stop resource for literature students, offering essential information and guidance needed at the beginning of a course through to more advanced knowledge and skills for the student more familiar with the particular topic. These volumes reflect current academic research and scholarship, teaching methods and strategies, and also provide an outline of essential historical contexts. Written in clear language by leading internationally-acknowledged academics, each book provides the following:

- Introduction to authors, texts, historical and cultural contexts
- Guides to key critics, concepts and topics
- Introduction to critical approaches, changes in the canon and new conceptual and theoretical issues, such as gender and ethnicity
- Case studies in reading literary and theoretical and critical texts
- Annotated bibliography (including selected websites), timeline, and a glossary of useful critical terms.

This student-friendly series as a whole has drawn its inspiration and structure largely from the latest principles of text book design employed in other disciplines and subjects, creating an unusual and distinctive approach for the undergraduate arts and humanities field. This structure is designed to be user-friendly and it is intended that the layout can be easily navigated, with various points of cross-reference. Such clarity and straightforward approach should help students understand the material and in so doing guide them through the increasing academic difficulty of complex critical and theoretical approaches to Literary Studies. These handbooks serve as gateways to the particular field that is explored.

All volumes make use of a 'progressive learning strategy', rather than the traditional chronological approach to the subject under discussion so that they might relate more closely to the learning process of the student. This means that the particular volume offers material that will aid the student to approach the period or topic confidently in the classroom for the very first time (for example, glossaries, historical context, key topics and critics), as well as material that helps the student develop more advanced skills (learning how to respond actively to selected primary texts and analyse and engage with modern critical arguments in relation to such texts). Each volume includes a specially commissioned new critical essay by a leading authority in the field discussing current debates and contexts. The progression in the contents mirrors the progress of the undergraduate student from beginner to a more advanced level. Each volume is aimed primarily at undergraduate students, intending to offer itself as both a guide and a reference text that will reflect the advances in academic studies in its subject matter, useful to both students and staff (the latter may find the appendix on pedagogy particularly helpful).

We realize that students in the twenty-first century are faced with numerous challenges and demands; it is our intention that the Handbook series should empower its readers to become effective and efficient in their studies.

Philip Tew and Steven Barfield

1 Introduction

Gary Day

Chapter Overview

Most of the chapters in this handbook concentrate on British literature, but the period known as the Enlightenment whose motto, summed up by the philosopher Immanuel Kant (1724–1804) was 'dare to know' (see Chapter 6, Key Critical Concepts and Topics page 119–20) was a European and American phenomenon. Accordingly, I will refer to thinkers from different countries in this introduction. My aim is to compare how the eighteenth century viewed history, literature and education to how we see them. The limitations of space mean that this comparison will be more of a sketch than a detailed examination but I hope it will be suggestive nevertheless. The eighteenth century can seem rather remote but by pointing out similarities and differences we may not only get to know it a little better but even learn from it.

When was the Eighteenth Century?

The 'long eighteenth century', which covers the period 1688 to 1832, begins with the Glorious Revolution when James II (1633–1701) was replaced by William III (1650–1702). James was a Catholic and that, together with his pro-French policies, convinced critics that he was going to undermine Protestantism and parliament. William was given the throne on condition that, among other things, he guaranteed the continuity of Parliament, ensured religious liberty for protestants and called elections every three years. The period ends with the Reform Act of 1832 which was the first in a series of Acts that extended the franchise. The Act gave only one in seven males the vote and it did not resolve the problem of bribery, but it did pave the way for the Second Reform Act of 1867 which enfranchised all male householders. Women had to wait until 1918 and 1928 before they could visit the ballot box.

There are alternative ways of organizing the eighteenth century. For example, some historians prefer to start with the restoration in 1660 and to end with the French Revolution in 1789. Others agree it should begin with the Glorious Revolution but argue that it ends when Victoria ascends the throne in 1837. It all depends what aspects of history we wish to emphasize. The concept of the long eighteenth century, for example, stresses political continuity and gradual progress and downplays the upheaval of revolution. Although many of the chapters in this handbook focus on literature and culture in the 1700s, the authors are working within a time frame that stretches from 1660 to 1837.

The Eighteenth Century and the Contemporary

The point is that our idea of a period is always open to revision. It is good to be aware that there are no fixed boundaries separating one period from another, but the subject of this book is only partly about constructions of history; its main focus is on literature and culture. And the first thing to say is that eighteenth-century literature can be difficult to understand. The subject-matter seems remote and the style of writing is very different from our own. More generally, we live in a culture that looks to the future, not the past, and so to peruse the works of, say, Alexander Pope (1688–1744) seems irrelevant to the concerns of the contemporary society, if not downright indulgent.

But, as this handbook shows, the way in which we see our world today is partly determined by what happened three hundred years ago. The principles of the American Declaration of Independence (1776) continue to animate political life in the USA. Some of the lines penned by Pope, such as 'a little learning is a dangerous thing' ('Essay on Criticism' 1711), have become part of common speech. And the 2004 film *Eternal Sunshine of the Spotless Mind*, starring Jim Carrey and Kate Winslet, takes its title from a line in Pope's poem 'Eloisa to Abelard' (1717). Our modern notions of Englishness, too, have their roots in this period. The rules of cricket, for example, were codified in the eighteenth century. One such was that the width of the bat should be restricted to four and a half inches after Thomas 'Shock' White turned out for Reigate with a bat as wide as the stumps.

Every age separates itself from those that have gone before it. But not every age sees itself as an improvement on its predecessors. Many thinkers in the middle ages, for example, believed that there was nothing new to be known and so all that was left to them was to transmit the wisdom of their forefathers. How, then, did eighteenth-century writers and philosophers view the past?

Answering that question helps us to understand how we may view the 'long eighteenth century'. A strong consciousness of change characterizes eighteenth-century conceptions of history. That societies develop may seem obvious to us but it was only in the Renaissance that commentators began to grapple with the idea that earlier ages were different from their own.

Eighteenth-Century History: A Brief Introduction

One of the first thinkers to consider the nature of history in our period was the Italian Giambattista Vico (1688–1744). He stated that human society had passed through three stages, religious, heroic and human. The first was characterized by a religious rule, the second by aristocratic rule and the third by monarchical rule. Adam Smith (1723–90) had a similar model of history, but he emphasized economic development as mankind moved from hunter, to shepherd, to farmer, to trader. Vico takes a scientific approach to history. He classifies the different stages through which it has passed and describes their characteristics. For example he assigns different forms of language – sign, symbol and legal – to each period. Vico thought that the symbolic language of poetry was a poor attempt to explain the world and that it would be superseded by scientific description of nature and the place of humans in it. You might like to consider whether this conception of poetry is a trifle narrow.

The Tory statesman, and friend of Pope and Jonathan Swift (1667–1745) Henry St John, Lord Bolingbroke (1678–1751) did not share Vico's scientific outlook. He thought we should study history because it taught us how to conduct ourselves in public and private life. But he also has a more nuanced understanding of the past than Vico. It is not merely a series of stages, it is something with which we have a living relationship. We have to recognize that we are different to those who came before us but we should also be aware that there are certain general principles and rules of life which must always be true. The study of history consists in being able to tell the difference between them. We would not, for example, sacrifice oxen to ensure success in battle but we would still agree with the ancient Athenians that courage is an admirable quality.

The philosopher David Hume (1711–76) picks up on this latter point when he claims that human nature remains the same throughout different ages. The sentiments of the Romans are the same as those of a modern Englishman, he opines. History reveals us to ourselves. Hume does not dwell on the notion of progress, a topic which preoccupies the French statesman, economist and political writer Anne-Robert-Jacques Turgot (1727–81). The world of nature is always the same, spring follows winter and water boils at one hundred degrees Celsius.

But human society, says Turgot, is an ever changing spectacle. In making the distinction between nature and culture he moves away from the purely scientific view of history that we find in Vico. But he would agree with the Italian that history is about progress. If we compare past and present, we see the growth of knowledge, a gradual improvement in manners and the drawing together of nations through commerce. In sum, the human race, despite some backward steps, marches always towards still higher perfection.

But there were those who took a different view. The English historian Edward Gibbon (1737–39) did not see the rise of Christianity as an improvement on the Roman Empire whose decline and fall he so memorably chronicled. Voltaire (1694–1778), the universal genius of the Enlightenment, described history as 'a long succession of useless cruelties' (in Kramnick, 1995: 371) with the only distinction between past and the present being their different ways of ordering evil.

Perhaps the most outspoken critic of the idea of history as progress was Jean-Jacques Rousseau (1712–78) who advanced the novel notion that the development of the arts and sciences had corrupted our nature. Delicacy of taste, perfection of manners and a consciousness of fashion give the appearance of virtue but not the reality. We have passed from authenticity to affectation and Rousseau locates the origin of this transition in the triumph of Athens with its love of learning over Sparta with its love of fighting.

Rousseau died before the French Revolution (1789–99) but not the American one (1775–83). The English radical Joseph Priestley (1733–1804) greeted both with enthusiasm. He believed that they heralded a new era in which national prejudice and religious dogma, so often a cause of wars, would be swept away forever. In their place we would have universal peace and goodwill to all men.

His optimism was shared by Marie Jean Antoine Nicolas de Caritat, Marquis de Condorcet (1743–94) one of the French *philosophes*, a group united by their belief in reason and their dislike of oppressive tradition. The marquis argued that the French Revolution represented a decisive break with the past, ushering in a dawn for the human race, one which 'the present state of knowledge assures us will be happy' (in Kramnick, 1995: 395). He died in prison in mysterious circumstances after having been arrested by the revolutionary authorities.

What emerges for this brief survey is that eighteenth-century thinkers viewed history in a variety of ways. One version emphasizes change, another continuity. The hope is that history will culminate in human happiness and perfection but the reality is that it can go backwards as well as forwards. The key point is that these different commentators were exercised about their relation to the past and they believed that they could learn from it.

This differs from contemporary conceptions of history. Broadly speaking, we are not interested in history as 'grand narrative'. The discipline is divided into specialisms with the result that we no longer have the overview that eighteenth-century writers did. On the other hand, we are more aware than they of the complexity of history, of its omissions, of how it is told from certain points of view, of the impossibility of our ever getting to know the past as it really was.

But if we say that our conception of history is more sophisticated than the eighteenth-century one, then we too are claiming, just as eighteenth-century historians did, that the history records the spread of Enlightenment. That similarity should not obscure the host of differences between twenty-first and eighteenth-century history, but neither should it be ignored. We may be closer to the past than we think. The eighteenth century, for example, saw a huge increase in publications as a result of the lapse of the Licensing Act in 1695. This print explosion in some way parallels the rise of the internet in our own age where information is available at the click of a mouse.

Eighteenth-Century Literature: A Brief Introduction

We have looked briefly at some eighteenth-century views of history but what about attitudes to art? In general, writers of the eighteenth century saw it in rather different terms to us. For the first part of the period they believed that it should imitate nature (see Glossary page 201) but from the mid-century onwards there was a growing interest in the imagination. This change is accompanied by another in the conception of art. The traditional view, which stemmed from the Roman poet Horace (65–8 BC), was that it should delight and instruct, but after about 1750 art is increasingly seen as a form of creation or self-expression.

The term neo-classical (see Chapter 6, Key Critical Concepts and Topics page 119) refers primarily to the debate about whether dramatists should observe the Aristotelian unities of action, time and place in their construction of plays. John Dryden (1631–1700) discusses the matter in his *Essay on Dramatic Poesy* (1668). The debate revolves around whether adhering to the unities, as French dramatists do, gives a more accurate picture of nature than the English method of introducing sub-plots, of compressing the passage of years into hours and of frequent changes of scene.

The principles of neo-classicism did not really take root in England. If they had Laurence Sterne (1713–68) could never have written *Tristram Shandy* (1759–67) generally regarded as the progenitor of the twentieth-century stream of consciousness novel. Nevertheless, classical authors were esteemed as guides to writing especially in the early part of our period. From the early to the mid-eighteenth-century writers looked back with admiration at Virgil (70–19 BC), Horace and Ovid (43 BC–AD 18), poets who flourished under the emperor Augustus (27 BC–AD 14). His goal was the moral regeneration of the Roman state by reviving the customs and traditions of the past. Hence he embarked on a massive programme of restoration, public works and spectacle in which poets, too, played their part. Horace was commissioned to write a poem on the 800th anniversary of Rome's founding.

While Augustus himself was seen as a tyrant whose destruction of the constitution marked the beginning of Rome's decline, his promotion of a civic culture, in which the arts played a central part, was recognized as a worthy achievement. Imposing architecture and Virgil's poetry portrayed an ideal of Rome which sought to diminish the divisions that had led to so many civil wars, the last and latest being Augustus' own (32–30 BC) against Mark Antony (83–30 BC).

The lesson was not lost on eighteenth-century writers. Dryden, Pope and Samuel Johnson (1709–84) were only too aware that the tensions which had led to the outbreak of the English Civil War (1642–48) might again boil over if measures were not taken to tone down political and religious differences. The famed eighteenth-century culture of politeness (see Glossary page 205) played a key role in this process by encouraging the upper and middle class to focus on self-cultivation rather than party politics.

The fear of renewed conflict explains the emphasis on order in early to mid-eighteenth-century writing. The heroic couplet, so called because it was, for a long time, the verse form for relating the deeds of great men, is a good example of order since it balances opposing views, as in these lines from Pope's 'Essay on Man' Epistle 2 (1733–34). Man is:

Plac'd on this isthmus of a middle state,
A being darkly wise, and rudely great
With too much knowledge for the sceptic side,
With too much weakness for the stoic's pride,
He hangs between; in doubt to act, or rest;
In doubt to deem himself a god, or beast;
In doubt his mind or body to prefer . . . (l. 3–9)

Pope writes about mankind in general as does Johnson in 'The Vanity of Human Wishes' (1749). This approach shows what people have in common rather than what divides them and so contributes to social cohesion.

Where poets write about individuals, as Dryden does in 'MacFlecknoe' (1682), or as Pope does in 'The Dunciad' (1743), the intent is usually satiric, with the aim of showing, through comic exaggeration, how they deviate from the norm in politics or poetry. The subject of Dryden's satire, for example, the dramatist Thomas Shadwell, is attacked both for his association with Anthony Ashley Cooper, first Earl of Shaftesbury (1621–83) who was a leading figure in trying to prevent the Catholic James from succeeding to the throne, and for the quality of his verse: 'The rest to some faint meaning make pretence / But Shadwell never deviates into sense' (l. 19–20). More generally, the dominance of satire can be related to the growth of public credit, commerce and government financial institutions. Those who were enriched by such developments sought entry to established society. But their efforts to fit in were often ridiculed. Satire, in short, can be seen as an attack by the landed interest on the new moneyed interest.

Broadly speaking, the poetry of the early to mid-eighteenth century deals more with public than with private matters. It offers advice on everything from how to write criticism to coping with the vicissitudes of life. At the end of 'The Vanity of Human Wishes', for example, Johnson counsels the reader to trust in God and accept whatever happens as being for the best, a notion give philosophical weight in the writings of Gottfried Wilhelm Leibniz (1646–1716) and ridiculed by Voltaire in *Candide* (1759).

Johnson's response to the novel (*Rambler* No. 4 [1750]), a genre which comes to prominence in this period, sums up a number of early to mid-eighteenth-century attitudes to art. He praises the novel because it exhibits life in its true state and eschews the improbabilities of romance. But, he continues, accurate representation is not the most important consideration for a writer of fiction. Since he or she is writing mainly for the young and impressionable, he or she has a duty to portray good characters on whom they can model their thought and behaviour.

Johnson here touches on a tension in Augustan (see Glossary page 201) thinking about art, namely that it should imitate nature but, as that would mean copying both its good and bad aspects, it must select its materials carefully. In other words, art is torn between truth and ethics. It cannot do justice to one without violating the other. Anthony Ashley Cooper, the third Earl of Shaftesbury (1671–1713), attempted to resolve this problem by arguing that as nature was the expression of the divine mind, there was nothing truly bad about it. Pope put the matter succinctly when he wrote:

> All Nature is but Art unknown to thee;
> All chance direction, which thou canst not see;
> All discord, harmony not understood;
> All partial evil, universal good:
> And spite of Pride, in erring Reason's spite,
> One truth is clear, *Whatever is, is right*.
> ('Essay on Man', Epistle 1 l. 289–94).

The Augustans were trying to strengthen the social order, to dampen the divisions which had led to the civil war. 'Avoid extremes', Pope wrote in his 'Essay on Criticism'. But the growth of trade demanded a new, more open kind of society. And this was partly reflected in a new kind of poetry, one that rejected the formal character of verse for a freer kind of expression. James Thomson (1700–48) best exemplifies this new development. His masterpiece 'The Seasons' (1726–30) was loosely structured and roamed widely over a wide range of topics from politics to the weather. But perhaps its most important feature was the way Thomson used the natural world to express his thoughts and feelings. It was this quality, indeed, that made the poem so popular with the Romantics.

The success of Thomson's poem signalled an important shift in the conception of the artist. Simplifying greatly, they were no longer to be judged on their intellect but on their sensibility (see Chapter 6, Key Critical Concepts and Topics page 132), no longer to be seen as the manipulator of inherited forms but as the creators of new ones. And if satire pitted the upper class against the middle class, the literature of sensibility, for example the sentimental novel, pitted the rich and affected against the poor and genuine. As the milkmaid turned poet Ann Yearsley (1752–1806) wrote:

Does Education give the transport keen,
Or swell your vaunted grief? No, Nature feels
Most poignant, undefended, hails with me
The Pow'rs of Sensibility untaught. ('Addressed to Sensibility' 1787 l. 78–82)

The Enlightenment quest for knowledge has been abandoned for the pursuit of feeling. Well, not quite. If we look at Pope's 'Eloisa to Abelard' we can find as much, if not more interest in emotion, as in Henry Mackenzie's *The Man of Feeling* (1771); it is just that the affective nature of humans is emphasized later in the period rather than earlier.

There was also a national dimension to the 'cult of sensibility'. According to John Brewer, such literature was 'offered embodiments of Britain: men who are earnest, sincere, pious and Christian, women who believe in their natural duties rather than public show' (1997: 120). This aspect of sensibility complements the search for an authentic national literature. An interest in older English poetry, for example Edmund Spenser (1552–99), author of *The Faerie Queene* (1589 and 1596), replaced an interest in the classics.

The literature of sensibility also has affinities with the Gothic (see Chapter 6, Key Critical Concepts and Topics page 125). One of its characteristic themes, the persecution of a virtuous woman, which forms the subject matter of Samuel Richardson's *Clarissa* (1747–48), is a major motif in gothic tales like *The Mysteries of Udolpho* (1794) by Ann Radcliffe (1764–1823).

Not everyone approved of the fashion for sensibility. Its effect on women was particularly noted. Sentimental novels encouraged them to indulge their feelings and made them easy to seduce, thereby threatening the home and family. Others saw it as a foreign import, designed to undermine the social order. The relation between reason and feeling at this point in history is masterfully explored by Jane Austen (1775–1817) in *Sense and Sensibility* (1811).

Even from this brief survey it should be evident that some of themes which pre-occupied eighteenth-century writers also concern us. The cult of sensibility, for example, and the reactions to it mirror contemporary discussion about whether Britons have learned to be more in touch with their feelings since the death of Princess Diana (1997). Equally, eighteenth-century readers had a taste for Gothic horror in much the same way that contemporary audiences do for similar fare today. There are also the same worries about how art affects young people and whether or not it should be censored in any way. And do we not think, as writers did at different times during the eighteenth century, that art is both a reflection of the world and the expression of our feelings about it?

But there are also, as we might expect, real differences between the contemporary world and that of the eighteenth century, particularly the early to mid-century part of it. We do not believe that art reflects *nature*; we are more likely to use the word *society*. And, in any case, we have a very different idea of nature to the one found in that period. To us, for example, it is a Darwinian struggle for survival; to our eighteenth-century counterparts it was a model of perfection.

But perhaps the biggest difference is that eighteenth-century literature was committed to ethics in a way that later literature is not. We are less certain about moral truth than the Augustans. To us, the claim that drama should 'render folly ridiculous, vice odious and virtue and nobleness amiable and lovely' (Richard Flecknoe [1620–78], in Spingarn, 1957: 96) sounds as quaint as it is absurd. Nor do we share their view that literature performs a kind of public service, supplying information, correcting opinion, refining taste and heightening expression.

Eighteenth-Century Criticism: A Brief Introduction

These differences are evident in the critical terms we use compared to our eighteenth-century counterparts. In addition to using words like 'nature' and 'truth' when assessing literary merit, they also praised it, at least in the early decades, for its degree of order, proportion and overall harmony. All these elements, together with an appreciation of how well an author had absorbed the classical past, went into the judgement of a poem or play, the novel still being in its infancy.

The critics of the early to mid-eighteenth century did not put a work into context, nor did they glory in its multiple meanings and nor did they consider whether it oppressed minorities. These are just some of the approaches we take to literature. But in the 1700s, they judged it.

Those who took up the quill were classified, criticized and compared. What kind of verse was this? – An elegy? (see Glossary page 202), A pastoral? (see Glossary page 204). Having decided to which genre the poem belonged, it would then be scrutinized for its excellences before being placed in a hierarchical relation to others of its kind. In these and other ways, criticism was the handmaid of art, inspiring would-be writers to match, if not surpass, the achievements of their predecessors.

Judgement was often contrasted with wit (see Glossary page 205). Addison says that wit unites ideas that appear to resemble one another, whereas judgement checks to see if that resemblance is accurate, thus preventing us from being misled by superficial likeness. Pope sees the two 'at strife' ('Essay on Criticism' page 182). Judgement is concerned with how well a work conforms to nature; wit is a form of invention that deviates from it. Judgement determines how well a copy resembles the original, wit determines what is original. But wit is also, as Pope memorably said, 'What oft was thought, but ne'er so well Exprest' ('Essay on Criticism' l. 297–8). The trouble with wit, though, is that the expression was sometimes more valued than the thought.

Criticism began to change in the later part of the period. One reason was that long standing poetic and dramatic genres were, by and large, falling into disuse. British society was changing, power relations were shifting and new ways were needed of seeing the new society.

In very general terms, the literary forms of the early part of the period were based on genres that had more relevance to antiquity than to the modern world. The closed form of the ode (see Chapter 6, Key Critical Concepts and Topics page 129) was ill-adapted to representing a dynamic modern society. Perhaps the sublime, with its suggestions of limitless immensity, would prove a better idiom for this new world? An example of the sublime in nature would be a desert or mountains while an example of the sublime in literature would be Milton's terrifying evocation of death in *Paradise Lost* (1667).

But since the sublime referred mostly to nature, it was not best suited to the task of conveying the experience of modern society. That job fell to the novel. Its narrative dealt not just with the hero's or heroine's travails but, more importantly, with their travels. The novel captures the feeling of people on the move, no longer tied to the place in which they were born.

One basic shift in eighteenth-century criticism is from an appreciation of formality and decorum in art, or beauty, to an appreciation of its power to overwhelm us, or sublimity. But this is only a part of the story. An appreciation of the beautiful often co-exists with an admiration of the sublime and neither of these terms was really useful for describing the novel.

A more profound change is in the conception of criticism from a mode of production to a mode of consumption. Traditionally, the purpose of criticism was to help authors improve their writing. There was a set of rules (for example, do not use high language for low characters) against which their work could be judged. But it was impossible to do this when the poet claimed that he was creating something new for which there was no precedent. How was the critic to assess 'unprescribed beauties and unexampled excellence' which were outside 'the pale of learning's laws' (Edward Young [1683–1765] in Ross, 2000: 200).

The short answer is that he or she could not. The guidelines have gone. New ones must be invented. This is where the concept of taste comes in. If neo-classicism was about helping authors to produce literature, taste was about helping readers to consume it properly. Joseph Addison (1672–1719) who, with Richard Steele (1672–1729), produced the influential *Spectator* magazine (1711–12) said that a person ought to be able to discern fine writing as they are able to identify different types of tea.

This comparison suggests that the senses as well as the intellect should play a part in our response to art. And indeed we see a growing emphasis on pleasure during the period. This was a relatively new phenomenon. Classical authors wrote that we should pursue goodness rather than pleasure while the Christian church taught that the flesh must be subdued if the spirit were to be saved. That changed in the eighteenth century.

The puritan conception of God as punitive figure who damned most of humanity, gave way to one who wanted them to enjoy the delights of his creation. The case was different in France where the philosopher Denis Diderot (1713–84) argued that since organized religion was incompatible with natural pleasure, its influence should be restricted. He upheld the lifestyle of the islanders of Tahiti as the one most likely to lead to human happiness.

And while there were many who worried about the growth of leisure, luxury and consumer goods, others held that it was the desire to gratify our appetites that stimulated progress and promoted social harmony. Chief among these was the Dutch physician Bernard Mandeville (1670–1733) whose poem, 'The Fable of the Bees' (1705 and 1714) argued that it was our vices that led to virtue and a happy, prosperous society.

> Thus every Part was full of Vice
> Yet the whole Mass a Paradise . . .
> And Virtue, who from Politicks
> Had learn'd a Thousand cunning Tricks
> Was, by their happy Influence,

Made Friends with Vice. And ever since
The Worst of all the Multitude
Did Something for the Common Good.
(1714 l. 155–6 and l. 163–8)

The aim of taste was to help a person to know the difference between instinctual indulgence and intelligent enjoyment. But it was not always an easy distinction to make. What is certain is that in this new, relaxed climate, art is as much a source of pleasure as a medium for education or ethics; if not more so. The concept of taste held in balance the two main tensions of English political life. On the one hand it corresponded to the aristocracy because it was something people were born with, on the other hand it corresponded to the 'middling sort' because it was something people could cultivate. The critic may still have helped them to develop their taste, but the end result would be that they can make their own judgements, which hopefully will agree with those of others.

Hume was one of a number of writers who wrote on taste. Like many he was worried that taste could mean no more than what a person liked. He therefore sought to establish a standard of taste. The first thing required is a receptive mind and the second is knowledge of the particular art you want to appreciate. The third thing is to compare different kinds of beauty in that art and the fourth is to rid your mind of prejudice. Yet even when we have done all this, two problems remain. One is that everyone is different and the other is that standards of taste vary from place to place.

This point is picked up by Adam Smith who declares that value in art is no more than a reflection of custom or even fashion. What the English regard as comedy, he observes, the French proclaim as tragedy. It is not too great a step from this argument to the assertion that art has very little worth indeed. This is Rousseau's claim. Theatre is his target because it encourages us to identify with fictional characters and to take more interest in a make-believe world than in the real one. It is a view that some in the business community have of 'arty' subjects in the curriculum; they do not prepare people for the world of work.

We are still living with the consequences of these developments in criticism. In particular we, like our eighteenth-century counterparts, have yet to establish firm grounds for the criticism – appreciation is a better word – of literature. Our vocabularies differ. We do not use terms like vice or virtue, and we rarely read of a work being described as 'beautiful'. But does that mean we do not think ethically? Or that we are not struck by the design of a work? Our critical vocabulary tends to be political (e.g. postcolonial) or technical (e.g. verse form) and so is not able to register those aspects of art enjoyed by eighteenth-century audiences.

The idea of taste still survives but in a somewhat debased form. It now means little more than an individual's preference. This is, in part, the result of a failure to ground taste in anything more substantial than our sense impressions. In the eighteenth century, the need to link pleasure to a higher purpose ensured that it was only one element in our response to art, but in contemporary culture we are happy to indulge ourselves.

Perhaps the biggest difference between us and our eighteenth-century counterparts is that they saw pleasure as the first step to refinement whereas for us, in our hedonistic, consumer culture, it is an end in itself. Certainly it would be hard to imagine, in the eighteenth century, a person who sought to improve their taste being accused of elitism If anything, taste was a democratic concept because it implied that everyone, if they were prepared to make the effort, could have something worthwhile to say about a work of art, not just critics.

Eighteenth-Century Education: A Brief Introduction

What happens in schools and universities is hotly debated in the media. Rarely a week goes by without some report or government initiative to improve education. On the whole, education is increasingly equated with training, with preparing students for the world of work. And, once again, we can trace this idea back to the eighteenth century if not beyond. One of the topics of Plato's *The Republic* (360 BC) is how the state should educate its citizens.

The idea that we should stop teaching, say, medieval history and equip people with skills for the economy is not new. An earlier version of it occurs in the writings of Joseph Priestley. As well as being a political radical he was also a schoolmaster at a Protestant Dissenting Academy. He complained that the present system of education offered little to those who were going into commerce. It may have been good preparation for those going into the learned professions, such as the church, but not for those going into business.

Priestley proposed introducing a number of new subjects into the curriculum which were more relevant to trade and finance than Latin. History, law, government and manufacture would not only increase prosperity but also make for a happy population at home and a formidable one abroad. Priestley argued that people should study history because it helped to form statesmen and produced intelligent and useful citizens.

Priestley seems to have a more positive – though some might say propagandist – view of history than contemporary politicians. In 2003 the then British Secretary of State for Education, Charles Clarke, famously dismissed the study of medieval history as 'ornamental' and a waste of public money. We have already compared ideas of history in the eighteenth century and views of history now. It is just worth adding that if children grow up ignorant of their country's history – and we can debate the idea of whose history – then that opens the way for the powerful to manipulate the past to their advantage.

Even though Priestley was concerned to meet the needs of the economy, he also felt that education should promote happiness. That is not a word that occurs too often in policy documents about schools and universities, nor is it particularly prominent in the philosopher John Locke's thoughts about education. Locke (1632–1704) thinks more in terms of 'virtue'. Virtue. That word again. Perhaps it is the term we find most alien from the period. There is an old saying, 'Virtue is its own reward'. It was current in the period. The dramatist John Vanbrugh (1664–1726), for example, writes in *The Relapse* (1696) that 'Virtue is its own reward. There's a pleasure in doing good which sufficiently pays itself' (5:2. l. 65–6). This sentiment contrasts strongly with our times where we often hear that companies must offer very attractive financial packages if they are to attract the right calibre of person; an argument that has been severely undermined by the credit crisis (2009). Such financial disasters, often from similar causes, were not unknown in the eighteenth century. The most famous was the collapse of the South Sea Company in 1720.

Back to education, what system would produce a virtuous person, one who is able to resist present pleasures for the sake of doing what is right? Not one that uses corporal punishment. If you beat children, writes Locke, you break their spirits and they will therefore amount to little in the world. But nor should you bribe them. Parents who reward their children with what most delights them accustom them to pleasure, the desire for which then becomes their motive for action. Thus are they encouraged to place their happiness in transient things rather than in doing their duty.

So, what is the answer? Treat children as rational creatures. If you can make them desire esteem and fear shame and disgrace, they will always do what is right. Rousseau disagrees. He thinks that children will not be able to understand fully what is said to them. This will breed resentment and cause them to rebel against their teachers. His proposal is that children should be left relatively free to enjoy their childhood. Let them play, let them explore, let them enjoy their games. When their faculties have developed, that is the time to begin their education.

Behind Rousseau's recommendations is a tragic view of life. Since only half of children reach adolescence, and since no-one knows when death may strike, it is better to let them have fun while they may. Rousseau is also conscious that he lives in an age of revolution and that the education children receive now may be quite irrelevant to any future social arrangement.

But we would be mistaken if we thought Rousseau simply wanted children to be happy in case their lives were cut short, or because the current curriculum may not survive political upheaval. Despite his support for childhood freedom – he compares pupils to 'galley-slaves' – he believes that the purpose of education is to suppress the individual so that he or she can better serve the state.

There were, then, a variety of views about education in the eighteenth century and as with their views of history, literature and criticism, we have only been able to touch on a few of them. Three things stand out. First there is an awareness that the curriculum needs to reflect to the modern world; second there is an assumption that education should inculcate love of country or, more chillingly, the state; and third that education should involve ethics and the cultivation of the whole person. The last two are possibly incompatible and the third has more or less dropped out of current educational debate.

Conclusion

This introduction has tried to deal with the apparent remoteness and difficulty that is often a student's first experience of the eighteenth century. My argument is that there are continuities between that period and our own though they may be expressed differently. Another way of putting this is to say that some of our current concerns about literature and culture have their origin in developments in the eighteenth century. Once we have established a connection with the period, we are then in a position to see what it can offer us. Is there anything in eighteenth-century culture from which we might learn? Stuart Sim has recently shown how a number of eighteenth-century novels negotiate the same sorts of problems as we face, such as anti-social behaviour and the nature of the family.

This handbook contains much information and many ideas to help you make up your mind. There is Kelly Kramer's timeline to guide you through the period. Ruth Larsen's chapter gives a historical overview while after that various authors focus closely on literary and cultural contexts. They are followed by two chapters dealing with case studies. The first, by Anne Chandler, concentrates on key primary texts while the second, by Steve Newman, looks at key critical texts that have helped to shape eighteenth-century studies. Richard Terry provides a useful list of terms which help clarify how eighteenth-century writers thought about literature and culture and this is complemented by a glossary, at the end of the handbook, of some terms occasionally encountered when studying the eighteenth century.

Philip Smallwood's chapter charts the changes in critical approaches to eighteenth-century literature while Bridget Keegan and Amber Haschenburger consider the nature and composition of the literary canon in the period. Chris Mounsey surveys ideas of sexuality in the period while Donna Landry provides a guide to current critical thinking about eighteenth-century literature and culture. Both lecturer and student will find the on line resource on teaching and learning useful and there is also an annotated bibliography.

Each chapter is self-contained, so there is no need to read through the book from start to finish. Of course it can be approached like that or it can be dipped into as the need arises. How it is used is entirely up to the individual reader.

Timeline

Kelly Kramer

Year	*Literary*	*National*	*Cultural*
1688	Alexander Pope born Aphra Behn, *Oroonoko*	'Glorious Revolution'; James II flees England; William of Orange arrives	
1689	John Locke, *Two Treatises of Government* (dated 1690)	Accession of William III and Mary II; Bill of Rights limits powers of crown and enshrines supremacy of parliament	John Dryden removed from post as poet laureate because of Catholic faith; replaced by Shadwell; death of Behn
1690	John Locke, *Essay Concerning Human Understanding* John Dryden, *Amphitryon*	Toleration Act	John Dunton, *Athenian Mercury* (periodical)
1691		Yorktown, Virginia founded	First meeting of the Society for the Reformation of Manners
1692	Dryden, *Cleomenes*	Massacre at Glencoe	
1693	William Congreve, *The Double Dealer* Locke, *Some Thoughts Concerning Education*		
1694	Mary Astell, *A Serious Proposal* Dryden, *Love Triumphant*	Bank of England founded; death of Mary II	
1695	Congreve, *Love for Love*	Bank of Scotland founded; Licensing Act lapses; Window Tax levied in England; Press Licensing Act fails	
1696	Elizabeth Singer (later Rowe), *Poems on Several Occasions*	Recoinage begins under Isaac Newton, Warden of the Mint	

Year	Literary	National	Cultural
1697	Dryden, *Alexander's Feast*		Recipients of Poor Relief forced to wear badges
1698	Aphra Behn, *Histories and Novels*	Blasphemy Act	
1699	Jeon Racine dies	Pirate Captain Kidd captured in Baston, John Bartam, father of American Botany, born	Shoplifting made a capital offence
1700	Behn, *The Dumb Virgin* Congreve, *The Way of the World*		*Norwich Post*, first provincial newspaper; death of Dryden
1701	Mary Chudleigh, *The Ladies' Defence*	Act of Settlement establishes line of succession and bars Catholics from the throne	Population of England and Wales: 5.8 million
1702		War of Spanish Succession; Anne ascends throne (sister of Mary II; daughter of James II)	First English language daily newspaper, *The Daily Courant* (until 1735)
1703	Chudleigh, *Poems on Several Occasions*		The Great Storm; Samuel Pepys dies
1704	Colley Cibber, *The Careless Husband* Jonathan Swift, *Tale of a Tub* Newton, *Opticks*	Gibraltar captured; battle of Blenheim	Daniel Defoe, *The Review* (until 1713); *Ladies' Diary* begins publication (until 1840)
1705	Delariviere Manley, *The Secret History of Queen Zarah*		Greenwich Royal Park opens; Newton knighted; Halley predicts return of comet
1706			
1707	Delariviere Manley, *The Lady's Packet of Letters*	Act of Union: Scotland, England, and Wales become 'Great Britain'	4 navy ships sink, killing 2,000, and resulting in a public outcry (22 October); Edward Lhuyd, *Archaeologia Britannica* (first volume)
1708		Jacobite invasion of Scotland attempted	United East India Company founded
1709	Manley, *The New Atlantis* Pope and Ambrose Phillips, *Poetical Miscellanies*	First Copyright Act; Naturalisation Act passed at Westminster	John Addison and Richard Steele, *The Tatler* (until 1711)

Year	*Literary*	*National*	*Cultural*
1710	Swift, *Journal to Stella* George Berkeley, *Treatise Concerning Principles of Human Knowledge*	British capture French Arcadia (Nova Scotia)	Swift, *The Examiner* (periodical); George Frederick Handel makes first visit to London
1711	Pope, *Essay on Criticism* Earl of Shaftesbury, *Characteristics of Men, Manners, Opinions, Times*		St Paul's Cathedral finished; South Sea Company founded; Handel's *Rinaldo*; Addison and Steele, *The Spectator* (1712)
1712	John Arbuthnot, *The History of John Bull* Pope, *The Rape of the Lock* (first edition) Swift, *Conduct of the Allies*	Patronage Act; repeal of Naturalisation Act	Last execution for witchcraft; Handel arrives in London; Thomas Newcomen's steam engine
1713	Ann Finch, *Miscellany Poems* Pope, *Windsor Forest*	Peace of Utrecht ends war of Spanish Succession	Theft by servants made capital offence
1714	John Gay, *The Shepherd's Week* Manley, *The Adventures of Rivella* Pope, *The Rape of the Lock* (revised)	Death of Queen Anne and accession of George I (beginning of Hanoverian monarchy); Schism Act	
1715	Nahum Tate, adapter of Shakespeare dies. William Wyderley, playwright dies.	First Jacobite uprising suppressed: 'Old Pretender' (son of James II) proclaimed James III by Louis XIV of France; Riot Act	Habeas corpus suspended; Society of Ancient Britons begun
1716	Gay, *Trivia*		Defoe, *Mercurius Politicus* (periodical)
1717	Pope, *Collected Works* Newton, *Opticks*		
1718	Thomas Parnell, memorist, literary historian, preacher, dies		Lady Mary Wortley Montagu introduces smallpox vaccination from Turkey
1719	Defoe, *Robinson Crusoe* Eliza Haywood, *Love in Excess* (to 1720) Swift, *Stella's Birthday Poems* (to 1727)	War with Spain; Jacobite invasion of England	Royal Academy of Music founded

Year	*Literary*	*National*	*Cultural*
1720	Manley, *Power of Love*	South Sea bubble scandal	Hell Fire clubs reported; Westminster Hospital founded (first subscription hospital)
1721		Robert Walpole becomes First Lord of the Treasury (Prime Minister), holds post until 1742; Calico Act bans wearing of calico	
1722	Defoe, *Moll Flanders; Journal of the Plague Year* Haywood, *The British Recluse* (dated 1723)		
1723	Haywood, *Idalia*	'Black Act' is passed; workhouses started ('English Act')	
1724	Defoe, *Roxana* and *A Tour through the Whole Island of Great Britain* (to 1726) Swift, *Drapier's Letters*	Levellers' Revolt in Scotland against enclosure	Death of Manley
1725	Francis Hutcheon, *Original of our Ideas of Beauty and Virtue*	Malt Tax riots in Scotland	
1726	Swift, *Gulliver's Travels* James Thomson, *Winter*	Middlesex JPs report on gin drinking	The case of Mary Toft, the 'Rabbit woman'; Academy of Ancient Music founded; Voltaire arrives in England
1727	Gay, *Fables* James Thomson, *Summer*	Accession of George II; Indemnity Act; Royal Bank of Scotland	
1728	John Gay, *The Beggar's Opera* Elizabeth Singer Rowe *Friendship in Death* James Thomson, *Spring* Pope, *The Dunciad*		(–1729) Land Tax reduced (reduced again in 1730–31, 1732)
1729	Gay, *Polly; an Opera* James Thomson, *Britannia* Swift, *A Modest Proposal*	Act regulating attorneys	*Polly* banned from production by Walpole; Parliament House (Dublin) begun; deaths of Congreve and Steele

Year	*Literary*	*National*	*Cultural*
1730	Henry Fielding, *Tom Thumb; Rape Upon Rape; The Author's Farce* Eliza Haywood, *Love Letters on All Occasions* James Thomson, *Seasons*		Colley Cibber made Poet Laureate; trial of Colonel Francis Charteris
1731	Pope, *Epistle to Burlington*		*Gentleman's magazine* (periodical) founded by Edward Cave; Dublin Society founded; death of Defoe
1732	William Hogarth, *The Harlot's Progress* Fielding, *Covent Garden Tragedy; Modern Husband; The Mock Doctor* Swift, *The Lady's Dressing Room*	Act requiring property qualification for English and Welsh JPs	Vauxhall Gardens opened; Burlington's Assembly Rooms (York); Covent Garden Theatre built
1733	Pope, *Essay on Man; Epistle to Cobham* Swift, *On Poetry, A Rhapsody* George Cheyne, *The English Malady* Voltaire, *Letters Concerning the English Nation*	Excise Crisis	Succession Church formed in Scotland; charter schools in Ireland established
1734	Mary Barber, *Poems on Several Occasions* Fielding, *Don Quixote in England* [Lady Mary Wortley Montagu], *Verses Addressed to the Imitator of . . . Horace*		Society of Dilettanti formed; George Sale's translation of the Koran
1735	Hogarth, *Rake's Progress* Alexander Pope, *Epistle to Dr. Arbuthnot; Epistle to a Lady*		Bristol Hospital Founded; Carl Linnaeus, *Systema Plantarum*
1736	Haywood, *Adventures of Evoaai*	Gin Riots; Witchcraft Act decriminalizes witchery	William Warburton, *Alliance between Church and State;* Joseph Butler, *The Analogy of Religion*; Linnaeus, *Systema Natura*
1737	Pope, *Horatian Epistles*	Theatre Licensing Act; Hardwick named Lord Chancellor	Thomson granted annual pension by Fredrick, Prince of Wales

Year	Literary	National	Cultural
1738	Singer Rowe, *Devout Exercises*		John Wesley's conversion experience in London – publishes *Songs and Hymns*; last report from Society for Reformation of Manners; Handel, *Saul*; Thomson's *Edward & Eleanora* banned from production
1739	Swift, *Verses on the Death of Dr. Swift* Mary Collier, *The Woman's Labour* David Hume *Treatise on Human Nature*	War of 'Jenkins' Ear' with Spain; Gaming Act	Samuel Johnson, *Compleat Vindication of the Licensers of the Stage*; Foundling Hospital, London; Dick Turpin hanged at York; Fielding and James Ralph, *The Champion* (periodical, until 1741)
1740	Samuel Richardson, *Pamela; or, Virtue Rewarded*	Food Riots; Horse Racing Act	(–1741) Irish famine decimates population; London Hospital founded; hard winter leads to harvest shortages; Thomas Arne sets Thomson's *Britannia* to music; George Anson's circumnavigation of the globe (report published 1748)
1741	Fielding, *Shamela* Haywood, *Anti-Pamela* Richardson, *Pamela, Part 2; Familiar Letters* Hume, *Essays Moral and Political* (–1742)	Legislation against sheep stealing	Harvest shortages; grain riots in England and Scotland; Handel, *Messiah*
1742	Fielding, *Joseph Andrews* Pope, *The New Dunciad* Edward Young, *The Complaint, or, Night-thoughts* (–1745)	Place Act; Convocation allowed to sit for the last time	Portsmouth shipyard riot; James Bradley appointed Astronomer-Royal
1743	Fielding, *Jonathan Wild* (published in his *Miscellanies*, 3 volumes) Robert Blair, *The Grave*	Treaty of Worms; Henry Pelham made 1st Lord of the Treasury (Prime Minister)	
1744	Sarah Fielding, *David Simple* Johnson, *Life of Richard Savage*	War with France; habeas corpus suspended	Death of Alexander Pope; Eliza Haywood, *The Female Spectator* (periodical, to 1746)

Year	Literary	National	Cultural
1745	Hogarth, *Marriage a la Mode*	'The Forty-Five': Young Pretender in Scotland takes Edinburgh (Bonnie Prince Charlie)	Bartholomew Mosse founds 'Lying-in' hospital in Dublin
1746	Tobias Smollett, *The Tears of Scotland*	Jacobites defeated at Culloden	*The Museum* (periodical, –1747)
1747	Richardson, *Clarissa* Hogarth, *Industry and Idleness* Johnson, *Plan of a Dictionary of the English Language* Sarah Fielding, *Familiar Letters between the Characters in David Simple* Gray, *Ode on Eton College*	Peace of Aix-la-Chapelle; Scottish heritable jurisdictions abolished	Garrick attempts to refuse spectators seats on the stage at Drury Lane Theatre; Henry Fielding, *The Jacobites Journal* (periodical, to 1748)
1748	Hume, *Essay Concerning Human Understanding* Mary Leapor, *Poems on Several Occasions* Smollett, *Adventures of Roderick Random* John Cleland, *Memoirs of a Woman of Pleasure* (*Fanny Hill*) (–1749)		
1749	Henry Fielding, *Tom Jones* Sarah Fielding, *The Governess* Johnson, *The Vanity of Human Wishes*	Embezzlement criminalized; British settlement at Halifax, Nova Scotia	*Monthly Review* (periodical) established, ceased 1845
1750	Charlotte Lennox, *The Life of Harriot Stuart*		London earthquake; excavation begins at Pompeii; Johnson, *The Rambler* (periodical, to 1752)
1751	Hogarth, *Beer Street; Gin Lane* Thomas Gray, *Elegry written in a Country Churchyard* Haywood, *The History of Miss Betsy Thoughtless* Smollett, *The Adventures of Peregrine Pickle*	Calendar Act; Gin Act	Frederick, Prince of Wales, dies; St Luke's hospital for the insane opened
1752	Lennox, *The Female Quixote* Christopher Smart, *Poems on Several Occasions*	Riots over adoption of Georgian calendar, and 11 'lost days'; Murder Act; Bawdy House Act	*The Adventurer* (periodical, to 1754)

Year	Literary	National	Cultural
1753	Hogarth, *The Analysis of Beauty* Richardson, *Sir Charles Grandison* (–1754)	Jewish Naturalization Act; Hardwick's Marriage Act; Apostolicum Ministerium of Benedict XIV organizing Roman Catholic church in England	British Museum and its Reading Room established
1754	Jane Collier and Sarah Fielding, *The Cry* John Duncombe, *The Feminead, or, Female Genius*	Repeal of Jewish Naturalization Act	Hume begins *History of England* (completed 1761)
1755	Johnson, *Dictionary of the English Language* Jean-Jacques Rousseau, *Discourse on Inequality*		Smollett, trans. of *Don Quixote*
1756		Beginning of Seven Years' War with France; 'Black Hole of Calcutta' – 123 British soldiers die	Joseph Black argues existence of 'fixed air', appointed Professor of Anatomy in Glasgow; *Critical Review* established (periodical; Smollett editor until 1763)
1757	Edmund Burke, *A Philosophical Enquiry into our ideas of the Beautiful and Sublime* Sarah Fielding, *The Lives of Cleopatra and Octavia* Tobias Smollett, *A Complete History of England* (–1758)	Militia Act riots; East India Company victory at the battle of Plassey	Death of Colley Cibber
1758	Lennox, *Henrietta*		Magdalen Hospital founded; Halley's comet returns (predicted by Halley in 1705); Samuel Johnson, *The Idler* (periodical, to 1760)
1759	Johnson, *The History of Rasselas* Adam Smith, *Theory of Moral Sentiments* Laurence Sterne, *Tristram Shandy* (completed 1767)	'Year of Victories': Quebec, Guadeloupe, Minden, Lagos, Quiberon Bay	Death of Handel; British Museum opened to the public

Year	*Literary*	*National*	*Cultural*
1760	James Macpherson, (Ossianic poems) *Fragments of Ancient Poetry*	British control Canada; destroy French power in India; death of George II, accession of George III	Society of Artists of Great Britain formed
1761	Frances Sheridan, *The Memoirs of Miss Sidney Bidulph*	General election; Pitt resigns	Death of Richardson
1762	Rousseau, *The Social Contract* Charlotte Lennox, *Sophia* James Macpherson (Ossian) *Fingal* Mary Collier, *Poems*	Spain joins war against British; British capture Martinique	Mystery of the Cock Lane ghost; Johann Christian Bach arrives in England; Samuel Johnson granted a government pension; death of Lady Mary Wortley Montagu
1763	Frances Brooke, *The History of Lady Julia Mandeville* Catharine Macaulay, *The History of England* (volume 1) Christopher Smart, *A Song to David; Poems by Mr Smart*	Peace of Paris	
1764	Oliver Goldsmith, *History of England* Rousseau, *Emile* Walpole, *The Castle of Otranto*	John Wilkes expelled from parliament; Sugar Act	James Watt invents separate condenser; James Hargreaves' spinning jenny invented (patented 1770)
1765	James Fordyce, *Sermons to Young Women* Macpherson, *Works of Ossian*	Stamp Act; Regency Act; American Mutiny Act	General warrants made illegal; Sir William Blackstone, *Commentaries on the Laws of England* (–1769)
1766	Goldsmith, *The Vicar of Wakefield*	American Declaratory Act; repeal of Stamp Act	Widespread food riots
1767	Frances Sheridan, *The History of Nourjahad*	New York assembly suspended	Joseph Priestley, *The History and Present State of Electricity*
1768	Laurence Sterne, *A Sentimental Journey* Gray, *Poems*		St George's Fields massacre; Royal Academy of Arts founded; first edition of *Encyclopaedia Britannica* published (–1771)
1769		Crown Lands Act	Wilkesite petitioning for parliamentary reform begins; first address by Sir Joshua Reynolds from *Discourses* at the Royal Academy (to 1790)

Year	Literary	National	Cultural
1770	Burke, *Thoughts on the Cause of the Present Discontent* Goldsmith, *The Deserted Village*	Falkland Islands crisis	
1771	Elizabeth Griffith, *The History of Lady Barton* Henry Mackenzie, *The Man of Feeling* Smollett, *The Expedition of Humphrey Clinker*		Printers' controversy regarding the publication of parliamentary debates; Captain James Cook returns from the Pacific; deaths of Gray and Smollett
1772		Royal Marriage Act	Food riots; financial crash
1773	Anna Letitia Aiken (later Barbauld), *Poems* Goldsmith, *She Stoops to Conquer*	'Boston Tea Party'; Tea Act	Food riots
1774	Mary Scott, *The Female Advocate* *Letters written by the Earl of Chesterfield to his Son* Thomas Wharton, *The History of English Poetry* (–1781, unfinished at author's death)	'Coercive Acts'; Madhouse Act; Quebec Act; Copyright law settled by House of Lords	Priestley isolates 'dephlogisticated air' (oxygen); death of Goldsmith
1775	Johnson, *Taxation No Tyranny* Richard Brinsley Sheridan, *The Rivals*	Beginning of War of American Independence; proclamation of American rebellion issued by Britain	
1776	Edward Gibbon, *Decline and Fall of the Roman Empire* Thomas Paine, *Common Sense* Richard Price, *Observations on Civil Liberty* Adam Smith, *The Wealth of Nations*	American Declaration of Independence	Garrick retires from the stage; death of David Hume
1777	Sheridan, *The School for Scandal* John Howard, *The State of Prisons in England and Wales* Clara Reeve, *The Champion of Virtue* (later, *The Old English Baron*)	General Burgoyne surrenders at Saratoga	Bath Society founded

Year	Literary	National	Cultural
1778	Anna Letitia Barbauld, *Lessons for Children* Frances Burney, *Evelina*	France sides with American colonies against Britain; Catholic Relief Act	
1779	William Alexander, *History of Women* Johnson, *Lives of the Most Eminent English Poets* (–1781)	Dissenters' Relief Act; Spain joins war against Britain	Samuel Crompton invents spinning mule; death of Garrick
1780	Immanuel Kant, *Critique of Pure Reason*	Holland joins war against Britain; Gordon riots; Irish Trade Act	Sunday schools begin; Duke of Richmond calls for manhood suffrage and annual parliaments
1781		Lord Cornwallis surrenders to American forces at Yorktown	Herschel discovers Uranus
1782	Burney, *Cecilia* William Cowper, *Poems; Table Talk* Hannah More, *Sacred Dramas*		
1783	Sophia Lee, *The Recess, or, A Tale of Other Times* (finished 1785)	Treaty of Versailles ends American War	Food riots; public executions moved from Tyburn to Newgate; Montgolfier brothers demonstrate hot air balloon in France
1784	Charlotte Smith, *Elegiac Sonnets and Other Essays*	Pitt the Younger endorsed in general election, begins financial and administrative reform	Death of Johnson
1785	Ann Yearsley, *Poems on Several Occasions* Clara Reeve, *The Progress of Romance*	Pitt's parliamentary reforms defeated	Thomas Warton made poet laureate; *Daily Universal Register* established (renamed *The Times* in 1788); Royal Irish Academy founded
1786	William Beckford, *Vathek* Robert Burns, *Chiefly in the Scottish Dialect*	Sinking Fund set up to pay National Debt	
1787	Mary Wollstonecraft, *Thoughts on the Education of Daughters* Ann Yearsley, *Poems on Various Subjects*	Impeachment of Warren Hastings begun (acquitted by House of Lords in 1795)	Association for Abolition of the Slave Trade founded; first convicts leave for Botany Bay

Year	Literary	National	Cultural
1788	Charlotte Smith, *Emmeline*	Regency Crisis instigated by George III's first bout of illness	
1789	Jeremy Bentham, *Introduction to the Principles of Morals and Legislation* William Blake, *Songs of Innocence* Olaudah Equiano, *The Interesting Narrative of the Life of Olaudah Equiano* Charlotte Smith, *Ethelinde* Ann Radcliffe, *A Sicilian Romance*	Outbreak of French Revolution	
1790	Hannah More, *Slavery, a Poem* Edmund Burke, *Reflections on the Revolution in France* Wollstonecraft, *A Vindication of the Rights of Men* Joseph Warton dies	Nootka Sound crisis between Britain and Spain	Henry James Pye named poet laureate
1791	Anna Laetitia Barbauld, *Epistle to William Wilberforce* James Boswell, *Life of Johnson* Erasmus Darwin, *The Botanic Garden* Thomas Paine, *The Rights of Man* (part 1)	Haitian revolution led by Toussaint L'Ouverture (first successful slave revolution in the west); Catholic Relief Act	Death of Wesley; anti-dissenter riots directed at Joseph Priestley as a Unitarian
1792	Wollstonecraft, *A Vindication of the Rights of Woman*	Proclamation against seditious publications; Catholic Relief Act (Ireland); Libel Act	London Corresponding Society founded; death of Sir Joshua Reynolds
1793	William Godwin, *Political Justice* Wordsworth, *Descriptive Sketches* Charlotte Smith, *The Old Manor House*	War with Revolutionary France	Eli Whitney invents the cotton gin
1794	Blake, *Songs of Experience* William Godwin, *Caleb Williams* Thomas Paine, *The Age of Reason* Ann Radcliffe, *The Mysteries of Udolpho*		Treason trials; death of Edward Gibbon

Year	Literary	National	Cultural
1795		'Gagging Acts' against seditious meetings passed	Food riots and anti-war demonstrations; Orange Order founded; death of James Boswell
1796	Matthew Lewis, *The Monk* Elizabeth Inchbald, *Nature and Art* Burney, *Camilla*		Edward Jenner tests smallpox vaccinations; Samuel Taylor Coleridge, *The Watchman* (periodical); death of Robert Burns and James Macpherson
1797	Wilberforce, *Practical View* Ann Radcliffe, *The Italian* Wordsworth, *The Borderers* (published 1842)	Bank Restriction Act suspends cash payments until 1821	Death of Wollstonecraft, Horace Walpole, Edmund Burke; *The Anti-Jacobin* (periodical, –1798)
1798	T. R. Malthus, *Essay on Population* Wordsworth and Samuel Taylor Coleridge, *Lyrical Ballads* William Godwin, *Memoirs of the Author of the Vindication of the Rights of Woman*	Irish rebellion; Nelson's victory at the Nile	
1799	Mary Hays, *The Victim of Prejudice*	Income Tax introduced; West India Dock Act; Combination Act	Napoleon's forces discover the Rosetta Stone
1800	Maria Edgeworth, *Castle Rackrent*	Act for Union of Britain and Ireland; Malta captured	Food riots; Richard Trevithick's high-powered steam engine patented
1801	Robert Southey, *Thabala*	Union of Britain and Ireland implemented; Pitt resigns over the issue of Catholic emancipation	First census undertaken – total population of Great Britain: 10.5 million
1802	Walter Scott, *Minstrelsy of the Scottish Border* William Wordsworth, *Preface to Lyrical Ballads*	Peace of Amiens	*Edinburgh Review* established; Society for the Repression of Vice founded
1803	William Cowper, *The Life and Posthumous Writings*	War with Napoleonic France; Maratha War (–1805) extends power in central India	
1804	Blake, *Milton; Jerusalem* (begun; until 1820)	Pitt returns as Prime Minister	

Year	Literary	National	Cultural
1805	Wordsworth, *The Prelude* Scott, *The Lay of the Last Minstrel*	Battle of Trafalgar (Nelson receives wounds that lead to his death)	
1806	Charlotte Dacre, *Zofloya*		Death of Pitt and Charlotte Smith
1808	Scott, *Marmion*		Leigh Hunt, *The Examiner* (periodical)
1807	George Gordon, Lord Byron, *Hours of Idleness* Charlotte Smith, *Beachy Head* Charles and Mary Lamb, *Tales from Shakespeare* Wilberforce, *A Letter on the Abolition of the Slave Trade*	Slave trade abolished	Geological Society of London established
1809		Curwen's Act against sale of seats in parliament	*Quarterly Review* established (periodical); London exhibition of paintings by Blake
1810	Scott, *Lady of the Lake* Southey, *The Curse of the Kehama*	George III falls ill; beginning of regency	
1811	Jane Austen, *Sense and Sensibility*	Prince of Wales made regent	Drury Lane Theatre burnt and rebuilt; Luddite machine-breaking riots begin; Glasgow weavers' riots; National Society for the Education of the Poor founded
1812		War with America; Act of Toleration	Gas Light and Coke Company formed in London
1813	Austen, *Pride and Prejudice* Percy Bysshe Shelley, *Queen Mab* More, *The Works of Hannah More* Lord Byron, *Pride of Abydos*	East India Company monopoly in Indian trade abolished; repeal of 1536 Statute of Artificers	Robert Southey named poet laureate
1814	Austen, *Mansfield Park* Scott, *Waverley* Wordsworth, *The Excursion*	Napoleon defeated; Peace Treaty of Ghent with America; Copyright Act extended	George Stephenson builds steam locomotive

Year	*Literary*	*National*	*Cultural*
1815	Scott, *Guy Mannering* Mary Hays, *The Brothers, or Consequences. A Story of What Happens Every Day*	Napoleon returns; 100 days' war; Battle of Waterloo; Peace Treaty of Vienna; Corn Law	
1816	Austen, *Emma* Coleridge, 'Kubla Khan' Scott, *The Antiquary* Byron, *Song for the Luddites* Coleridge, *Christabel*		Elgin marbles brought to England
1817	Coleridge, *Biographia Literaria* John Keats, *Poems*		*Blackwood's Edinburgh Magazine* founded; Habeas Corpus suspended; death of Jane Austen
1818	Mary Shelley, *Frankenstein* Austen, *Northanger Abbey* (written circa 1800) Keats, *Endymion* Scott, *Rob Roy*		
1819	Scott, *Ivanhoe*	Peterloo Massacre	
1820	Shelley, *Prometheus Unbound*	Death of George III; accession of George IV	Cato Street and Grange Moor conspiracies
1821	Thomas De Quincey, *Confessions of an Opium Eater* Percy Bysshe Shelley, *Defence of Poetry*	Sierra Leone, Gambia, and the Gold Coast form British West Africa	Death of John Keats; *Manchester Guardian* begins publication; famine in Ireland
1822			Death of Percy Bysshe Shelley; Rosetta Stone deciphered by Champollion in France
1823	Lord Byron, *Don Juan*		Rugby invented
1824			National Gallery opened; death of Lord Byron
1825			Trade unions legalized; John Milton's *De Doctrina Christiana* discovered and published
1826			

Year	Literary	National	Cultural
1827			University College London founded; death of Blake
1828		New Corn Laws relax tariff; repeal of	
1829	Thomas Carlyle, *Signs of the Times*	Catholic Emancipation Bill enacted	Governesses' Mutual Society founded; Metropolitan Police (London) established
1830	Alfred, Lord Tennyson, *Poems Chiefly Lyrical*	Death of George IV, accession of William IV	Petitions to both houses of parliament on abolition of slavery
1831			Charles Darwin's voyage on the *Beagle*
1832		Reform Act begins process of expanding political representation	Death of Scott
1833		Abolition of slavery in British Empire	Death of Hannah More
1834		New Poor Law Commission founds workhouses	First colony established in South Australia; Tolpuddle martyrs transported there; houses of parliament largely destroyed by fire; deaths of Coleridge and Charles Lamb
1835	John Clare, *The Rural Muse*	Assasination attempt on President Andrew Jackson	HMS Beagle, with Darwin on board, anchors off the Chonos Archipelago
1836	Charles Dickens, *Pickwick Papers*		
1837	Dickens, *Oliver Twist* Thomas Carlyle, *The French Revolution*	Queen Victoria ascends throne	

2 Contexts, Identities and Consumption: Britain 1688–1815

Ruth M. Larsen

Chapter Overview

This chapter explores a number of the central themes of the history of Britain between 1688 and 1815. It considers the political world exploring the impact of the Glorious Revolution, the development of party politics, and political representation. The essay then considers the importance of identity considering both national identities and social identities, looking at religion, gender, ethnicity and social rank. Finally, it highlights how this identity was expressed through culture and consumption. Eighteenth-century England has been described as the most modern country of its age, a time of great novelty and development (Baugh, 1976: 1). That novelty and wealth shaped the experiences of many across Georgian Britain, which have, in turn, shaped the modern world.

The Glorious Revolution and its Consequences

In terms of political history, eighteenth-century Britain was, in many ways, shaped by the 'Glorious Revolution'. This was the term given to the series of events which led to the Catholic James II (1633–1701) being replaced by his daughter Mary (1662–94) and her Protestant husband William of Orange (1650–1702). The overthrow of James was organized by William and a group of Parliamentarians who feared that England would become a Catholic country. As a grandson of Charles I (r.1625–49), William had a claim to the throne and so the Protestant couple proved to be an attractive alternative to the elites. He was invited to come to England to defend the Protestant faith, and following James' departure from his kingdom in December 1688, William was asked to take over the government. In February 1689 William and Mary formally ascended the throne to rule together.

The reign of William III and Mary II marked the end of the age of absolutism, that is, the notion that all authority was vested in the monarch because they were chosen by God. In 1690, a Bill of Rights was passed which formally recognized the power of Parliament and removed any possibility of a Catholic monarchy. The implications of this came into play following the death in 1714 of the next monarch, Anne (1665–1714), Mary's sister. Under the rules of the Bill of Rights, Anne was succeeded by George of Hanover, George I (1660–1727); while there were no fewer than 58 other individuals who had a closer kin relationship with Anne, he was the preferred choice because of his Protestantism.

The Bill of Rights also circumscribed the monarch's powers; the crown could no longer levy taxes, suspend laws or maintain a standing army during peacetime without Parliament's permission. It was this Bill which helped to create the modern constitutional monarchy that has continued in England, and later Britain, to the present day. In addition, some of the features of modern government emerged in this period, such as the Cabinet, the concept of a 'prime minister', party politics and the associated growth of political satire.

The two main political 'parties' in the eighteenth century were the Whigs and the Tories. These groups were, to some extent, differentiated by their social status. The gentry, small landholders dependent on agricultural income, tended to gather themselves around the Tory cause. Essentially loyal to the Stuarts in the early part of the eighteenth century, the death of Anne and the Hanoverian succession led to a decline in their fortunes. While they remained an important force in politics, active in their support of the Anglican Church and against high taxation, they spent much of the mid-eighteenth century in opposition. The Whigs were the moneyed elite: aristocratic landowners, the increasingly wealthy merchant classes, and the newly emerging professionals. They were concerned with upholding the Bill of Rights and ensuring the Protestant succession. They were also in favour of the Act of Union which, in 1707, formally tied Scotland, Wales and England together. The Whigs and Tories, however, were not formal, oppositional political parties as we know them in modern Britain. Instead, they offered a loose framework of ideas to which people aligned themselves as suited their needs. Politics was often about individuals gaining influence rather than furthering the party cause, and so people often worked across the political groupings in order to seek position and power.

The great age of the Whigs was from the early to the mid-eighteenth century. Although it was usual practice for the monarch to include representatives from both parties in their administration, due to the Tories' xenophobic anti-Hanoverian rhetoric and the 1715 Jacobite[1] uprising the government of George I became a Whig stronghold. Their position was strengthened from 1721 when Sir Robert Walpole (1671–1745) became the First Lord of the Treasury. Popularly known as the first Prime Minister, although he denied that he held that title, Walpole successfully managed both the House of Commons and the Court in order to ensure that he remained in power. His long period in office (1721–42) was known as the 'Robinocracy'[2] and he and the government were the subject of political satire in cartoons, the press and in plays, such as John Gay's *The Beggar's Opera* (1728). It has been argued that the Whig Oligarchy corrupted the party and led to the premature death of their liberal traditions: they kept a large standing army in times of peace; they suspended Habeas Corpus[3] on numerous occasions and introduced the Riot Act (1715).[4] However, the system that emerged under Walpole of mild but effective government was greatly admired by visitors to Britain. The stability of politics from 1714 to 1760 was also reflected in a period of stability in religion, society and literature, and so the 'Whig Ascendancy' had a long-term impact on the nature of life in eighteenth-century Britain.

Political Representation

One of the reasons for the success of the Whigs was their management of elections, and therefore Parliament. While technically members of the House of Lords were prohibited from interfering in elections for the Commons, in practice they were often closely involved. In many of the shires it was usual for the peers and local gentry to discuss who the Member of Parliament for that seat should be. If they reached an agreement, it was unusual for anyone else to nominate a candidate; an election would not occur, and the selected candidate would be seated unopposed.

Where there was an election, elites often continued to have great influence. The electorate formed a small proportion of the population; the right to vote was only granted to those who fulfilled the property requirements of that seat; in the counties of England and Wales it was the ownership of a freehold property worth forty shillings or more. Tenants could also vote if they had a 'lease for life', that is if they held a plot – land – for the duration of their life. Women did sometimes fulfil these requirements and they appeared on electoral rolls, although it appears that in practice they often sent a male proxy to vote in their place; they were formally disenfranchised in 1832. Due to the public nature of elections, the individual voter did not always have the freedom to vote as they pleased; the secret ballot was not introduced until 1872. While only a small number of tenants would have been forcibly coerced, many would have felt a degree of social obligation to the local landowner to vote for their candidate. This sense of deference was not confined to tenants; it may also have been felt by those who relied on the landed elite for business. This loyalty could also be bought: in 1727, Viscount Perceval (1683–1748) spent £900 on the 32 voters of Harwich, an exercise which had cost Samuel Pepys (1644–1703) just £5 5s 6d in 1689. The cost of electioneering increased further: at the end of the eighteenth century: the eleventh Duke of Norfolk (1746–1815) spent £70,000 in his failed attempt to control the borough seat of Horsham, West Sussex.

Aristocrats had direct influence over the electorate, over the Cabinet, the Lords and the Commons; it could be argued that eighteenth-century Britain was an oligarchy. It was thought that politics should be limited to those who had both the time and the motivation to be involved in Government, and it was thought that wealth, especially the ownership of land, gave people this. Involvement in elections in the eighteenth century was therefore mainly confined to the wealthy: the franchise was limited to those who fulfilled property requirements, and the membership of the Commons and the Lords was largely made up of the landed elite and their associates. There was little desire amongst the ruling elite to expand the franchise to give the lower orders a political voice, and there was little call for it from the masses. Due to the lack of repression of labouring traditions, the overall wealth of the nation and the general absence of famine, even when there were bad harvests, meant that the poor and lower classes were by and large a stable and conservative group. The agitation for enfranchisement and recognition that became a major part of the nineteenth century's political arena was a minority concern in the Georgian age.

War and National Identity

What was a major concern for the government, though, was the threat of invasion, mainly from the Dutch and the French, and the impact of war. This period saw the most sustained period of warfare in British history; between

1688 and 1815 the British state was either officially or unofficially at war for no less than 65 years either defending itself or protecting its wider empire and commercial interests. Britain was by no means successful in all of these wars; 1782–3 saw its greatest and most humiliating loss, that of the American colonies, followed swiftly by the successful claim by Ireland for semi-autonomy. At the start of the nineteenth century, though, Britain emerged as a great military power on the international stage.

The impact of war had numerous effects on the people living in the British Isles. The wars were costly; in 1761 the spending on the army, navy, militias and ordnance was in excess of £16 million. This needed funding, and taxation was the main source of revenue for the government. Much of the burden fell on consumers, with a substantial rise in excise duties on items such as beer, malt, leather and soap. It is therefore not surprising that there were numerous anti-recruitment and anti-tax riots as people reacted against the long-term costs of warfare. Nevertheless, the fear of an invasion, especially from France, did mean that there was generally an acceptance of these measures. In 1795, 60,000 people were reported to have attended the Leeds 'military festival', indicating how there was some public support for the war efforts and the armed forces.

War and the growth of the empire fuelled a sense of national identity. One of the results of Britain developing an empire was that its ideals (Protestantism, courage, mercantile enterprise, liberty, value of property) became part of the nation's ideals. England and Wales were only formally united with Scotland in 1707, with Ireland joining the Union in 1800, so a sense of 'Britishness' was just emerging. In the 1740s, when Britain was at war with Spain, France, Austria and the Jacobites, the official and unofficial (*Rule Britannia*!) national anthems were composed, reflecting the increasingly 'jingoist' sentiment of the era. These wars, and subsequent battles, gave the people of Britain a shared sense of enemy which helped to 'forge the nation' (Colley 1992). This, along with a growing sense of loyalty across Britain to the monarchy and the increasing centralization of the British government, especially following the abolition of the Irish Parliament in 1800, led to sense of a United Kingdom.

Religion

Religion also played an important role in the development of a sense of national identity. Despite the secular nature of Enlightenment thought, the country remained a Christian, and largely Protestant, one. In many cases the only books read by the literate poor would have been the Bible and the *Book of Common Prayer*, and if they were able to afford another volume, Bunyan's *Pilgrim's Progress* (1684) was a popular choice. Christian ideals featured in many literary texts, not only in formal religious writings, but also in didactic literature, poetry and novels; even apparently secular texts such as *Robinson Crusoe* (1719) and *Clarissa* (1747–48) had religious messages at their heart.

There was also active involvement in religious services amongst the wider population. Although many people moved away from the established Churches, they began to follow one of the increasingly popular dissenting religions. By 1812, there were 256 dissenting places of worship in London compared to just 186 Anglican churches. This did not mean, though, that dissenters had little contact with the established church. Not only was it part of the monarchical state, and its parishes formed the basis of local government, but the Church of England also worked with dissenting churches, such as the Baptists, Quakers, Unitarians, Presbyterians and, once they had separated from the established church, the Methodists. These Protestant dissenting groups were protected by the Toleration Act (1690), which gave them the freedom to worship but still limited their ability to hold public office. Roman Catholics were not included in this Act, and the long-term wars with France and other European Catholic countries along with the continuing popularity of Foxe's *Book of Martyrs* (1563) meant that papists were often seen as the enemy. The Protestant Association's leader Lord George Gordon (1751–93) led a campaign against the Relief Act, which rescinded restrictions on Catholic ownership and inheritance of land. His supporters began anti-Catholic demonstrations, the Gordon Riots, in 1780. In London the rioters burned down Catholic chapels, released Newgate prison's inmates and launched an assault on the Bank of England; as many as 450 people were reported to have been killed. However, despite this public hostility, Roman Catholic worship was largely accepted by successive governments, and the recusants were slowly granted more freedoms, including the franchise to forty-shilling freeholders in 1793. It was not until the 1829 Emancipation Act, though, that Catholics were able to sit in the United Kingdom parliament, and only slowly did they became a more accepted part of British society.

At the end of the century the Evangelical Revival began to have a major influence on various Christian denominations. Evangelicals promoted a practical, crusading religion and it was central to the development of Methodism, reshaped the Church of England, and influenced various dissenting groups including the Congregationalists, Presbyterians and Baptists. Evangelicalism had an impact beyond the religious world in the eighteenth and nineteenth centuries. It was the driving force behind political and social reforms, especially regarding education and the abolition of the slave trade. It encouraged families to place religion at the heart of their domestic world, and gave new authority to the concept of respectability. These ideas were part of the late eighteenth-century movement towards the promotion of social rules which upheld the ideals of an 'ordered society', with distinct roles for people of different classes and genders. Religion was a major factor not only in shaping an individual's own identity but also in shaping the social rules of how others perceived that individual.

Society and Social Structure

Social rank as well as religion was a significant factor in an individual's identity; wealth, occupation and status shaped their influence in the wider world. British society was strongly hierarchical. The term 'society' had a number of different meanings. It was seen in relation to the individual, and also referred to the people as opposed to the government. The term 'civil society' signified a certain level of civilization and refinement in contrast to 'primitive' societies and it also could denote societies governed by laws rather than by despots. Some believed that the origin of society lay in a desire to protect life and property, both of which were in danger in the lawless state of nature. Others believed that society was a corruption of the state of nature and pointed to the apparent contentment of 'savages' compared to the fretful existence of 'civilized man'. Dr Samuel Johnson (1709–84), conversationalist, literary critic and lexicographer, summed up the various tensions in the idea of 'society' when he noted that while we can enjoy its advantages, we must also suffer its inconveniences.

The basic social division at the beginning of the eighteenth century was between those who were 'gentle' and those who were 'common'. Henry Fielding (1707–54) wrote:

> To be born for no other purpose but to consume the fruits of the earth is the privilege (if it may be called a privilege) of very few. The greater part of mankind must sweat hard to produce them, or society will no longer answer the purposes for which it was ordained (1751: 5).

Fielding saw social division in terms of a potential conflict between those who worked and those who did not, while the poet and clergyman John Langhorne (1735–79) saw it in more complementary terms, with the rich taking a paternal interest in the poor: 'Soothed by his pity, by his bounty fed, / The sick found medicine, and the aged bread' (cited in Thompson, 1993: 23). Differences in income were a major factor of social division; in the mid-eighteenth century a labourer or a journeyman earned between £8 and £35 per annum while most aristocrats would have had an annual income of at least £10,000. However, the fact that some commercial traders were reported to have earned £100,000 in a good year complicated the simple binary view of society. Increasingly, most contemporaries tended to think that there were at least three groups: the upper orders, the middle ranks and the rest. Within these groups there was a great deal of internal diversity. The aristocracy was divided into Dukes, Marquises, Earls, Viscounts and Baronets; the middle ranks included, among others, businessmen, merchants, professionals, shopkeepers and tradesmen; while the lower orders embraced a variety of occupations including weavers, sailors, ostlers, shepherds, hawkers, crossing sweepers and coal miners. The variety within these groups led to a constant struggle over status differentiation. As Porter remarks, 'the distinction between being a servant in or out of livery . . . mattered no less at their own levels than the pecking order between baronets and earls' (1990: 49).

People were not tied to the rank of their birth, though: social mobility could be considerable. William Strahan (1715–85), an Edinburgh printing apprentice, went to London in 1738 where he made social contacts with writers and published the works of Johnson, the historian Edward Gibbon (1737–94) and the economist and moral philosopher Adam Smith (1723–90). He became the king's printer and died worth £95,000. Josiah Wedgwood (1730–95) was born the twelfth son of a mediocre potter but died worth £500,000 due to the success of his pottery industry. Others benefited from direct patronage; talented writers from agricultural or impoverished backgrounds, such as Stephen Duck (1705–56), Robert Bloomfield (1766–1823) and Ann Yearsley (1752–1806), could earn considerable money from their writings if they had sufficient support from elites or royalty. Those with talent or an enterprising spirit could move from the poorest levels of society to enjoy the lifestyle of the wealthy (see p. 126, Chapter 6, Key Critical Concepts and Topics: Labouring-class poets).

Despite the successes of 'practical men of enterprise' (Porter, 1990: 80), entering the formal circles of the social elite was more difficult. While the landed gentry enjoyed the benefits of the national wealth and the services that the merchants, manufacturers and professionals provided, members of this group, however rich they were, were often socially excluded from elite circles because of their involvement in these activities. Overseas traders, fashionable physicians, and agricultural capitalists did find more favour, but it was not until the later eighteenth century that the wealthy provincial merchants began to find some level of acceptance in genteel society. Wealth alone was not enough to gain access to the highest echelons of society; one needed to have the country estate, political influence and a network of elite contacts. It could take many generations to gain these social markers: Henry Lascelles (c. 1690–1753), a West Indies merchant who made his fortune through slavery, bought the Gawthorp estate in Yorkshire in 1739. His son was ennobled as Lord Harewood, but it was not until 1812 that the family gained the title of Earl of Harewood.

It was the 'middling sort', the group that came to prominence during the period, which enjoyed the greatest social mobility. The number of people who fell into this classification grew significantly between 1700 and 1801, in some estimates growing from 170,000 to 475,000. Professionals, merchants, manufacturers, financiers and trades-people all became wealthier, and with the 'petit bourgeois' of successful shopkeepers, craftspeople and victuallers, they emerged to form a proto 'middle class'. These different groups mainly settled in urban areas, and it was the towns which both gave them their financial success and allowed them to develop their own communities. A significant minority were dissenters and some were influenced by the Evangelical Revival, becoming a vocal group against social injustices, such as Hannah More (1745–1833) who campaigned against the poor state of female education. Many radicals were also from this social group: the literate, intellectual and inquisitive who desire change, typified by Mary Wollstonecraft (1759–97), author of *A Vindication of the Rights of Women* (1792). Others, however, were much more conservative in their viewpoints. While the 'middling sort' were not a hegemonic group, the majority would have enjoyed a comfortable lifestyle, were concerned with self improvement and were relatively cultured. They were the 'polite and commercial people' who became increasingly important through the century.

The majority of people in the eighteenth century would have fallen into the group described by Daniel Defoe (1660–1731) as 'mere labouring people' (in Speck, 1977: 31). As we have seen the 'labour' that people were involved in was diverse, including trades, agricultural work, employment in the armed forces, and domestic service. Before the industrialization of the later eighteenth century, when people began to work in factories, seasonal work was the norm and many people undertook a wide range of jobs over a year. There was also a real sense of the household economic unit, where all members of the family, young and old, were involved in earning their keep. Children would have supported their parents in their work or were employed by manufacturers and industrialists when they needed cheap and easily controlled labour. Despite this diversity of work and the difficult fiscal situations many people found themselves in, there is some evidence of a collective spirit. In urban areas pubs and gin houses provided locations for community gatherings. When faced with perceived injustices they got together to rally around the cause, such as food riots campaigning against high food prices, one of the main bases of plebeian politics in small towns. There was a real sense of ceremony to many riots, with the beating of drums or ringing of bells, and there was a tendency for the rioters to legitimize their actions by appealing to traditions of fair prices, fair practices or fair pay. Some protests had a specifically political bent; for example in 1765 there were riots to support John Wilkes (1725–97), a campaigner against government interference in the press and elections. The harshness of their working lives, the development of community based facilities and festivals, and the ability to come together to try and make their voices heard in a political system that was weighted against them helped to give the labouring classes a sense of shared identity. However, theirs was not a unified working class, and across the social spectrum, status was a mix of family, privilege, wealth, occupation, religion and residency; it was these that formed an individual's identity and their place in the social hierarchy.

Gender

Gender was also an important factor in determining personal and social identity (see p. 170, Chapter 9, 'Gender, Sexuality and Ethnicity'). There was significant debate about the nature of gender roles during the period, and didactic literature and periodicals, including *The Tatler* and *The Spectator*, were central to the creation of ideals of masculine and feminine behaviour. While, in practice, there was not a single form of hegemonic 'masculinity' or 'femininity', common ideals appeared in these texts. Women were expected to be passive, concerned with performing the domestic duties of a good daughter, wife or mother, and to be accomplished rather than educated. Men were expected to be knowledgeable and eloquent, involved with fiscal success while prudent, and to be a competent manager of both their household and their wider interests. However, the mid-eighteenth century saw a rise in sociability, which shaped the male and female roles in polite society; it was more important to be sincere than to adhere to an ideal. Alongside this was the growing emphasis on sensibility, the ability to express openly one's feelings which countered some ideals of masculinity. While for most of the eighteenth century there appears to have been a relatively tolerant attitude towards 'deviant' expressions of gender, such as foppery and cross-dressing, there is some evidence that in the later part of the century there was a 'gender panic' (Wahrman 2004: 42–4). This, along with the Evangelical revival, led to a return of some conservative attitudes towards gender.

Some scholars have pointed to the eighteenth century as the time when the concept of gendered 'separate spheres' emerged. A dichotomy between the public and the private spheres was used by contemporary commentators, and some historians have tried to apply these concepts as ideals which limited men and women to the public and private spheres respectively. However, recent studies have found that the actual separation between the spheres was often indistinct and subject to personal interpretation. Amanda Vickery has argued that only rarely did the Georgian use of the terms 'public' and 'private' match their understandings of 'male' and 'female', and that women had access to many public areas, including the opera, urban walks, concerts, libraries and pleasure gardens (Vickery, 1998: 288 ff.). It was not gender so much as wealth and social status that made the real difference in terms of access to public life. A number of elite women were actively involved in the most public arena: politics. Georgiana, Duchess of Devonshire (1757–1806) acted as an unofficial party whip to the Whigs in the late eighteenth century, and Frances, Viscountess Irwin (1734–1807) was actively involved in electioneering in Horsham. Elite men were likewise concerned with the domestic and the familial, involved with their children's upbringing and wellbeing. Some could be exceptionally permissive, such as Henry Fox, Baron Holland (1705–74), who allowed his son to fulfil his wish to dance in a large bowl of cream during a formal dinner for foreign ministers. For the labouring class, adherence to any concept of separate spheres was something that they could not afford. Although poor women were excluded from the political process they were often a powerful force within their own family, and did not conform to gender-specific behaviour to the same extent as women from other social classes; they did what was necessary to survive. Industrialization widened the range of work available to women and they increasingly moved away from home work into the factories and small industries developing in the later eighteenth century. In many ways it was the middling sort of people who were subject to the most significant familial scrutiny. Their roles as wives, mothers, daughters and sisters, or fathers, husbands and public servants were often shaped by culturally specific expectations, and so they were still expected to fulfil the ideals of masculine and feminine behaviour.

Race and Slavery

(See p. 168, Chapter 9, 'Gender, Sexuality and Ethnicity'; see p. 187, Chapter 10, Mapping the Current Critical Landscape)

From the early eighteenth century, a number of successful plantation owners began to return to London from the West Indies; they not only brought back their fortunes but also their personal slaves. Reflecting the Enlightenment fascination with both the 'exotic' and the 'noble savage', young black servants dressed in a metal collar and extravagant Oriental costume became popular fashion accessories for members of the urban elites, a trend ridiculed in William Hogarth's (1697–1764) satirical engravings *Marriage a la Mode* (c.1743) and in James Townley's (1714–78) play *High Life Below Stairs* (1759). There was an internal trade among these servants, and there were adverts in newspapers for the sale of slaves; in 1771 a 'negro boy' was sold in Richmond for £32. However, these black servants were often in an ambiguous situation as the law neither recognized the legality of slavery in England nor formally granted them freedom from it. The complexity of their legal status became the basis of Granville Sharp's (1735–1813) abolitionist campaign, and he developed contacts with former slaves who provided him with evidence about the atrocities of the slave trade. Black writers also spoke out against slavery, such as

Olaudah Equiano (c.1745–97) and his friend Ottobah Cugoano (c.1757–date of death unknown) whose *Sentiments on the Evil and Wicked Traffic of the Commerce of the Human Species* (1787) was the first abolitionist publication in English by an African.

However, not all black people living in Britain in the eighteenth century were slaves, and nor were their political and social interests confined to the abolitionist movement. When two black men were confined to Bridewell Prison in 1773 for begging, it was reported that three hundred black people came to visit them in order to offer economic and emotional support. In the later eighteenth century non-conformist chapels, pubs and community meeting places were being built by and for the black community in London, especially in St Giles, St Paul's and in Wapping. However, these were not racial ghettos, but the home of the urban poor, both black and white, and the high number of interracial marriages reflects how the two communities integrated.

It is unclear how many black people lived in Britain during this time period, but with estimates between ten and twenty thousand resident in London during the later eighteenth century, it was of a significant size. Many were former soldiers and sailors, who following the conclusions of the Seven Years War in 1763 and the American War of Independence in 1781, were discharged into Britain's ports. They found work in a range of urban occupations, including porters, watermen, basket women, hawkers and chairmen. Others took advantage of the public fascination with the 'negro': boxers Thomas Molyneaux (c.1785–1818) and Bill Richmond (1763–1829) were famed for their talent, while child prodigy George Bridgetower (1780–1860) developed a friendship with Beethoven and gave a series of popular concerts in the 1790s. This interest did not always bring financial success to the individual. Bridgetower died in poverty and the most famous black woman of the late eighteenth century was Suartjie Baartman (d. 1815), the (probably unwilling) performer known as the 'Hottentot Venus', who was treated as a scientific curiosity.

Consumption, Coffee and Culture

The popularity of African servants and black performers was part of the growing consumerism of the eighteenth century. The spread of commerce, the growth of empire and industrialization all stimulated a 'consumer revolution' where the purchase of goods and services that were previously limited to the wealthiest became available to many more people. The robustness of the eighteenth-century economy, and especially the decline in the cost of food, meant that for many people there was additional money that could be spent not just on necessities but also on some luxuries. This consumerism was further encouraged by the ideological shift away from Calvinist taboos against indulgence, and the popularity of the idea that spending was good for the economy, promoted by writers such as Bernard Mandeville (1670–1733) and Adam Smith (1723–90). Amongst the items that became popular were wallpaper, china, clothes, framed prints and cushioned chairs. Urban dwellers of all social groups became active consumers, enjoying the assembly rooms, cafes, theatres and promenades which were all part of the eighteenth-century 'democratization of consumption' (Appleby, 1976: 515).

An important feature of the urban consumer environment was the coffee house. This acted as an important space for consumption, leisure and sociability, although, excluding the female staff and visiting prostitutes, most had a male-only clientele. The first coffee houses, which also sold chocolate and tea, opened in London and Oxford in the 1650s. These houses offered their customers a taste of the East with added health benefits, as the drinks were supposed to improve digestion as well as provide stimulation, and a location for discussion and debate. Writers, politicians, artists and merchants gathered in the small premises, and there was often reading material available for them to digest and discuss. Newspapers, periodicals, pamphlets and handwritten manuscripts describing recent events were provided by the proprietor, and these were often embellished by the customers' oral accounts of gossip, rumours and scandalous tales.

This coffee house culture of drink, discussion and display moved beyond these mainly male environs during the eighteenth century, and the consumption of caffeine shaped many formal and informal gatherings in Georgian polite society. Refreshments were an important part of the visit to pleasure gardens, and the cost of tea, coffee, bread and butter was covered by the entry fee to Ranelagh Gardens. The association of the garden with polite refreshments began to grow and specialist parks were created, including the Bayswater Teagarden in London. Tea was a central part of domestic sociability too, and became especially associated with the ritual of visiting. It offered an arena for women to engage in intelligent conversation and polite behaviour, while the hostess could demonstrate her status through the fashionability of her chinaware, the decoration of her parlour and the quality of her tea.

During the eighteenth century culture became 'a commodity' (Brewer, 1995: 345); culture was available to anyone who could pay. There was little sense of high or low culture or separation of types of culture; periodicals such as the *Gentleman's Magazine* featured essays on the arts, mathematics, town gossip, updates of scientific discoveries, medicines, recipes and domestic advice. There was also a sense that culture could be a means of self-improvement. The portrait painter Jonathan Richardson (1665–1745) argued in his *Two Discourses* (1719) about the benefits of the art of painting, and argued how 'much more it might be made to the Publick in the Reformation of our Manners,

Improvement of our People and Increase of our Wealth, all which would bring proportionable Addition of Honour, and Power to this Brave Nation' (1719: 64).

This desire for improvement was manifest in the scientific, philosophical and debating societies which were a central part of urban society. Some of these were deliberately exclusive, which only the invited could join, such as the Royal Society and the Royal Academy which were formed to further scientific research or artistic developments respectively. Others were more covert, such as the Lunar Society, a Midlands-based group of thinkers and inventors, including Erasmus Darwin (1731–1802) and Joseph Priestley (1733–1804). Open and closed debating groups, including the increasing number of Ladies Debating Societies, took advantage of the British tradition of freedom in debate, a liberty noted by visitors to the country. The French philosopher Voltaire (1694–1778) wrote in 1726 that in England: 'one can think freely and nobly, without hesitations caused by servile fear' (in Baugh, 1976: 2).

This freedom was central to the intellectual world of the eighteenth century, which was greatly influenced by both the recent European renaissance and the ancient classical world. Amongst the renaissance heroes for the intellectual elite of eighteenth-century Britain was Sir Isaac Newton (1642–1727), who was described in the *Spectator* as 'the Miracle of the present Age' (in Sambrook, 1993: 2). Raphael (1483–1520) and Michelangelo (1475–1564) were especially inspirational to the artist and first president of the Royal Academy Sir Joshua Reynolds (1723–92), and the builders of eighteenth-century country houses were likewise influenced by the Renaissance architect Inigo Jones (1573–1652). However, the classical world was also a strong source of inspiration and ideology to painters, architects and thinkers alike. In modern Britain the legacy of this can still be seen in the buildings designed by Georgians, many of which were either directly or indirectly influenced by the designs of Vitruvius (first century), the Roman architect. In art the ancient world was also important; 'history' paintings of biblical or classical scenes were thought to be the noblest form of art, and those which portrayed a moral choice were particularly favoured. The Augustan Roman age was a source of inspiration for early eighteenth-century writers, especially Alexander Pope (1688–1744), and the history of the age was the topic for a number of popular texts, especially Edward Gibbon's (1737–94) six volume *The History of The Decline and Fall of the Roman Empire* (1776–89). The inspiration for Gibbon, as it was for many other eighteenth-century cultural producers, was the Grand Tour. The tradition of travelling across Europe, especially to Rome, tightened the enlightened age's ties with the classical world and allowed Britons to experience the ancient civilizations they so admired, hopefully morally and intellectually inspired by them.

Conclusion

In the eighteenth century identity was shaped by gender, social rank, ethnicity and wealth. Talent, luck and determination, though, could allow a great deal of social mobility, to move from an apprentice to the king's printer, from a slave owner to an earl. The period was one of real economic strength, bolstered by financial, agrarian, consumer and industrial 'revolutions'. However, it was also an age of war, where the threat from France and beyond began to unite the people of the newly formed kingdom. Scholars argue as to the identity of the eighteenth century: was it an age of politeness or pleasure; war or peace? What is clear, though, was that it was an age of increasing freedom – to travel, to spend, to improve one's situation. It was also a time of an increased freedom to write, to read and to think; it was a time to enjoy, in the words of Archibald Alison (1757–1839), the 'pleasures of the imagination' (in Brewer, 1997: xv).

Notes

1 The Jacobites were the adherents of James II (1633–1701) and his heirs, who wanted the restoration of the (Catholic) Stuart monarchy. There were a number of Jacobite rebellions, most notably the battle of Culloden (1745) which saw the defeat of Charles Edward Stuart (Bonnie Prince Charlie) (1720–88). This effectively crushed the Jacobite cause which thereafter dwindled into insignificance.

2 This term was used by Walpole's opponents to refer to his practice of buying the loyalty of members of Parliament through his control of government offices and perks. 'Rob' is short for Robert while 'cracy', from the Greek *kratia*, means 'rule' or 'governing body'. 'Robin' sounds, as it was probably meant to, like 'robbing'.

3 The term which literally means 'I have body' is a writ which requires a person detained by the authorities be brought before a court of law so that the legality of the detention may be examined.

4 The Riot Act was an attempt to strengthen the power of the civil authorities when threatened with riotous behaviour. The act made it a serious crime for members of a crowd of twelve or more people to refuse to disperse within an hour of being ordered to do so by a magistrate.

3 Literary and Cultural Figures, Genres and Contexts

Gavin Budge, Michael Caines, Daniel Cook, Bonnie Latimer

Chapter Overview

Figures

Frances (Fanny) Burney (1752–1840)
(See p. 87, Chapter 4, Case Studies in Reading 1: Key Primary Literary Texts)

Major Works: *Evelina: Or The History of A Young Lady's Entrance into the World* (1778), *Cecilia* (1782), *Camilla: Or A Picture of Youth* (1796), *The Wanderer: Or Female Difficulties* (1814).

Frances or 'Fanny' Burney was one of the best-known late-century novelists. A courtier and the daughter of a well-known scholar, Burney used her experiences to paint scathing portraits of fashionable society. Repeatedly, her novels interrogate the failure of male family-members to protect the women over whom they exercised so much power.

Burney's first novel, the epistolary *Evelina* (1778), was an instant success; it tells of a young woman's entrance into fashionable society. Not always a likeable character, the heroine, Evelina, assesses all she finds with blunt honesty and experiences a series of social embarrassments, showcasing Burney's skill at comic caricature. The novel also reveals Burney's signature concern with names and inheritance: Evelina's father has disowned her now-dead mother, so everyone believes that Evelina is a bastard. Until the happy conclusion, she cannot use her father's name, and her surname, Anville, is invented. This novel begins Burney's career-long concern with awkward heroines whose plights highlight legal and social injustices against women.

Burney's second novel, *Cecilia* (1782), turns on similar themes; its heroine is an orphaned heiress who travels to London to live with the guardians named in her father's will. These turn out to be singularly unsuitable: one is a miser, another is a pompous yet cash-strapped aristocrat, and the third is a gambler. The reader quickly sees that Cecilia has more sense than the men who control her money. Things become complicated when she falls in love with Mortimer Delvile, the son of her aristocrat-guardian. This is problematic: her father's will states that if she wishes to inherit his property, she must marry a man who will adopt her surname. The proud Delviles, however, will never allow their son to give up his family name. In the end, Cecilia sacrifices her inheritance to marry Mortimer on his terms. The novel ends on a bittersweet note, emphasizing the arbitrary nature of legal restrictions on women.

Camilla (1796) represents a new departure in that it does not feature a coolly intelligent heroine. Instead, Camilla's impulsive nature and heedlessness form the basis for the plot. She loves her childhood companion Edgar Mandelbert; Edgar, however, is under the guidance of the misogynistic Dr Marchmont, who counsels Edgar not to marry Camilla, but to scrutinize her behaviour to see how truly virtuous she is. Camilla's frequent misjudgements, fuelled by her uncertainty over Edgar's true feelings, lead Edgar to believe her unworthy. Matters are eventually resolved, but this is another innovative novel which satirizes the eighteenth-century novelistic theme of 'trying' (or testing) women's virtue.

Burney's last novel, *The Wanderer* (1814), was published after a long, self-imposed exile in France. It was not well received, but it does feature familiar elements: the heroine, Juliet, returns to England from the continent and lives under a false name, occupying a lowly position within high society. Juliet's story once again invites reflection on women's financial predicament and the significance of names.

Critical interest in Burney has recently blossomed, and with good reason: her contributions to the eighteenth-century novel include development of the sentimental novel with sophisticated, darker tales and an insistent focus on social injustices against women.

Bonnie Latimer

Daniel Defoe (1660–1731)

Major Works: *The True-Born Englishman* (1701), *Robinson Crusoe* (1719), *Moll Flanders* (1722), *A Journal of the Plague Year* (1722), *Roxana* (1724), *The Complete English Tradesman* (1726).

Journalist, pamphleteer, propagandist, freedom fighter, and perhaps arguably the first English novelist: the impact of Daniel Defoe on English society cannot be denied. A passionate Londoner, Defoe's writings are saturated with the capital and its frenzied history, even if his novels in particular have always held great universal appeal. In his journalism and fiction he wrote on a bewilderingly large array of topics, including politics, crime, marriage, nationalism, and the supernatural, as well as the historical events of fire, plague and civil war.

Although he would remain a lifelong believer in the freedom of religion and speech, he followed his father into trade instead of entering nonconformist ministry. He did soon begin to write political essays in the 1680s but his only real success at the time was *The True-Born Englishman*, a critically acclaimed poem printed in 1701 that reached fifty editions by the middle of the century. By this point known to contemporaries as a political agitator, Defoe's fortunes began to plummet and he soon ended up in Newgate Prison for business debts. After his release he published *A True Collection of the Author of the True Born English-Man* (1703) and *The Second Volume of the Writings of the Author of the True-Born Englishman* (1731) in a desperate attempt to remind the reading public of his bestselling work. Defoe undertook some significant enterprises in journalism, such as *The Review*, which has been credited by modern historians with introducing new propagandist potential into the one-man editorials. Working by now as a spy for the government, his political writings continued to appear alongside his 'secret histories' and conduct books.

His modern biographer Maximillian Novak highlights the years 1715 to 1724 as Defoe's most creative period. After all, it was during these years that Defoe published his first novel – at around the age of 59 – in 1719. *Robinson Crusoe*, a tale of a stranded traveller, is based on real-life travel narratives by Alexander Selkirk, Henry Pitman and others, and examines a number of the socio-political and religious debates that had long occupied him. The book was a great success and Defoe followed it up that same year with *Farther Adventures of Robinson Crusoe* and, in 1720, *The Life, Adventures, and Pyracies, of the Famous Captain Singleton*. Direct imitations of *Robinson Crusoe* appeared immediately, such as Lucy Aikin's curious *Robinson Crusoe in Words of One Syllable*, which ran to a second edition within months. Aside from loose translations, other imitations were more general, such as Ambrose Evans's *The Adventures and Surprizing Deliverances of James Dubourdieu and his Wife*. Only the Bible was translated into more languages than *Robinson Crusoe* and in our century Defoe's novel continues to be copied and recycled in all manner of TV, movie and new media formats.

With his success in mind, Defoe continued to work in the travel narrative genre, such as in his *Colonel Jack* (1722) and *A New Voyage Round the World* (1724). Additionally he produced *Moll Flanders* in 1722, a first-person novel from the vantage point of a woman forced into a life of crime, which many commentators have read as an essay on human transportation and public welfare. In the same year appeared *Journal of the Plague Year*, an imaginative return to the catastrophe-hit London of the 1660s that sought to help repeal the Quarantine Act of 1721. Throughout the 1720s the restless Defoe continued to write in a series of genres and styles, all with the welfare and mercantile hopes of his society firmly in mind. His final novel, *Roxana* (1724), recounts the moral and spiritual decline of a high society courtesan, while his *Memoirs of a Cavalier* (1720) revisits the English Civil Wars. Never had England been served so generously by so versatile a writer.

Daniel Cook

Henry Fielding (1707–54)

Major Works: *Tom Thumb* (1730 & 1731), *An Apology for the Life of Mrs Shamela Andrews* (1741), *The Adventures of Mr Joseph Andrews and of his friend Mr Abraham Adams* (1742), *The Life and Death of Jonathan Wild the Great* (1743), *The History of Tom Jones, a foundling* (1749), *Amelia* (1751).

A novelist, playwright, theatre manager, journalist, barrister, and later a magistrate, even the founder of the Metropolitan Police, Henry Fielding is best known in literary circles for creating perhaps the most enduring comic masterpiece in the English tradition, *The History of Tom Jones, a foundling* (1749).

Fielding's plays, by contrast, have fared less well today, even though his first play, *Love in Several Masques*, was performed with great success at Drury Lane in 1728 when he was not yet 21. In the 1730s he had some successes with farces, heroic comedies and ballad operas, often produced under the name Scriblerus Secundus and thereby forming a kinship with Pope, Swift and Gay – great wits collectively known as the Scriblerus Club (see Glossary page 205). In 1737, however, Robert Walpole's government passed the Theatrical Licensing Act. This limited performances and imposed censorship. With his theatre career under threat, Fielding began preparing for the bar, to which he was admitted three years later. Following a series of personal and professional setbacks, the early 1740s was a very productive period for Fielding, especially as a novelist.

Fielding's *Shamela* (1741) set the way for a number of lesser 'anti-Pamelas', parodic imitations of Samuel Richardson's popular if naïvely moralizing *Pamela, or, Virtue Rewarded* (1740). With a new comic theory of the novel in his mind, Fielding soon followed this with *Joseph Andrews* (1742), which told of the adventures of Pamela's supposed brother, who himself deflects onslaughts on his chastity in much the same way as Richardson's heroine. Fielding's novel was defined as 'a comic Epic-Poem in Prose' in the preface, this time in imitative homage to Cervantes's *Don Quixote*. At this point Fielding signed a lucrative deal with the bookseller Andrew Millar, who would publish most of his major works. The *Miscellanies* duly appeared in three volumes in 1743 and included his poetry, comedies and essays. After the death of his wife, and a number of professional disappointments, however, Fielding's productivity waned.

And yet, one more masterpiece was to come: *Tom Jones*. This novel in particular has been the most frequently adapted, imitated and filmed piece of his fiction in the twentieth and twenty-first centuries and continues to attract the most critical attention. But when the novel first appeared in 1749 it incited much bemusement and outrage since it focuses on the bawdy adventures of a foundling of mysterious origins. Despite this, many commentators have treated *Tom Jones* as a moralizing novel, or simply as a ripping yarn. In such a way, the seeming simplicity of the story is betrayed by the vastly different readings that have been made over the centuries. The plot itself is simple. In the first sections (Books 1–6) Tom is raised to manhood in the home of the just and fair Squire Allworthy. Tom falls in love with Sophia Western but is expelled from the home for bad behaviour as claimed by Blifil, a love rival. In the second section (Books 7–12) Tom – and the others separately – undergoes a series of journeys and adventures, usually brawls and wanton pursuits. In the final section (Books 13–18) everyone gathers in London. Tom enjoys (somewhat guiltily) his affair with Lady Bellaston while searching for Sophia. Also on the road is Sophia, who is being forced to marry Blifil by her father and aunt. Lady Bellaston, for her part, wants Sophia to accept Lord Fellamar. At the same time the treachery of Blifil becomes known and Allworthy takes Tom back into his favour. Tom's infidelities are forgiven and he and Sophia are married. By way of comic mishaps and misadventures, order has been restored.

Daniel Cook

Samuel Johnson (1709–84)

(See p. 77, Chapter 4: Case Studies in Reading 1: Key Primary Texts: Samuel Johnson)

Major Works: *Irene* (1736), *London* (1737), *The Vanity of Human Wishes* (1749), *A Dictionary of the English Language* (1755), *Rasselas, Prince of Abyssinia* (1759), *A Journey to the Western Islands of Scotland* (1775), *The Lives of the English Poets* (1779–81).

Samuel Johnson was one of the first English writers to become a celebrity, something reflected in the famous biography of him published in 1791 by his friend James Boswell (1740–95), which recorded his life in unprecedented detail. Born the son of a bookseller in Lichfield, his extraordinary memory and mastery of classical languages seemed to destine him for an academic career, but lack of money, owing to the failure of his father's business, forced him to abandon his degree at the University of Oxford. Johnson subsequently attempted to establish himself as a schoolmaster, a career in which his lack of success was probably due to his personal uncouthness, since, throughout his life, he was subject to odd nervous tics which may have been symptoms of Tourette's syndrome. He moved in 1737 to London where, for the next few years, he scratched a living by writing pamphlets and biographical prefaces commissioned by publishers, a period reflected in his *Life of Savage* (1744), which commemorates Johnson's friendship with an eccentric minor hack writer.

In 1746, Johnson's close relationships with the publishing trade led to a commission to compile an English dictionary. Johnson made the highly innovative decision to base his word definitions around illustrative quotations from famous writers, so that when the dictionary was published in 1755 it enjoyed an unparalleled prestige, forming the basis for all English dictionaries published up until the mid nineteenth century, something reflected in the opening incident of the novel *Vanity Fair* (1847–48), where Thackeray makes his rebellious social-climber Becky Sharp throw Johnson's Dictionary out the window in order to signify her rejection of authority.

During his years of struggle to compile the dictionary, Johnson published his famous poetic imitation of Juvenal, *The Vanity of Human Wishes* (1749), and his impressive series of moralistic essays, *The Rambler* (1750–52), establishing a literary reputation which was cemented by the dictionary's appearance. Johnson's letter firmly rebutting attempts by Philip Dormer Stanhope, fourth Earl of Chesterfield (1694–1773), to claim credit for the dictionary's publication as its nominal patron, is often regarded as marking the breakdown of the system of aristocratic patronage, although Johnson later benefited from that same system by accepting a state pension.

In 1759, Johnson published his best known work, the allegorical oriental tale *Rasselas*, in order to defray the costs of his mother's funeral: this story of a group of travellers searching inconclusively for the best way to live has received widely divergent interpretations, but is often regarded as reflecting an underlying sceptical outlook on Johnson's part, despite the Christian piety to which the many prayers he composed testify. Johnson's scepticism about contemporary deistical thought is exemplified by his famously scathing review of Soame Jenyns's *A Free Inquiry into the Nature and Origin of Evil* (1757), where he poured scorn on the suggestion that individual suffering was necessary to universal happiness.

The major contribution to literary criticism of Johnson's later years, the *Lives of the Poets* (1779–81), originated as a series of prefaces to a collected edition of English poetry, and as a result is somewhat haphazard in its coverage.

Gavin Budge

Alexander Pope (1688–1744)

(See p. 70, Chapter 4, Case Studies in Reading 1: Key Primary Literary Texts)

Major Works: *An Essay on Criticism* (1711), *The Rape of the Lock* (1712–14), *Windsor-Forest* (1713), Translation of Homer's *Iliad* (1715–20), *Verses to the Memory of an Unfortunate Lady* (1717), *Eloisa to Abelard* (1717), *Moral Essays* (1731–34), *Essay on Man* (1733–34), *An Epistle to Dr. Arbuthnot* (1735), *The Dunciad* (1728–43).

Perhaps England's finest satirist, Alexander Pope has long been treated as the first recognizably professional poet in the English language. A canny exploiter of the burgeoning print culture, his dealings with dubious booksellers, such as Edmund Curll (?1683–1747) and others, marked a notable development in the profession of literature away from dependence on court patronage. Indeed, as a Catholic in a period of pronounced anti-Catholic bias, Pope was in many ways a political and social outsider, debarred from university and, in his words, from 'Posts of Profit or of Trust'. Yet, in spite of the many obstacles in his way, no less the severe physical discomfort caused by chronic ill-health, he was a prolific correspondent and generous host, and much admired – even if grudgingly – by his contemporaries.

Pope's metrical talents were evidenced early on, when his teenage *Pastorals* in the Virgilian tradition finally appeared in 1709. There soon followed *An Essay on Criticism* (1711), *Windsor-Forest* (1713) and *The Rape of the Lock* (1712–14), a stupendous mock-epic. The *Essay* in particular gained the attention of prominent literary men in London, such as Joseph Addison's circle. A didactic poem in heroic couplets, it outlines the rules of taste among the finest ancient writers. Confident in its delivery and bold in its assertions, it was a remarkable intellectual achievement for the young poet. *Windsor-Forest*, too, attracted fellow poets, most notably Jonathan Swift, with its dense and finely woven examination of tense political issues. These lengthy works were quickly followed by idiosyncratic translations of Homer's *Iliad* (1715–20) and the *Odyssey* (1725–26) and other classics.

In addition to his translations and editing, which included an edition of Shakespeare, Pope continued to produce mock-epics. In these works he conflated the mundaneness of the modern world with the heroic language and exploits of the ancients in order to make statements about the present. *The Dunciad* (1728–43) – perhaps Pope's greatest work – uses mock-heroic language and machinery in order to ridicule the vain and ignorant scholars and writers that Pope felt abounded in the literary marketplace. Throughout the poem the reign of Dulness is described, and a series of prophecies about the growth of indolence, the decline in educational standards, and the return of night and chaos are being fulfilled.

Pope also produced his philosophical poem *An Essay on Man* (1733–4) in this period. Its professed aim is to vindicate the ways of God to man, to prove that the universe is good despite the appearance of evil and that our failure to perceive the perfection of the whole is evidence of our own limited vision. The furore caused by *The Dunciad* was offset here by his shift of focus from the particular to the philosophical and general. Published anonymously, the poem was widely praised for its freshness and seemingly satire-free delivery. When Pope finally acknowledged the poem, his critics grudgingly conceded that his literary powers extended beyond satire.

It is as an exemplary satirist, nonetheless, that he will be justly remembered. Although he did not match the polymathic range of Samuel Johnson's prose and verse, and although he was not situated in the university scene as the Wartons and Thomas Gray were, Pope is the standout poet of the eighteenth century. A master of form and register, a maestro of metre, and a doyen of wit, Pope will remain among the most read and most imitated writers in the English language.

Daniel Cook

Samuel Richardson (1689–1761)
Major Works: *Pamela: Or, Virtue Rewarded* (1740–1), *Clarissa* (1747–48), *Sir Charles Grandison* (1753–54).

Samuel Richardson might have seemed to his contemporaries an unlikely candidate for enduring literary fame. A printer with little formal education, Richardson did not publish fiction until he was over fifty – and yet his work changed the course of the English novel.

Richardson began his first novel while composing a book of model letters, some of which branched off into an independent narrative, becoming *Pamela; Or, Virtue Rewarded* (1740). Its plot concerns a young servant, Pamela, whose master, Mr B, imprisons her, hoping to bully her into becoming his mistress. But Pamela refuses, believing that to surrender her 'virtue' outside marriage would be immoral. The narrative takes the form of a letter-journal written to pass the time of her captivity; the reader shares Pamela's resistance to Mr B and her disbelief when he announces that he wishes to marry her, 'rewarding' her virtue. Crude as this resolution may be, *Pamela* is a landmark text because it centralizes the rights of a working-class woman against an upper-class man's sexual demands.

Richardson wrote a sequel to *Pamela*, which is now little-read; however, his next novel, *Clarissa* (1747–48), became one of the defining fictions of its age. When Clarissa's relatives pressure her to marry the greedy Solmes, she panics and elopes with the charming, aristocratic libertine Lovelace, who falsely promises her marriage. Lovelace is fascinated by her but convinced that no woman is strong enough to withstand his seductive powers. He puts her to trial, imprisoning her and then raping her to make her capitulate. Contrite, he offers to repair her honour by marrying her, but Clarissa chooses death instead.

This plot provides the skeleton for an epistolary novel of incredible psychological intensity, as the reader witnesses Clarissa's growing paranoia in her letters to her best friend Anna. Clarissa's correspondence with Anna is paralleled by Lovelace's letters to his friend Belford; the overlapping of the two sequences of letters produces bitter ironies as Clarissa and Lovelace report the same events from completely different perspectives. It reveals their intense sexual attraction, frustrated by their failure to understand one another until it is too late. Lovelace and Clarissa remain two of the most memorable characters in eighteenth-century fiction, fiercely intelligent, witty, passionate, and self-willed. The novel itself stands as a meditation on the limits of the self and how far one should comply with the demands of others.

Richardson's final novel, *Sir Charles Grandison* (1753–54), continues this theme. Although many critics regard it as stuffy, it was popular at the time, and later novelists such as Jane Austen and George Eliot treasured it. It, too, is an epistolary novel; the clever, carefree heroine, Harriet, falls in love with Sir Charles Grandison before discovering that he is half-engaged to Clementina, an Italian Catholic. Clementina rejects Sir Charles on religious grounds, freeing him to marry Harriet, but Harriet must accept coming second and the requirements of eighteenth-century marriage, which positioned women as inferior. More positive than *Clarissa, Grandison* is still a reflection on how women handle the demands of their society.

Richardson's major contributions to the novel are the creation of seriously intelligent women characters, an unparalleled command of the epistolary form, and a psychological acuteness which directly influenced nineteenth-century novels.

Bonnie Latimer

Jonathan Swift (1667–1745)

Major Works: *The Battle of the Books* (1704), *A Tale of a Tub* (1704), *Journal to Stella* (1710–13), *Gulliver's Travels* (1726), *A Modest Proposal* (1729), 'Strephon and Chloe' (1731), 'A Beautiful Young Nymph Going to Bed' (1734).

An Anglo-Irish satirist and wit, Jonathan Swift, Dean of St Patrick's Cathedral, Dublin, was praised and chastised equally by his contemporaries. Even though he wrote a large number of works in verse, Swift has always been best known for his controversial prose satires, most notably *Gulliver's Travels, A Tale of a Tub* and *The Battle of the Books, A Modest Proposal, The Drapier's Letters* (1724–5) and *An Argument against Abolishing Christianity* (1708).

Swift is at once disarmingly witty and unflinchingly caustic. *Ridet et odit*: he laughs and loathes. Among the numerous targets of his satiric bite even the author himself is depicted as selfish and deplorable, as in his tongue-in-cheek *Verses on the Death of Dr. Swift, D.S.P.D.* (1739). In his anxiously masculine engagement with women we find endearing, if disturbing, love stories of great integrity and honesty. Couched in the language of traditional English love poetry, false modesty is soon cast asunder in his blunt poems to 'Stella' (Esther Johnson [1681–1728]). Similarly, the female mystique is explored with discomforting openness in his unusual love poems, such as in the *Strephon and Chloe* series, as well as 'The Lady's Dressing Room' (1732), and 'A Beautiful Young Nymph Going to Bed'. *Cadenus and Vanessa* (1713), and the letters collected in *Journal to Stella*, too, are, even at their most playful, alarmingly personal.

But, even if in the last twenty years or so serious discussion has been spent on Swift's poetry, it is the morally and politically complex prose satires that have always attracted scholars, especially his *Gulliver's Travels*. Pseudonymously published, this book recounts the memoirs of a castaway ship's surgeon, Lemuel Gulliver, who has undergone a series of fantastical adventures in various utopian and dystopian places. He awakes in Lilliput, a place inhabited by tiny and petty creatures. A second journey takes him to a land of giants, where again his disproportionate size affords him new insights into human nature. Cast adrift by pirates, he discovers islands in which learning is misdirected and immortality leads only to misery. Following his final adventure, Gulliver and his family, he comes to realize, are no different to the savage yet human-like Yahoos who cohabit with the idealized Houyhnhnms, talking horses of great integrity and reasoning. Contemporaries regarded Swift as misanthropic for this self-loathing hatred of mankind, though he often denied this. After all, the Houyhnhnms, 'perfection of nature', have no curiosity or drive and so cannot experience human relief and achievement. Humankind is not perfect but at least we have the capacity for freedom.

This humanistic imperative is present in Swift's complicated stance on Irish nationalism. *A Modest Proposal*, a mordantly ironic satire on the English oppression of Ireland remains, his most shocking such work. Logically speaking, the particulars of the modest proposer's argument for consuming the Irish babies to ease famine in Ireland and to supply an insatiable England cannot be faulted. On moral grounds it is downright abominable. And yet, in many ways, Swift presents the Irish as lacking in will and strength. How does society, how do governments, address such discrepancies in order to help the oppressed and underprivileged? Is the human endeavour doomed to failure, are we already beaten, or can we stomach a radical change in our sensibilities? Elsewhere, in *A Tale of a Tub*, his attack on religious excess, and *The Drapier's Letters* the collective name for a sustained attack on the inferior English coinage foisted on Ireland, and in a vast body of pamphlets, the tireless Swift seems to lead us on a social mission to save modern society. But, like a criminal, his intentions cannot be fully ascertained.

Daniel Cook

Genres

Eighteenth-century Poetry

For a time dismissed as a literary wasteland situated between the high achievements of the Restoration and Romantic periods, eighteenth-century poetry has, after the pioneering work of Roger Lonsdale, increasingly become again an exciting and varied field of study in recent years. Not only have talented, original and otherwise fascinating figures gained renewed attention, the recovery of completely unknown writers continues to challenge our expectations about poetry in the period. Traditionally eighteenth-century poetry has been associated narrowly with 'neoclassicism', with an attempt to recreate the polish and refinement of ancient Greek and Latin writers. Unquestionably, many eighteenth-century poets used neoclassical forms, such as the rhyming couplets of Alexander Pope. In comparison with Pope, on these terms, many would fall short. But, as David Fairer and Christine Gerard have said of Mary Leapor (1722–46), 'it is in her discomposure – her unexpected juxtapositions, her ear for lively rhythms, and her off-centre angles of vision – that much of her power lies'. This beautiful dissonance is everywhere in the eighteenth century, should we seek it out (see p. 130 and p. 133, Chapter 6, Key Critical Concepts and Topics: Poetic Diction and Versification).

Traditionally the canon comprises Alexander Pope (1688–1744), Jonathan Swift (1667–1745), Samuel Johnson (1709–84) and Thomas Gray (1716–71), and sometimes includes Oliver Goldsmith (c.1728–74), Christopher Smart (1722–71) and William Cowper (1731–1800). It might be said that these writers were gentlemen at the centre of polite society who mixed with scholars and men of means in their literary clubs and who dominated the bookshops and reading rooms. Yet, Cowper was exiled by his own descent into madness, and, although socially elevated, Pope and Swift were marginalized by their respective Catholicism and Irishness and, after the reign of Queen Anne, by their Tory sympathies. Samuel Johnson, arguably the greatest literary polymath of the century, and certainly no slouch in the study of classics, was a self-made man who rose from an apprenticeship in the world of hack writing represented by Grub Street (see Glossary page 203) to fame as the compiler of the definitive English dictionary, a feat that earned him an honorary doctorate. Goldsmith and Gray can appear quaint to modern readers, as writers of poems about deserted villages, drowning cats and crazy old beggars, but in these poems they were bearing witness to the radical social and political changes in English society caused by such issues as agricultural enclosure and economic luxury.

The dominance of Pope and Swift on the literary scene of the first half of the eighteenth century engendered a widely held assumption that the most pervasive literary mode was **satire**, in a misleading contrast with the critically disparaged works of the florid and emotional Romantics. Along with **John Gay** (1685–1732), author of *Trivia* (1716) and *The Beggar's Opera* (1728), Pope and Swift launched intellectual warfare on the corrupt and ignorant society that they perceived England to be in the eighteenth century. Perhaps best thought of as a 'mock-book' in its elaborate mimicking of scholarly footnotes and the like, Pope's *Dunciad* (1728–43) existed in a variety of forms but its essential attack on the hacks and ignorant scholars of the time lost none of its force. Other great practitioners of satire – and of many other forms of poetry – were Anne Finch (1661–1720) and Lady Mary Wortley Montagu (1689–1762), both of whom were greatly admired by their contemporaries.

But not all eighteenth-century poetry is satire, and not all is written in Popean couplets. The Pindaric ode, for instance, was irregular in metre and full of digressions in thought. And many poets, including Pope, Swift and the like, wrote hugely popular verse letters, pastorals, blank verse and mock-epics. In 1730, the same year that the peasant-poet Stephen Duck (1705?–1756) produced his multifarious *Poems on Several Subjects*, James Thomson (1700–48) completed *The Seasons*, a long Latinate poem that illustrates the beauties of nature in the plushest terms. Throughout the 1740s, William Collins (1721–59) produced his *Persian Eclogues* (1742), the same year in which Edward Young's (1683–1765) widely-read *The Complaint, or Night Thoughts* (1742–45) began to appear. This was followed by Mark Akenside's (1721–70) *The Pleasures of Imagination* (1744) and Robert Dodsley's important edited *Collection of Poems* (1748–58).

In contrast to the variegated works printed up until this point, the second half of the eighteenth century, at least up until the early 1790s, is often characterized as one of the least impressive periods in the history of English poetry. Nonetheless, this period witnessed an immense number of significant works. In 1751, Thomas Gray penned what is arguably the most imitated and widely read poem in the language, certainly one that influenced generations of poets after him: *Elegy written in a Country Church Yard*. In the 1760s and the 1770s, James Macpherson (1736–96) 'translated' the poems of the ancient Celtic bard 'Ossian' into a fashionably sentimental prose style, and the prodigious teenager Thomas Chatterton (1752–70) forged medieval verse under the name of Thomas Rowley, a semi-fictitious medieval priest, and others. This coincided with a rise of interest in Britain's vernacular traditions, in no small part influenced by Evan Evans's *Specimens of Ancient Welsh Bards* (1764) and Thomas Percy's frequently printed *Reliques of Ancient English Poetry* (1765). Gray, along with the Warton brothers, Thomas and Joseph, penned a number of mock-ancient poems and ballads alongside their neoclassical poems over a period of many years. At the same time, in the mid-century, a new gang of political satirists came briefly to prominence, most notably Charles Churchill (1732–64), Robert Lloyd (1733–64) and a number of men collectively known as the 'Nonsense Club'. Churchill's 1761 poem *The Rosciad* is perhaps the most notable of their productions, and deserves renewed attention.

Also during the second half of the century, George Crabbe (1754–1832) produced his anti-pastoral masterpiece, *The Village* (1783), and went on to realistic, sometimes grimly humorous narratives in couplets, of which the most famous has become 'Peter Grimes'. Throughout the 1770s and 1780s, especially, prominent female poets came to the fore, most notably Mary Robinson (1756/1758?–1800), Anna Laetitia Barbauld (1743–1825), Anna Seward (1742–1809), Charlotte Smith (1749–1806) and Helen Maria Williams (1761–1827). This period also witnessed Goldsmith's much-imitated *Deserted Village* (1770), James Beattie's *The Minstrel* (1771–74), William Cowper's *The Task* (1785), and a number of songs by Robert Burns (1759–96), such as the eternally popular 'Auld Lang Syne'. And, although largely defined as one of the major Romantics, William Blake (1757–1827) began his dual career as a poet and illustrator in the 1780s, with *Poetical Sketches* (1783) and *Songs of Innocence* (1789).

For many, the eighteenth century was a great age of prose, philosophical Reason, history writing and, no less, the rise of the novel. After all, it had even been suggested by a contemporary that Pope, the greatest poet of the century, wrote his drafts first in prose before translating his ideas into his artificial rhyming couplets. Yet, this is to overlook an immense and varied body of poetry. Even if the great eighteenth-century epic failed to appear, mock-epics, along with verse epistles, satires, pastorals and other forms matched and surpassed any in the language. This was truly a great age of poetry.

Daniel Cook

Eighteenth-century Novel

The novel is a defining genre of the eighteenth century and its rise to prominence is a focus of modern scholarship. Mid-twentieth-century criticism emphasized the prosperity of the eighteenth-century middle classes; as their wealth increased, they bought 'luxury' items such as books, and particularly novels. These offered, for the first time, prose fictions of the lives of recognizable, realistic individuals – frequently, women speaking in the first person. This concentration on women's voices in fiction was a radical change: previously, feminine experience had not been a mainstay of literature. Women also represent some of the most popular eighteenth-century novelists; scholarly comment in more recent years has often concentrated on gender and sought to reintroduce their work to the literary canon.

Many of the earliest novels are exciting tales, related to criminal biographies and 'secret histories' (thinly disguised comment on public figures). Picaresque novels (see Glossary page 204), for instance, typically follow the exploits of adventurers. The work of Daniel Defoe (1660–1731) is related to this tradition: his novels *Robinson Crusoe* (1719), *Moll Flanders* (1722) and *Roxana* (1724) tell of irreligious protagonists who meet with various adventures before repenting. Defoe's novels are complex, leaving to question how far his characters are telling the truth.

Another early subgenre is the 'amatory' novel, whose most famous practitioner is Eliza Haywood (1693–1756); she burst upon the literary scene with *Love in Excess* (1719) and was very prolific throughout the 1720s and early 1730s. Her novels depict young women's experiences of erotic love and refer explicitly to female sexual pleasure. Like Defoe's, Haywood's work is far from simplistic: she offers sharply satiric portraits of heterosexual relations. Haywood was widely regarded as scandalous and as popular literature became increasingly moralistic, her 'amatory' fiction fell out of favour, to be replaced in the middle of the eighteenth century by the sentimental novel.

The first major sentimental novel was Samuel Richardson's *Pamela* (1740). Richardson (1689–1761) deliberately reworked the racy popular novel to inculcate religious lessons. His heroine, Pamela, is a servant-girl threatened with seduction by her upper-class master. Unlike the lusty heroines of amatory fiction, though, Pamela does not surrender; the novel is revolutionary in its focus on a working woman who asserts and values herself. A woman's right to defend herself against sexual encroachment and the loose morals of the aristocracy would become major themes of the sentimental novel.

Richardson's work helped to begin a trend for sentimental fiction, which absorbs the reader in sympathetic feelings for the suffering, virtuous protagonist. In this sense, it is frequently didactic, or concerned to edify. Often, it is written in the epistolary mode (in letters); this form makes the protagonist's private emotions and experiences central. Notable sentimental novelists include Sarah Fielding (1710–68) and Oliver Goldsmith (1730?–74); both write of good-hearted men who suffer at the hands of aristocratic villains but who are morally vindicated in the end.

Sentimental novels did provoke responses: Henry Fielding (1707–54), Sarah's brother, particularly mocked Richardson's combination of ripping yarns and strict morality in *Shamela* (1741) and *Joseph Andrews* (1742). There were also less directly parodic reactions: in *Memoirs of a Woman of Pleasure* (1748–49), John Cleland (1709–89) co-opts features of the sentimental novel to tell a prostitute's life. The result is a wickedly satiric reworking of the virtuous-heroine trope as well as a celebrated piece of erotica. Laurence Sterne (1713–68), too, provides slyly mocking explorations of sentimentality in his *Sentimental Journey* (1768). These novelists revise the assumptions of the sentimental novel by pointing out its covert eroticism and poking fun at the idea of learning virtue from a novel. The mid-century period also saw other comic novels, often based on adventure or travel themes, such as Henry Fielding's *Tom Jones* (1749), or *The Expedition of Humphry Clinker* (1771) by Tobias Smollett (1721–71).

As the century wore on, the sentimental mode became exhausted. Major novelists who used it now often did so with a degree of irony: Charlotte Smith (1749–1806), whose work is currently attracting fresh scholarly attention, employed sentimental elements in this way. Frances Burney (1752–1840), one of the most successful novelists of the century, played knowingly with the sentimental format of a woman entering society, producing rich novels that recount the costs to women of living in a male-dominated world.

The final decades of the century saw the rise of the gothic mode, which eschewed the psychological realism of earlier sentimental novels and featured melodramatic or supernatural elements. The first real gothic novel is the early *Castle of Otranto* (1764) by Horace Walpole (1717–97); it was the precursor to a craze for 'horrid' novels, gory fictions which gained popularity during the 1790s. The most sensational gothic novel is *The Monk* (1795) by Matthew Lewis (1775–1818); it became infamous for its blasphemy and violence. The most influential writer in this genre, however, is Ann Radcliffe (1764–1823), who first achieved fame with *The Romance of the Forest* (1791). Radcliffe is often read as reacting to contemporary political debates, especially over the French Revolution, the increasing bloodiness of which shocked English people in the 1790s. Many novels of this 'revolutionary decade' participate in cultural debate; the radicalism of this decade reopened questions of women's rights and those of marginalized groups. Non-gothic writers such as Elizabeth Inchbald (1753–1821), Mary Hays (1759–1843), William Godwin (1756–1836) and Mary Wollstonecraft (1759–97) used the novel to address issues of social and political injustice.

It is worth emphasizing some final points. Firstly, the term 'novel' can be a muddy one: it is possible to group disparate texts under the banner of 'the novel' and the term is often applied retrospectively. It gained credibility slowly during the century: Clara Reeve (1729–1807), who offered the first major critical assessment of the form in *The Progress of Romance* (1785), actually used the term 'romance' rather than 'novel' in her treatise. Earlier 'novelists' like Defoe had in fact referred to their own work as 'histories' or 'accounts'. Secondly, the novel form had a serious impact on British culture. With its prioritization of a protagonist's psychology and choices, the novel added to a distinctively modern concern with the individual and the self. It legitimized the use of fiction to talk about the private and the domestic – and particularly women's experiences of these things. In this way, the eighteenth-century novel can be seen as a forum for debate about a newly constituted realm of privatized experience, as well as the beginnings of one of the most popular genres in modern literature.

Bonnie Latimer

Eighteenth-century Theatre

There is a famous scene set in a theatre in Henry Fielding's novel *Tom Jones* (1749). The greatest actor of the day, David Garrick (1717–79), is appearing in one of his greatest roles, as Shakespeare's Hamlet, and Fielding's hero Tom and Tom's travelling companion Partridge are watching from 'the first row . . . of the first gallery' in London's prestigious, venerable Theatre Royal in Drury Lane. Partridge 'immediately declared it was the finest place he had ever been in', as many non-fictional visitors to the capital must have done before him. He is even more impressed, however, by the scene between Hamlet and the ghost of his father. Though Partridge knows it is a play, and scoffs at the ghost itself, he nonetheless falls 'into so violent a trembling, that his knees [knock] against each other'. Why? Because he thinks Garrick himself is afraid. 'Nay, you may call me a coward if you will; but if that little man there upon the stage is not frightened, I never saw any man frightened in my life'.

When it comes to the grave-digging scene, Partridge expresses surprise at the number of skulls excavated from beneath the stage, until Jones tells him that it is one of the London's most famous burial places. 'No wonder then', says Partridge, 'that the place is haunted'. Once the tragedy is over, he declares the actor playing the king to be his favourite, despite Garrick's reputation as the best in the business: 'why, I could act as well as he myself. I am sure, if I had seen a ghost, I should have looked in the very same manner, and done just as he did. And then, to be sure, in that scene, as you call it, between him and his mother, where you told me he acted so fine, why, Lord help me, any man, that is, any good man, that had such a mother, would have done exactly the same'. The king, on the other hand, well, 'he speaks all his words distinctly, half as loud again as the other. – Anybody may see he is an actor'.

In a sense, this scene is Fielding's compliment to Garrick: his style of acting is so unostentatious, so 'natural', that it looks, to a simple fellow like Partridge, like it is not acting at all. Yet if Garrick dominated the theatre in the middle of the eighteenth century (he made his London debut in 1741 and retired in 1776), there was no shortage of rival stars (such as Colley Cibber [1671–1757] and Robert Wilks [?1665–1732] before Garrick, and the siblings John Philip Kemble [1757–1823] and Sarah Siddons [1755–1831] after him) and no shortage of rival entertainments pitched closer to Partridge's level. A correspondent to the *Scots Magazine* could complain in 1799 that

> The visitor of the Theatre now no longer sees a rational entertainment, or receives lessons of morality, but is doomed to sit all the night long beholding what is hardly a suitable amusement for the nursery; camels and elephants moving with solemn steps across the stage, noise and pageantry substituted in the place of a regular plot, the house ringing with balderdash and declamation, and superb scenery presented for the pleasure of the eye. . . .

Show business was turning into big business, employing thousands of people in specialized roles, and catering – by the end of the century – for tens of thousands of customers. Its nature changed accordingly. London's Theatres Royal, Drury Lane and Covent Garden, held between them the exclusive right to perform spoken drama (that is, Shakespeare, Restoration comedy, etc), but this could be easily circumvented. And it was at Covent Garden that pantomime, under the management of John Rich, evolved into a distinctly English blend of music, mime and special effects. The craze for Gothic fiction became, from the 1770s onwards, a craze for spectacular, sometimes ingeniously staged Gothic dramas. The theatres were adapting to attract a growing, diversifying audience (one playwright, Hannah Cowley [1743–1809], gave it all up in disgust). Drury Lane and Covent Garden each trebled their capacity between 1700 and 1800; their rivals included the so-called illegitimate theatres, such as Astley's Amphitheatre and Sadler's Wells, and Italian opera at the King's Theatre. And there were still traditional opportunities for performers such as Bartholomew Fair, with its booths and puppet shows. In London as elsewhere in the British Isles, the eighteenth century saw an exhilarating proliferation of show *businesses*. But what was showing?

The audience, for one thing. People came to the theatre, as they had always done, to see one another and be seen. The rowdy auditorium was its own form of entertainment, offering opportunities for unabashed exhibitionism, flirtation and prostitution, possibly thievery and rioting. When the patent theatres tried, in 1762, to abolish the custom of half-price entry for those who arrived after the third act of a play, they paid the price in broken benches, smashed scenery and terrorized actors. In *Amusements Serious and Comical* (1700), Tom Brown called the theatre 'the *Land of Enchantment*, the *Country of Metamorphosis*', but he was thinking of audiences, not plays – of those 'Persons of all Degrees and Qualities whatsoever, that have a great deal of Idle Time lying upon their Hands, and cannot tell how to employ it worse', from '*Lords* [who] come to Laugh, and to be Laugh'd at for being there' to country gentlemen who 'trouble the Pit with their Impertinence about Hawking, Hunting, and their Handsome Wives' and ladies with 'Scab'd, or Pimpled Faces, [who] wear a thousand Patches to hide them', as well as fops, mild citizens and drunken bullies.

If the theatregoer succeeded in drawing his attention away from these curiosities, he might have seen much the same characters on stage. Lords, country gentlemen, loose-moralled ladies and others constituted the stock types that eighteenth-century playwrights inherited from their seventeenth-century predecessors. Indeed, the witty comedies of John Vanbrugh (1664–1726) and William Congreve (1670–1729) proved immensely popular with eighteenth-century audiences – though they were generally performed without the bursts of profanity and immorality that had so inflamed the Reverend Jeremy Collier (1650–1726) against the stage in the 1690s.

There was greater diversity in the eighteenth-century repertoire, however, than this would suggest. There were adaptations of Shakespeare (such as Nahum Tate's *King Lear* with a happy ending) and his contemporaries; sentimental comedies such as *The Conscious Lovers* (1722) by Richard Steele (1672–1729); the vastly successful *Beggar's Opera* (1728) by John Gay (1685–1732), in a category of its own; the bourgeois tragedy of *The London Merchant* (1731) by George Lillo (1693–1739); the rise of the 'afterpiece', usually a comic or musical supplement to the main event; not to mention the seeming revival of 'laughing comedy' with *She Stoops to Conquer* (1773) by Oliver Goldsmith (?1730–74), and *The Rivals* (1775) and *The School for Scandal* (1777) by Richard Brinsley Sheridan (1751–1816). The list could go on . . .

One name that could be added to it is that of Henry Fielding, who was, before he wrote *Tom Jones*, a playwright. As manager of the Haymarket Theatre in the 1730s, Fielding had staged plays that repeatedly (and popularly) satirized the Prime Minister, Robert Walpole (1676–1745) – prompting the latter to introduce the Licensing Act in 1737. Fielding's brief success turned out to be, in the long term, disastrous. From then on, the law required that all plays for performance had to be submitted to the Lord Chamberlain's Office, where they could be examined for sedition and libel – and dramatic literature would thus receive the censorious attentions of the authorities for the next two centuries (the statute was abolished in 1968) (see p. 122, Chapter 6, Key Critical Concepts and Topics: Copyright and Censorship). The eighteenth century's great entertainments, it is worth remembering, could be cancelled at the touch of a censor's pencil.

Michael Caines

Contexts

Eighteenth-century Print Culture

For some people, by the end of the eighteenth century, there were simply too many books and too much printed material. 'Oh ye great authors luminous, voluminous!', Byron wrote mockingly in Canto IX of *Don Juan* (1819–24). 'Ye twice ten hundred thousand daily scribes, / Whose pamphlets, volumes, newspapers illumine us!' Newspapers alone had, by then, spread to every corner of England, Scotland and Ireland, so that, outside London, there were fifty in England alone by the 1780s, selling millions of copies. London itself had daily papers, as well as a weekly, specialist and Sunday press. By 1800, about 6,000 books were being published in a year, rising from 1,800 in 1700. The number of paper mills had doubled in the same period. Circulating libraries had appeared. The historian Edward Gibbon (1737–94), trying to keep track of his collection of some 5,000 or 6,000 books, invented the card index, writing the book details on the backs of playing cards.

Statistics tell one version of the story; they begin to make more sense when it is remembered that print and periodical culture in the British Isles underwent this great transformation thanks to a gradual legal revolution (see p. 122, Chapter 6, Key Critical Concepts and Topics: Copyright and Censorship). 'To kill a man', John Milton (1608–74) had written in *Areopagitica* in 1644, 'is to kill a reasonable human being; but to kill a book is to kill reason itself'. Reason,

Milton had argued, was God-gifted – so the age of censorship that the English Parliament had created with the Licensing Order of 1643 (in the wake of the abolished royal mechanisms of pre-publication censorship) could be seen as a violation of that divine right. But the violation would continue until the 1690s, when the Order was debated, briefly renewed and finally permitted to lapse. Though what Milton had called 'the liberty of unlicensed printing' could still be curtailed and challenged, if required, by post-publication censorship – trial for obscenity or sedition, for example – this was to prove an essential advance.

There were further changes in the law to come. In 1710, the 'Statute of Anne' granted authors and their chosen publishers exclusive ownership of their works for fourteen years, after which time they could either renew their contract or allow their intellectual property to enter the public domain (at least, this was how the theory went; reality could prove more complicated). And much later, in 1774, perpetual copyright – a concept that harked back to the glory days of the Stationers Company, with its monopoly on classical and Renaissance texts – was abolished.

The result of this reasonable progress – and the broader trends in society as a whole – was that the individual author and the enterprising bookseller had a much greater degree of freedom and more opportunities for unfettered profit than did (for one pertinent example) their French counterparts. Throughout the century, the French Office of the Book Trade operated an efficient and increasingly ruthless regime, that burned and banned some of the more threateningly radical books produced by French Enlightenment thinkers, and saw, by the 1730s, more than 100 writers, printers or their business associates under lock and key in the Bastille.

Not everybody thought that booksellers and authors doing such good business was good per se. And it should be remembered that out of a tradesman's income of £40–50 per annum, an addiction to poetry or novels could prove prohibitively expensive (five shillings being a stretch, ten being a luxury). But this did not stop Samuel Johnson saying to two Scottish friends, James Boswell (1740–95), who wrote down what was said, and Allan Ramsay (1686–1758), over dinner on 29 April 1778, 'We must read what the modern world reads at the moment'. Johnson identified both good and bad aspects to the eighteenth-century publishing explosion:

> It has been maintained that this superfoetation, this teeming of the press in modern times, is prejudicial to good literature, because it obliges us to read so much of what is of inferiour value, in order to be in the fashion; so that better works are neglected for want of time, because a man will have more gratification of his vanity in conversation, from having read modern books, than from having read the best works of antiquity. But it must be

> considered, that we have now more knowledge generally diffused; all our ladies read now, which is a great extension. . . .

This 'great extension' was certainly not welcomed by all. Not 'all the ladies' were thought to benefit, for example, from reading romances, either the titillating pulp fictions of Eliza Haywood (?1693–1756) (*Love in Excess* [1719–20], *Fantomina* [1725], *The History of Miss Betsy Thoughtless* [1751]) or the more antiquated, pre-eighteenth century variety. The consequences of such reading became a literary trope that tapped conventional anxieties about the dangers of over-literal reading, as demonstrated by the title of Charlotte Lennox's most popular work, *The Female Quixote* of 1752, and Lydia Languish, the book-brained heroine of Richard Brinsley Sheridan's comedy *The Rivals* (1775).

Booksellers knew exactly how to exploit eager demand for reading matter. Haywood's *Miss Betsy Thoughtless*, for example, first appeared in 1751, published by T. Gardner. Four more editions appeared, as well as a theatrical adaptation and translations into French and German, before the novel appeared again in 1783, this time as the thirteenth volume of a magazine. Comparably, Tobias Smollett's *Complete History of England* was first published in four volumes in 1757–58, but when the author embarked on a *Continuation* a couple of years later, the instalments began to appear in weekly numbers, for sixpence each, thus putting them within the financial reach of the less well-off. This form of publishing, in 'fascicles' of sixteen or thirty-two pages, could be a highly profitable enterprise; Smollett himself is thought to have made an impressive £2,000 from the *History* and its *Continuation*.

In short, as far as books were concerned, the eighteenth century could be thought of as a richly various and jostling marketplace, in which authors struggled to appear the most important figures – the eighteenth century also had its extraordinary readers, editors, critics, booksellers (not least Pope's old foe, the wily Edmund Curll [1683–1747] and book collectors Topham Beauclerk [1739–80], for instance, owned a library of some 30,000 titles). Milton might not have approved of everything that was published, but the principle of the freedom to publish he would have understood.

Michael Caines

Eighteenth-century Science

What we now call 'science' was in the eighteenth century known as 'natural philosophy', a difference in terminology which reflects the lack of any special professional status in the period for those who studied the natural world. This lack of specialization is reflected in the diverse range of achievements of figures such as Joseph Priestley (1733–1804), the discoverer of oxygen but also central to the theological development of rational dissent, and Erasmus

Darwin (1731–1802), whose interests ranged from botany to atmospheric physics, poetry and medical theory.

It was impossible in the eighteenth century to make a living purely as an experimental scientist and, for this reason, science was closely allied with medicine, which offered substantial financial rewards for doctors who succeeded in building up a wealthy clientele: Erasmus Darwin's scientific interests were underwritten by his medical practice, as was the work of pioneering comparative anatomist and surgeon John Hunter (1728–93), whose collection of anatomical specimens (called the Hunterian Museum) can still be visited at the Royal College of Surgeons. Even those scientists who made a living from teaching did so in a context which was largely shaped by the demands of medical students, something true as much of the renowned chemist Joseph Black (1728–99), holder of professorships at Glasgow and Edinburgh, as of the many travelling lecturers the importance of whose contribution to the development of scientific knowledge has been highlighted by recent scholarship.

The tendency to regard science as a form of philosophy testifies to the influence of philosophical empiricism on eighteenth-century thought, an outlook identified with the philosopher John Locke (1632–1704). Locke's extensive scientific interests influenced the key philosophical claim of his *Essay Concerning Human Understanding* (1690) that words were meaningless unless they corresponded to an idea in the mind which ultimately originated in sense-perception. Locke was hostile to rhetoric because he suspected it obscured the correspondence between words and ideas which constituted truth, and this emphasis on the intellectual value of the plain style, which was extremely influential in the eighteenth century, can be traced back to the *History of the Royal Society* (1667) by Thomas Sprat (1635–1713).

In *Gulliver's Travels*, Jonathan Swift satirized the empiricist claim that words and ideas must correspond, by portraying the philosophers of the academy of Lagado as so distrustful of language that they have to carry round heavy backpacks containing objects at which to point. It has been suggested that Daniel Defoe was influenced by the Royal Society's promotion of the plain style, as reflected in the relentlessly observational journal entries with which his novel *Robinson Crusoe* abounds. Although Locke himself explicitly excluded the revealed language of the Bible from his requirement that all words should be derivable from sensory ideas, some of his followers were not so cautious, with religious freethinkers such as John Toland (1670–1722) and Anthony Collins (1676–1729) controversially advocating natural religion on the basis of a Lockean argument that, since the meaning of words derived from the senses, religious ideas could not legitimately claim to transcend the natural world.

The mathematical formulation of the principle of gravity by Isaac Newton

(1643–1727) was the paradigmatic scientific discovery of the eighteenth century, a breakthrough hailed by Alexander Pope in a near-blasphemous rewriting of Genesis, 'Nature and nature's laws lay hid in Night. / God said, "Let Newton be!" and all was light.' Newton was taken as having defined the scientific method, and as a consequence most eighteenth-century thinkers asserted their own Newtonianism through devising explanatory systems based on a small number of simple principles: the economics of Adam Smith (1723–90), for example, can be seen as a Newtonian system, and Smith himself in his essay on the history of astronomy explained the development of science in these Newtonian terms, as motivated by the search for increasingly simple and elegant intellectual systems.

The influence of Newtonian method can be seen in the philosophy of David Hume (1711–76), which seeks to explain mental processes through the transmission of force (or 'vivacity') between ideas. Priestley regarded the Newtonian appeal to an immaterial force, in the form of gravity, as implying a far-reaching unification of the realms of matter and spirit. Commentators have noted that this agenda of problematizing the distinction between materiality and the immaterial underlay both Priestley's scientific study of electricity and gases and his radical unitarian theology. Priestley was an active popularizer of an Enlightenment model of science as an intellectual pursuit accessible to the educated general public, but in the aftermath of the French Revolution, his approach to science became suspect as a result of its association with his political radicalism, and was gradually replaced by a more specialized and laboratory-based approach.

Priestley was a member of the Lunar Society, a Birmingham-based group who shared an interest in science and its application, and who brought about a number of far-reaching technological innovations which led to the Industrial Revolution. One of the most significant of these was the condensing steam-engine, developed by the Scottish engineer James Watt (1736–1819) in partnership with Birmingham entrepreneur Matthew Boulton (1728–1809). The adoption by Lancashire factory pioneer Richard Arkwright (1732–92) of this engine revolutionized the textile industry.

The prominent industrialist Josiah Wedgwood (1730–95), whose pottery business is regarded as having pioneered consumerist culture, was also a member of the Lunar Society, and as well as being an early adopter of the steam-engine promoted canals as a means of transport for freight. Another important member was Erasmus Darwin, whose medical friend Thomas Beddoes (1760–1808) drew on Lunar Society patronage and the chemical engineering expertise of Watt in setting up his Pneumatic Institute in Bristol, a clinic for the study of the medical effects of gases which provided the young Humphrey Davy (1778–1829) with his first scientific post.

Gavin Budge

4 Case Studies in Reading I: Key Primary Literary Texts

Anne Chandler

Chapter Overview

Alexander Pope's *Essay on Criticism* (1711)

(See p. 53, Chapter 3, Major Figures, Institutions, Topics, Events, Movements: Alexander Pope and Eighteenth-Century Poetry; See p. 122, Chapter 6, Key Critical Concepts and Topics: Criticism)

The most influential poem of the early eighteenth century asks us to view 'criticism' not as a fault-finding mission, but as an earnest search for beauty and coherence in art. Thus, Pope's opening complaint about the threat of frivolous commentary to serious literature leads to a broader wish that our faculties of 'wit' and 'judgement' could be made to work in concert with the higher truths governing the universe, truths he collectively designates 'Nature'. The mediating force between intellect and Nature was, for Pope, the literary-humanist tradition founded in ancient Greece, and such is Pope's conviction about the emotive power of this tradition that the poem still speaks clearly to students of the liberal arts.

(1)

'Tis with our judgements as our watches, none
Go just alike, yet each believes his own.
In poets as true genius is but rare,

True taste as seldom is the critic's share;
Both must alike from Heaven derive their light,
These born to judge, as well as those to write.
Let such teach others who themselves excel,
And censure freely who have written well;
Authors are partial to their wit, 'tis true,
But are not critics to their judgement too? (l. 9–18)

Comment

By the time we reach this second verse paragraph of the poem, we might feel dizzy from the crisscrosses Pope has used in lines 1–8 to argue that the self-generating nature of criticism – a multitude of voices, finding easy expression in print – dwarfs any initial problem critics claim to address. Everyone believes in the validity of his own opinion, but if 'true genius' is a rare commodity in literature, 'true taste' in critical judgement is equally rare. Those who would harangue others about style, he says, had better be stylists themselves. Pope's rhetorical balancing of authors and critics is meant to even out a burden of proof that he feels has been assigned disproportionately to authors. He reinforces this point through implicit reference to Locke's *Essay Concerning Human Understanding* (1690), where 'wit', the ability to make clever verbal associations, is deemed a lesser faculty than 'judgement', the ability to make logical or qualitative distinctions. Elsewhere in the poem, Pope (no special proponent of Locke) casts doubt on this cognitive hierarchy; here, he merely indicates that a contest between wit and judgement would be a meaningless tug-of-war if viewed within the confines of the individual psyche, critic's or writer's. Rather, 'Both must alike from Heaven derive their light'.

(2) Nature to all things fixed the limits fit,
And wisely curbed proud man's pretending wit.
As on the land while here the ocean gains,
In other parts it leaves wide sandy plains;
Thus in the soul while memory prevails,
The solid power of understanding fails;
Where beams of warm imagination play,
The memory's soft figures melt away.
One science only will one genius fit;
So vast is art, so narrow human wit:
Not only bounded to peculiar arts,
But oft in those confined to single parts.
Like kings we lose the conquest gained before,
By vain ambition still to make them more;

Each might his several province well command,
Would all but stoop to what they understand. (l. 52–67)

Comment

In positing a divinely ordained limit to human knowledge, Pope's subtext of intellectual pride aligns this passage with Milton's *Paradise Lost*. What hubris is for the tragic hero, what kryptonite was for Superman, the hazy, self-serving memory is for the scholar. Pope's territorial analogy sees memory, understanding and imagination competing to occupy the same finite mental ground: the sea encroaches, and the land disappears. This phenomenon is compounded by the sad reality that most of us are doomed to be good at only one thing in the grand scheme of intellectual endeavour. Art is 'vast', a universe (and in line 74, linked to Nature); 'human wit' is 'narrow' (line 61). To pretend otherwise is to be like a grasping monarch with imperial ambitions. Why do critics, or would-be scholars, Pope asks, so often claim more intellectual turf than they can defend?

(3) First follow Nature, and your judgment frame
By her just standard, which is still the same.
Unerring Nature, still divinely bright,
One clear, unchanged, and universal light,
Life, force, and beauty must to all impart,
At once the source, and end, and test of art. (l. 68–73)

Comment

This directive is one of the most inspiring moments of the poem, and one of the hardest to pin down. Clearly Pope is upping the ante from 'judgement' in the sense of discrimination to a 'just standard' aligned with Nature herself. But what is that standard, and how do you 'frame' your judgement with it? Granting that Nature could always remain the same, how might it also serve as a 'test' of art? As if to forestall these questions, Pope turns, in lines 74–87, to analogies which may or may not clarify the matter – figurations of 'Nature' feeding art much as the soul nourishes the body, and of judgement reining in a superabundance of wit as a trainer would tame a stallion.

In lines 88–117, Pope spells out the proper relation of criticism to literary tradition. 'Those rules of old discovered, not devised, / Are Nature still, but Nature methodised' (l. 88–9) refer to classical precepts of literary decorum, which envision a close fit between form and content. Great writers 'follow Nature' while also paying their respects to man-made traditions. Pope argues that his culture has lost its sense of how criticism should, in its turn, 'follow' literature. The Greeks had it right, he says, because writers and critics sought the 'universal light' through the inspiring example of *their* predecessors

(l. 98–9), and 'The generous critic fanned the poet's fire / And taught the world with reason to admire' (l. 100–1), much as a handmaiden would dress her mistress to advantage (l. 102–3). Now, though, critics perform not as disinterested arbiters but as vindictive 'wits' – 'woo[ing] the maid', i.e. critical commentary, when they cannot 'win the mistress', i.e. recognition for their own artistic abilities (l. 104–5).

(4) Be Homer's works your study and delight,
Read them by day, and meditate by night;
Thence form your judgement, thence your maxims bring,
And trace the Muses upward to their spring. (l. 124–7)

* * *

Perhaps [Virgil] seemed above the critic's law,
And but from Nature's fountains scorned to draw;
But when to examine every part he came,
Nature and Homer were, he found, the same.
Convinced, amazed, he checks the bold design,
And rules as strict his labored work confine
As if the Stagirite o'erlooked each line.
Learn hence for ancient rules a just esteem;
To copy Nature is to copy them. (l. 132–40)

* * *

Oh, may some spark of your celestial fire,
The last, the meanest of your sons inspire
(That on weak wings, from far, pursues your flights,
Glows while he reads, but trembles as he writes) . . . (l. 195–8)

Comment

These passages are distinguished by their concentration of imperative and exclamatory statements; by their varied use of water motifs as related to inspiration (leading to the famous 'Drink deep' injunction of Part II); and by their extravagance in praising Homer, Aristotle ('the Stagirite') and Virgil. It is important that Aristotle was an ancient writer to Virgil, and Homer even more so. Pope promotes a sense of historical consciousness that differs from a simple model of progressive change. Excitement, speed and discovery all reside in classical antiquity.

The devotional tone of these passages suggests that Pope sought not only to correct others, but to internalize for himself the 'celestial fire' of the ancients. 'Read them by day, and meditate by night' – 'Convinced, amazed, he checks the bold design' – 'Glows while he reads, but trembles as he writes': these are expressions of almost religious fervour. Receptive to the lessons of his forebears, Pope embraces the task of 'copying' them much as a monk, transcribing a fragile manuscript, would have been conveying its knowledge to future generations. Yearning to join the pantheon, 'glow[ing]' with excitement as a reader, Pope is at pains to say that he 'trembles' with a due sense of humility when he puts pen to paper.

(5) A little learning is a dangerous thing:
Drink deep, or taste not the Pierian spring.
There shallow draughts intoxicate the brain,
And drinking largely sobers us again.
Fired at first with what the Muse imparts,
In fearless youth we tempt the heights of arts,
While from the bounded level of our mind
Short views we take, nor see the lengths behind;
But more advanced, behold with strange surprise
New distant scenes of endless science rise!
So pleased at first the towering Alps we try,
Mount o'er the vales, and seem to tread the sky,
The eternal snows appear already past,
And the first clouds and mountains seem the last;
But, those attained, we tremble to survey
The growing labors of the lengthened way,
The increasing prospect tires our wandering eyes,
Hills peep o'er hill, and Alps on Alps arise! (l. 215–32)

Comment

These metaphors initiate a second line of argument, equally applicable to poets and critics, which states that the 'rules' must be supplemented by individual discipline, desire and talent. Pope's first formulation is paradoxical but finally self-explanatory: the waters of knowledge intoxicate us only at first taste, before we know very much. His second, really an epic simile of changed perspective through learning, is the most dramatic of the poem's analogies. Where the earlier territorial metaphor concerned the mental limitations of humankind, this analogy treats the dynamics of individual aspiration. In Pope's day, climbing the Alps was a largely imaginary enterprise, the province of philosophic reveries and theological topographies. Only later, with the help of Edmund Burke's 1757 treatise on aesthetics, would landscape sublimity come to be widely viewed as a medium for self-discovery. Pope's anticipation of that later movement in this passage is exciting, and it partly accounts for the lingering influence of the poem. Mainly he urges the chastening effect of wider views – note the recurrence of the word 'tremble' – yet there is 'glowing' here, too, something thrilling about the 'strange surprise' and the Icarus-like treading of the sky. Even as the 'increasing prospect tires our wandering eyes', Pope gives no signal that the climber should turn back.

The mandate to keep going is followed by a rehabilitation of 'wit' as the vehicle for Nature's coherence: 'In wit, as nature, what affects our hearts / Is not the exactness of peculiar parts; / 'Tis not a lip, or eye, we beauty call, / But the joint force and full result of all' (l. 243–6). Pope is now doing for wit what he first did for judgement, which is to make it a transcendent and semi-mystical force, at least within the microcosm of human creativity. Turnabout is fair play: if writers must look upward and align themselves with pre-existing standards of judgement, critics must meet wit halfway too, reading for the spirit as well as the letter, and accepting the communal dimension of 'what affects our hearts'.

(6) False eloquence, like the prismatic glass,
Its gaudy colors spreads on every place;
The face of Nature we no more survey,
All glares alike, without distinction gay.
But true expression, like the unchanging sun,
Clears and improves whate'er it shines upon;
It gilds all objects, but it alters none.
Expression is the Dress of Thought, and still
Appears more decent as more suitable . . . . (l. 311–19)

Comment

This passage exemplifies a longer sequence (l. 285–383) in which Pope discusses three misapprehensions of wit – as clever conceit, as ornamental diction, and as mechanistic versification – by critics who view poetry in narrowly formalist terms. (Later, in lines 394–473, he tackles the problem of political prejudice in criticism.) As if to illustrate the problem, Pope introduces two conceits of his own – involving qualities of light and aspects of 'dress' – and runs through so many permutations (positive and negative connotations of each; light leading to dress, or vice-versa) that no cumulative meaning can be derived. The most famous lines, 'True wit is Nature to advantage dressed, / What oft was thought, but ne'er so well expressed' (l. 297–8), follow Pope's hypothetical case of the artist who relies on heavy drapery to hide his ignorance of anatomy, but really stand better by themselves, as an aphorism with just a hint of metaphor. Such memorable turns of phrase illustrate Pope's breathtaking command of the heroic couplet. Similarly, the lines quoted above, which use the light conceit (as well as a graceful triplet) to disparage stylistic posturing, do not deliver new information, but rather confirm that Nature, in this metaphorical setting, can still be revealed through wit.

The movement of lines 311–18 is a miniature version of what Pope will go on to do in the master-class format of lines 337–83, where he demonstrates the clumsy results of a rigid adherence to the rules of poetic form, and then goes on, beautifully, to show how a real artist breathes life into those principles. Here, lines 311–14 purposefully scan poorly, but lines 315–18 scan perfectly, as Pope leaves 'false eloquence' behind and turns to characterize 'true expression', an advancement even from wit.

(7) Ah, ne'er so dire a thirst of glory boast,
Nor in the critic let the man be lost!
Good nature and good sense must ever join;
To err is human, to forgive divine. (l. 522–5)

All seems infected that th'infected spy,
As all looks jaundiced to the jaundiced eye.
Learn then what morals critics ought to show,
For 'tis but half a judge's task, to know.
'Tis not enough, taste, judgement, learning, join;
In all you speak, let truth and candor shine:
That not alone what to your sense is due
All may allow, but seek your friendship too. (l. 558–65)

Comment

These passages represent a transition from pessimism to optimism, in which Pope's earlier complaints are converted into an appeal to humanistic large-mindedness as opposed to academic specialization or political partnership. This is consistent with Pope's suggestion, in intervening lines, that critics look to the political scene, not to art, for 'crimes' to prosecute (l. 528–9); and he develops a picture of 'dullness' and 'obscenity' (l. 531) as twin scourges that found cultural purchase during the reign of Charles II (1660–85). As elsewhere in the poem, Pope uses metaphors of humoral excess. Humoral medicine derived from the ancient Greek idea that health and personality depended on relative proportions of blood (exuberance); phlegm (sluggishness); choler (irritability) and black bile (melancholy). Pope uses the metaphor of humoral excess to condemn the sort of one-track thinking that purports to be varied and new: the 'jaundiced eye' (a combination of irritability and melancholy) of critical antagonism is not merely impaired, but diseased.

Lines 560–65 return to Pope's positive view of criticism in surprisingly restrained terms. Indeed, the poem will close with a review of literary history that must be called reflective rather than rousing. Briefly, Pope will voice exasperation in the spirit of Diogenes: 'But where's the man, who counsel can bestow, / Still pleased to teach, and yet not proud to know?' (l. 631–2 ff.). But the more pervasive spirit of the final sequence is one of calm resolution. Pope appeals here to a notion of critics and writers as allies. Although 'friendship' in the early eighteenth century tended to connote sponsorship or familial protection, there is a voluntary sense of community implied in Pope's idea that writers might actually 'seek' interaction with critics who operate in good faith. To urge that 'In all you speak, let truth and candor shine' is to link critical analysis with the larger principle of Nature as the 'universal light', and to offer critics themselves – if they will accept it – the 'celestial fire' of inspiration.

Samuel Johnson's *Rambler* No. 4 (1750)

(See p. 52, Chapter 3, Literary and Cultural Contexts: Samuel Johnson)

Johnson's periodical-essay series *The Rambler* (1750–52) and *The Idler* (1758–60) insist upon the moral *and* material dimensions of literature. Johnson's methods of illustration range from the humorously anecdotal to the earnestly sermonic; he often cites foibles recognizably his own, expressing his religious conviction that all humans in this vale of tears are flawed, self-deceiving and prone to error. Still, as a true child of the eighteenth century, he also applies a kind of anthropological eagerness to his essays, even those employing the traditional device of the archetypal character-study. Johnson forefronts *experiential* evaluations of art and ideas, and this injects a sense of boundless curiosity into the voice of his essayistic persona.

The much-anthologized *Rambler* No. 4 (31 March 1750) typifies this blend of humanism and didacticism. Widely understood as a critical response to Henry Fielding's novel *Tom Jones* (1749), the essay never names Fielding (1707–54) (or any other living writer); it therefore transcends a standard 'review' format, existing more truly as a meditation on the moral issues raised by various types of novelistic realism (see p. 50, Chapter 3, Literary and Cultural Contexts: Henry Fielding). According to Boswell, Johnson preferred the mode of psychological realism offered by Samuel Richardson (1689–1761) in *Pamela* (1740–41) and *Clarissa* (1747–48); he characterized Richardson as a watchmaker, and Fielding as someone who merely tells the time. Whereas Richardson's epistolary fiction clearly signposts virtue and vice through characters' own words, Fielding's omniscient narrator assumes a 'comic epic' view of the proceedings, archly subverting our expectations of moral and poetic justice. What happens, Johnson asks, when such relativism meets with our natural urge to view characters as real people? Since modern novelists can safely assume a widening and educationally diverse readership, famously described by Johnson as 'the common reader', they must ensure they take a morally responsible stance towards this new market. Backed by these questions, *Rambler* No. 4 serves both to examine the rise of the novel and to explore the psychology of reading.

(1) Epigraph and First Paragraph

> *Simul et jucunda et idonea dicere vitae.*
> ('And join both profit and delight in one') Horace, *Ars Poetica*

> The works of fiction, with which the present generation seems more particularly delighted, are such as exhibit life in its true state, diversified only by accidents that daily happen in the world, and influenced by passions and qualities which are really to be found in conversing with mankind.

Comment

Johnson's epigraph lends the essay familiar Augustan (see Glossary, page 201) parameters, but is then applied to contemporary fiction in unexpected ways. Johnson is not merely seconding Horace's formulaic blend of usefulness and pleasure, but making his own statement about where 'the present generation' locates these values. His modifiers 'true', 'only', 'daily', and 'really' connote practicality and forthrightness, with the implication that domestic realism will promote clear thinking. This is in contrast to romances whose absurdities, such as giants snatching ladies away as they are about to be married, develop a state of mind not suited to dealing with the real world. 'Why this wild strain of imagination found reception so long, in polite and learned ages', Johnson goes on to say at the beginning of paragraph 4, 'it is not easy to conceive'. The remark flatters the modern reader's sense of artistic progress. But Johnson will soon go on to show that the distinction between realism and romance is not as clear cut as he at first states it to be. What matters is not how credible a story is but how it affects behaviour.

(2) Paragraphs 5 and 6

> The task of our present writers is very different; it requires, together with that learning which is be gained from books, that experience which can never be attained by solitary diligence, but must arise from general converse and accurate observation of the living world. . . . They are engaged in portraits of which every one knows the original, and can detect any deviation from exactness of resemblance. Other writings are safe, except from the malice of learning, but these are in danger from every common reader. . . .

> But the fear of not being approved as just copiers of human manners, is not the most important concern that an author of this sort ought to have before him. These books are written chiefly to the young, the ignorant, and the idle, to whom they serve as lectures of conduct, and introductions into life. They are the entertainment of minds unfurnished with ideas, and therefore easily susceptible of impressions; not fixed by principles, and therefore easily following the current of fancy; not informed by experience, and consequently open to every false suggestion and partial account.

Comment

Paragraph 5 begs the question of how important mimesis actually is to the experience of novel-reading, but for now that question is quietly stowed under the rug, as Johnson turns in paragraph 6 to what has been his real subject all along. A novelist's 'most important concern', he says here, is not that an imperfect realism will be scorned by the 'common reader', but that this same reader is vulnerable – by virtue of realism's powerful sway – to the novelist's own moral compass, or lack thereof. Johnson manages this transition in an interesting way. Rather than introduce the issue as a moral problem for those readers who are susceptible of being led astray, he presents it, first, as a moral problem for authors: they will be the *agents* of this manipulation. The erstwhile victim of an ill-informed reading public is now the potential victimizer of 'the young, the ignorant, and the idle'.

Johnson's depiction of impressionability is uncharacteristically elitist and deliberately overstated. He conjures up a naïve reader whose need for guidance goes unmet by the witty sophistication of a novelist like Fielding. Such a reader, smitten by Fielding's attractive hero, might seek out the amorous adventures that come Tom's way, and expect to be exonerated as Tom is. (For the added imputation of sexual curiosity in youthful readers, see paragraph 7.) This argument resembles modern indictments of animated cartoons as dangerous to children; indeed, Johnson will later say that in fiction, 'vice ... should always disgust'.

The sentence beginning 'They are the entertainment ...' represents Johnsonian syntax, in its virtuosic use of grammatical parallelism. Here, the orator's 'rule of three' drives home the point that the young lack judgement and will therefore indiscriminately imitate characters they encounter in fiction. Johnson's dazzling sentences mark a world of critical thinking into which he seeks to usher as many of his fellow 'common readers' as possible – an effort that becomes clearer in his later paragraphs.

(3) Paragraphs 9 and 10

> [W]hen an adventurer is levelled with the rest of the world . . . [,] young spectators fix their eyes upon him with closer attention, and hope by observing his behaviour and success to regulate their own practices, when they shall be engaged in the like part.
>
> For this reason these familiar histories may perhaps be made of greater use than the solemnities of professed morality, and convey the knowledge of vice and virtue with more efficacy than axioms and definitions. But if the power of example is so great, as to take possession of the memory by a kind of violence, and produce effects almost without the intervention of the will, care ought to be taken that, when the choice is unrestrained, the best examples only should be exhibited. . . .

Comment

Here, common reader meets common protagonist, and Johnson stresses the interpersonal nature of that connection. He imagines 'young spectators' scrutinizing the hero expressly to plan their own movements. Then, while noting the 'power of example', Johnson verges, himself, into a view of the character as a palpable, charismatic presence, capable of ravishing the mind. A contrasting view of readerly identification is expressed in *Rambler* No. 60, which argues that biographies (which 'enchain the heart by irresistible interest') edify readers precisely by showcasing the common emotions that humanize greatness: 'We are all prompted by the same motives, all deceived by the same fallacies, all animated by hope, obstructed by danger, entangled by desire, and seduced by pleasure'. Why this inconsistency? Johnson may have felt that such an appeal to commonality was superfluous for novels, many of which fabricate the struggles of the low-born in great detail; indeed, the exaggerated 'commonness' of Tom Jones, a foundling, may fuel Johnson's complaint, as it enables the storyline's comic mitigations of moral responsibility.

(4) Paragraph 11 and following

> The chief advantage which these fictions have over real life is, that their authors are at liberty, tho' not to invent, yet to select objects, and to cull from the mass of mankind, those individuals upon which the attention ought most to be employ'd; as a diamond, though it cannot be made, may be polished by art, and placed in such a situation, as to display that lustre which before was buried among common stones.

Comment

In paragraphs 11–13, Johnson floats three alternatives to the paradigm of realism. First, his assertion that novelists can 'cull' the finest moral examples from the 'mass of mankind' resembles a Renaissance humanist's view of the literary imagination, notably as expressed in Sidney's *Defence of Poesy* (1598). This view privileges poetry over all other forms of writing for its capacity to create a new, golden world: an idealized version that people can imitate in the service of goodness. Johnson's second option, presented in paragraphs 12 and 13, is to view the novel in more starkly didactic terms, so that it resembles a medieval morality play or Puritan spiritual allegory: 'The purpose of these writings is . . . to teach the means of avoiding the snares which are laid by Treachery for Innocence'.

But the leading metaphor, and the third alternative, is quasi-scientific: the writer's task, Johnson says, is akin to diamond-mining. This conceit balances what is found, with what is created by the author: the diamond 'cannot be made' but 'may be polished'. The irresponsible novelist, by contrast, might offer readers a miscellaneous bag of 'common stones', justifying his haphazardness with the truism that it takes all sorts to make a world. We can see common stones anywhere, Johnson seems to say; art should show us rarer, more beautiful specimens. Later, in paragraph 12, Johnson pits this idea against the convention of art as mimetic: 'If the world be promiscuously described, I cannot see of what use it can be to read the account; or why it may not be as safe to turn the eye immediately upon mankind, as upon a mirror which shows all that presents itself without discrimination'. Unlike a mirror, a cut diamond refracts light in a way strategically planned by a craftsman; the 'polished' diamond is thus a figure for moral 'discrimination' in art.

(5) Paragraphs 14 and 16

> Many writers, for the sake of following nature, so mingle good and bad qualities in their principal personages, that they are both equally conspicuous; and as we accompany them through their adventures with delight, and are led by degrees to interest ourselves in their favour, we lose the abhorrence of their faults. . . .
>
> * * *
>
> Some have advanced . . . that certain virtues have their correspondent faults, and therefore that to exhibit either apart is to deviate from probability. Thus men are observed by Swift to be 'grateful in the same degree as they are resentful'. This principle, with others of the same kind, supposes man to act from a brute impulse . . .; for otherwise, though it should be allowed that gratitude and resentment arise from the same constitution of the passions, it follows not that they will be equally indulged when reason is consulted. . . .

Comment

Setting aside the problem of the feckless hero, Johnson suggests that Pope's 'First follow Nature' dictum (*Essay on Criticism* l. 68) unfortunately has provided false justification for the portrayal of fascinating villains. No calculus of good and evil, he argues, can trump narrative 'delight', which inexorably favours the colourful character. Further, Johnson warns, the notion of temperamental symmetry degrades the power of reason in moral choice. Johnson implies that whereas the real can be processed by reason, the merely realistic tends to impair reason because it is always infused with a *theory* of human nature that engages the indiscriminately curious part of our minds. By extension, he suggests here that it is actually the educated reader who is most susceptible to novelistic gamesmanship, most likely to misconstrue the novelist's clever admission of artifice as a sign of trustworthiness. This subtle problematic applies more accurately to Fielding than does Johnson's earlier alarm about the character as negative influence.

Returning in paragraph 18 to the fallacy of 'good and evil as springing from the same root', Johnson condemns 'all those [writers] ... who confound the colours of right and wrong, and ... mix them with so much art, that no common mind is able to disunite them'. Johnson's new term 'common mind' sheds the elitist connotations of the phrases 'common reader' and 'common stones', grounding his universalist appeal in the physiology of perception.

(6) Final paragraph

> In narratives where historical veracity has no place, I cannot discover why there should not be exhibited the most perfect idea of virtue; of virtue not angelical, nor above probability, for what we cannot credit, we shall never imitate, but the highest and purest that humanity can reach, which, exercised in such trials as the various revolutions of things shall bring upon it, may, by conquering some calamities, and enduring others, teach us what we may hope, and what we can perform. . . .

Comment

Johnson knows perfectly well why fiction does not always 'exhibit' the ideal: his essay has not only dealt with the range of motives that take novelists in other directions, but also, in the process of challenging these motives, has shown that a right-minded attitude to realism is a difficult feat of balance. In general, he recommends allegorically that fiction show a believable 'virtue' being tested by 'various' circumstances, with commensurately variable results. Interestingly, this prescription applies as well to Fielding as to Richardson – and also, incidentally, to the documentary loquacity of failed businessman, successful writer and sometime spy Daniel Defoe (1660–1731) – as to the symbolic economy Johnson would go on to cultivate in *Rasselas* (1759). But Johnson stipulates, in closing, that this believable virtue should appear as 'the highest proof of understanding', and 'vice' as 'the natural consequence of narrow thoughts'.

Thomas Gray's *Elegy Written in a Country Churchyard* (1751)

Addressing the universal question of what any human life can mean to the world, Gray's tremendously popular *Elegy* privileges the dignity of quiet dutifulness over the quest for public recognition. 'The paths of glory lead but to the grave', the poem intones (line 36), but Gray refurbishes the theme of death as the great leveler by appealing to the rich intensity of a sequestered life and its localized remembrance.

Gray's educated speaker evaluates his relation to the unschooled inhabitants of a rural village – people whose histories are made public only through the carvings on their gravestones. Thoughts on class, literacy and communal memory lead him to consider his own mortality, and to wonder how a villager might memorialize him if a fellow-outsider, a 'kindred spirit' (line 96), were later to visit the churchyard. This stunning shift in point-of-view turns the camera on the speaker and incorporates him into the scene he has been observing. The poem's closing 'Epitaph' hints that the primary speaker's lifework resided less in poetry than in friendship.

When viewed alongside Gray's *Sonnet on the Death of Mr. Richard West* (1742), a heart-rending lament on the untimely death of a friend, the *Elegy* is tantalizingly autobiographical. Like *Ode on a Distant Prospect of Eton College* (1742), too, the *Elegy* can be read as an attempt to find solace through distance. Yet that distance is also part of the composition of this poem, which took shape in the years 1746–50. Like Milton's pastoral elegy *Lycidas* (1638), Gray's *Elegy* may be said to link private grief with a larger sense of alienation or cultural loss.

(1) The curfew tolls the knell of parting day,
The lowing herd wind slowly o'er the lea,
The ploughman homeward plods his weary way,
And leaves the world to darkness and to me. (l. 1–4)

Comment

Startlingly telescopic in their focus, these lines evoke communal vitality through dying light and fading sounds. Gray has set aside the 'Graveyard School' motif of the crumbling mansion; his churchyard is a living, breathing institution. The tolling bell does, admittedly, signal a deathlike homecoming, and the consonance and assonance of 'lowing o'er the lea' imitate a lulling effect felt by the observant speaker. But then comes a thrill: the echoic progression of the last phrase, 'to darkness and *to me*'. In the context of Augustan poetry, where personal revelations are muted, Gray's self-reference is electrifying. 'The world' – vacated by other participants – is being bequeathed 'to me', alone in the darkness. The intimacy of this introduction is virtually unmatched in the poetry of the previous eighty years. The sight of the ploughman inspires a spiritual centering-down that anticipates the Wordsworthian idea of a 'wise passiveness'. Accordingly, Gray shuns the rapid shifts of Augustan heroic couplets for more ruminative quatrains.

(2)

Beneath those rugged elms, that yew-tree's shade,
Where heaves the turf in many a mouldering heap,
Each in his narrow cell for ever laid,
The rude forefathers of the hamlet sleep (l. 13–16)

* * *

Let not Ambition mock their useful toil,
Their homely joys, and destiny obscure;
Nor Grandeur hear with a disdainful smile,
The short and simple annals of the poor. (l. 29–32)

Comment

Stanzas 4–9, excerpted above, negotiate between conventional and fresh considerations of rusticity: the speaker is not witnessing but reconstructing scenes of village life, and this process involves literary and verbal association. Thus, while 'rugged elms' aptly shelter 'rude forefathers', the 'heav[ing]' ground shows the eruption of these imagined lives into Gray's consciousness. The family scenes of the intervening sixth stanza conjoin the sentimental tableau with the pastoral idyll to emphasize warmth and energy: 'blazing', 'busy', 'run', 'climb' (l. 21–4). The farmers appear as stout-hearted conquerors of field and forest (l. 25–8), befitting the poem's paradoxical stance towards heroism. But are these archetypes meant to be received as truly heroic, or as cartoonish? Is the speaker's 'Let not . . .' admonition addressed to someone else, to us, or to himself? Possibly these lines rehearse his own shifts in attitude; to eighteenth-century readers, the use of allegorical entities ('Ambition', 'Grandeur') would have been an understandable means of modulating moral and emotional distance from the issue at hand.

Line 32 provocatively implies that gravestone inscriptions are the most meaningful texts that could exist for uneducated people – possibly, for any person.

(3) Perhaps in this neglected spot is laid
Some heart once pregnant with celestial fire . . . (l. 45–6)

* * *

Chill Penury repressed their noble rage,
And froze the genial current of the soul.

Full many a gem of purest ray serene,
The dark unfathomed caves of ocean bear:
Full many a flower is born to blush unseen,
And waste its sweetness on the desert air. (l. 51–6)

Comment

Lines 45 through 60, especially the lines quoted above, bemoan the crushing of individual initiative by material circumstance. 'Noble rage' predictably falls to class oppression, but the 'genial current' is an unexpected casualty: altruism, open-handedness, good humour are also killed by hardship. Almost viscerally – it is warm blood, by implication, that is 'chill[ed]' and 'froze[n]' by poverty, and hot-blooded anger that is 'repressed' – these lines credit the passions of now-unknowable human beings and the living actuality of their place in the community. The sense of life is more palpable here than in the later speculations on the unknown Hampdens, Cromwells and Miltons who never made it out, because those later lines (l. 57–60) may be read as tinged with condescending irony. Lines 53–6 are obvious in message, but again Gray's figurations are noteworthy. To the domestic ordinariness of the village, he has juxtaposed exotic, colourful locales. (Although the adjectival 'desert' or 'desart' connoted desolation as much as aridity, its opposition to 'ocean' invites a momentary picture of the Sahara.) The phrases 'Full many' and 'unfathomed caves of ocean', as well as the image of the buried 'gem', are distorted echoes of Ariel's ditty: 'Full fathom five thy father lies . . . Those are pearls that once were his eyes' (*The Tempest* I.ii.397–9). Gray's gem sounds more like an Arabian Nights treasure, now 'serene' in its removal from human commerce. But if the flower is *born* to blush unseen, what does this say about the 'obscurity' of the poor? Can the implied class difference between polished 'gem' and wild 'flower' successfully signify that nature's laws apply equally to all?

These emblems also relate ambiguously to the speaker. The villagers' isolation resembles the speaker's aloneness, though his state seems semi-voluntary. On one hand, then, these lines might refer to Gray's own experiences of social alienation. The individual friendship alluded to in the poem is not quite the same thing as the steadier social context enjoyed by the villagers; at some level, perhaps, they may be envied. On the other hand, Gray's speaker seems placidly uninformed about the daily lives of agricultural workers. While 'their lot forbade' them (line 65) from engaging in the dramas of national history; the poem is so vague about what would constitute political action for such people that it almost undermines the speaker's respectful attitude towards them.

(4) Far from the madding crowd's ignoble strife,
Their sober wishes never learned to stray;
Along the cool sequestered vale of life
They kept the noiseless tenor of their way. (l. 73–6)

* * *

Their name, their years, spelt by th'unlettered muse,
The place of fame and elegy supply:
And many a holy text around she strews,
That teach the rustic moralist to die. (l. 81–4)

Comment

Lines 73–6 have been repeatedly mined for literary irony; Thomas Hardy titled his bleak chronicle of agricultural depression *Far from the Madding Crowd* (1874). In context, though, the lines can serve simply as rhetorical amplifications of the poem's theme. Their ironic potential is suggested later, in lines 81–4, which again suggest that the speaker and the villagers may have different outlooks on the 'teaching' power of the written word. Is the term 'unlettered muse' gratuitously slighting? Are the scriptural quotations that 'teach the rustic moralist to die' to be understood as tributes to spiritual purity, or, since they seem randomly 'strew[n]', as symptoms of primitive ignorance? The memorials have been described as 'frail', 'uncouth' and even 'shapeless' (l. 78–9). The class gap here can be narrowed, perhaps, if we credit the speaker with an upwelling of affection for the villagers, or if we view these lines as setting up the final 'turn' of the poem.

(5) For thee, who mindful of the unhonoured dead
Dost in these lines their artless tale relate;
If chance, by lonely Contemplation led,
Some kindred spirit shall inquire thy fate,

Haply some hoary-headed swain may say,
'Oft have we seen him at the peep of dawn
Brushing with hasty steps the dews away
To meet the sun upon the upland lawn. . . .' (l. 93–100)

Comment

These lines show the speaker returning to the here-and-now. If he is addressing himself as 'thee', then the 'mindful' writer of 'these lines' that we are reading is also himself. Alternatively, some critics have read 'thee' as referring to the rural artisan responsible for the gravestone inscriptions. In that reading, the stonecutter's graven 'lines' make him a local historian and self-taught poet – thus lending nuance to the class politics of the poem, by lessening its reliance on pastoral cliché. But a reading of 'thee' as self-referential resonates more felicitously with the possibility that Gray's persona is experimenting with several attitudes towards himself, trying to locate his own place in humanity. Thus the colleague he imagines inquiring about his fate is not an 'unlettered muse' (l. 81), but another educated poet. In that event, perhaps ('haply') some ageing peasant will recall having seen the ruminative young man, and will also recall his subsequent burial. The oddness of a privileged youth's burial in the parish grounds is admitted in the suggestion that the villagers were spectators, not participants, in his funeral: 'we saw him borne', says the hypothetical swain (l. 114), implying that nobody among 'us' bore his coffin. Further separation is conveyed in the poem's third appeal to literacy as class marker: 'Approach and read (for thou canst read)' the inscription, says the native to the newcomer (l. 115). The final irony, then, could be that the villagers are just as detached from the main narrator's consciousness as he has been from theirs. It is such unsettling possibilities that ensure the *Elegy*'s continued freshness and profundity.

Frances Burney's *Evelina* (1778)

(See p. 48, Chapter 3, Literary and Cultural Contexts: Frances Burney)

Burney (1752–1840), who enjoyed a friendly acquaintceship with Samuel Johnson among other prominent writers, exploits an aesthetic shift distinct from the one Johnson delineates in *Rambler* No. 4, not simply from romance to realism, but from one kind of realism to another. Like Defoe in *Moll Flanders* (1722), she examines what the patriarchal marriage imperative means for one woman's emotional and material welfare. Unlike Defoe, however, and more concertedly than Richardson or Fielding, Burney highlights continuity in human relationships, and allows the protagonist's maturation to shape the narrative. This paradigm of the *Bildungsroman* or 'novel of education' later prevailed in the Romantic and Victorian eras. Burney's early, influential mode of psychological realism inflects British 'Sentiment' with the confessional approach of Continental writers like Jean-Jacques Rousseau (1712–78) and Johann Wolfgang von Goethe (1749–1832), and thus it fascinatingly mingles ironic self-deprecation with egotistical yearning. *Evelina* registers the consequences of patriarchy rather than agitating for change, but its study of gender and class identity-formation is rich in documentary detail.

Evelina uses a family-romance plot, wherein an impoverished orphan regains nobility. Evelina's father, Sir John Belmont, abandoned her mother (who then died), and now denies paternity; her surrogate parent, the Reverend Mr Villars, fears that a lawsuit against Belmont would fail, and has temporarily provided Evelina the false surname 'Anville'. The fragility of Evelina's social status motivates Villars to resist her inclusion in a London junket proposed by a family friend. Once permitted, the journey is inevitably lengthened, zigzagging between city and country settings, and between rough and refined company, until at last Evelina returns home to 'the best of men'.

(1) From Vol. I, Letter XII (Evelina to Mr Villars)

Thursday morning

The very first person I saw [at Ranelagh] was Lord Orville. I felt so confused! – but he did not see me. After tea, Mrs. Mirvan being tired, Maria and I walked round the room alone. Then again we saw him, standing by the orchestra. . . . He bowed to me; I courtesied, and I am sure I coloured. . . .

I cannot but be hurt at the opinion he entertains of me. It is true my own behaviour incurred it – yet he is himself the most agreeable, and, seemingly, the most amiable man in the world, and therefore it is that I am grieved to be thought ill of by him: for of whose esteem ought we to be ambitious, if not of those who most merit our own? – But it is too late to reflect upon this now. Well I can't help it. – However, I think I have done with assemblies.

This morning was destined for seeing sights, auctions, curious shops, and so forth; but my head ached, and I was not in a humour to be amused, and so I made them go without me, though very unwillingly. They are all kindness.

And now I am sorry I did not accompany them, for I know not what to do with myself. I had resolved not to go to the play to-night; but I believe I shall. In short, I hardly care whether I do or not.

* * *

I thought I had done wrong! Mrs. Mirvan and Maria have been half the town over, and so entertained! – while I, like a fool, staid at home to do nothing. And, at the auction in Pall-mall, whom should they meet but Lord Orville. . . .

I may never have such another opportunity of seeing London; I am quite sorry that I was not of the party; but I deserve this mortification, for having indulged my ill-humour.

Thursday Night
We are just returned from the play, which was King Lear, and has made me very sad. We did not see any body we knew.

Well, adieu, it is too late to write more.

Friday
Captain Mirvan is arrived. I have not spirits to give an account of his introduction, for he has really shocked me. I do not like him. He seems to be surly, vulgar, and disagreeable.

. . . [T]hat kind and sweet-tempered woman, Mrs. Mirvan, deserved a better lot. I am amazed she would marry him. . . .

Comment

Evelina's early letters to Villars, in Richardsonian 'journal' style, illustrate the dynamics of epistolary revelation. At an earlier ball, Lord Orville tried gallantly to remedy Evelina's error of engaging with a predatory dance partner, but then was heard marvelling at her rusticity. Briefly daunted, Evelina still senses a mutual attraction and resumes her analysis of Orville's every gesture. Admitting her earlier mistakes, she insinuates that Orville could have been more tolerant. Then, like many a confessional letter-writer, she affects flippancy in closing.

Her harried request for solitude shows a flash of self-possession, but shortly thereafter she feels lost without the group. Her fluctuating responses 'writing to the moment', in Richardson's coinage – render all events as judgements upon herself, and this sense is compounded as she records Orville's absence from the theatre: the play, *King Lear*, moves her to scrawl a homesick good-night to Villars.

Starkly contrastive is Evelina's condemnation of her chaperone's husband. Mirvan's boorishness is disturbing because he is the son-in-law of Lady Howard, a model of gentility whose rallying letters to Villars show us the more gregarious side of human decency. Evelina's ensuing misadventures (including a brief entanglement with London prostitutes) will be punctuated by Mirvan's jingoistic vendettas and practical jokes.

(2) From Vol. II, Letter II (Evelina to Mr Villars)

I was both uneasy and impatient to know the fate of Madame Duval . . . I desired the footman to show me which way she was gone; he pointed with his finger by way of answer, and I saw that he dared not trust his voice to make any other. I walked on at a very quick pace, and soon, to my great

> consternation, perceived the poor lady seated upright in a ditch. I flew to her with unfeigned concern at her situation. She was sobbing, nay, almost roaring, and in the utmost agony of rage and terror. As soon as she saw me, she redoubled her cries; but her voice was so broken, I could not understand a word she said. I was so much shocked, that it was with difficulty I forebore exclaiming against the cruelty of the Captain . . . and I could not forgive myself for having passively suffered the deception. I used my utmost endeavours to comfort her. . . .
>
> Almost bursting with passion, she pointed to her feet, and with frightful violence she actually tore the ground with her hands.
>
> I then saw that her feet were tied together with a strong rope . . . I endeavoured to untie the knot; but soon found it was infinitely beyond my strength. I was, therefore, obliged to apply to the footman; but, being very unwilling to add to his mirth by the sight of Madame Duval's situation, I desired him to lend me a knife: I returned with it, and cut the rope. . . . But what was my astonishment, when, the moment she was up, she hit me a violent slap on the face! . . . [S]he then loaded me with reproaches, which, though almost unintelligible, convinced me that she imagined I had voluntarily deserted her; but she seemed not to have the slightest suspicion that she had not been attacked by real robbers.

Comment

Here Mirvan has victimized Evelina's maternal grandmother Madame Duval, the ex-barmaid who remarried and settled in France after her first husband's death (thus acquiring a comically Franglish accent). Uncouth, yet vulnerable – seeking reinstatement in Evelina's family – Madame Duval exasperates protagonists and readers alike, even as a feminist lens reveals her position as similar to Evelina's own.

Mirvan's staged hijacking evokes the aftermath of a rape, leading Evelina to feel 'shock' and compassion. She also perceives the 'mirth' of Mirvan's confederates – and, though anxious to undo their work, she does not deny the risibility of the older lady's plight. Indeed, several such episodes operate in their very 'violence' – a term used twice here – almost as slapstick comedy. Madame Duval's animalism, ingratitude and gullibility serve to mitigate the latent 'horror' of the event. Later, Madame Duval misses her hairpiece, lovingly designated 'my curls'; the footman, snickering, retrieves them from the ditch, and she clings to them despite their dirtiness ('I was amazed she would take [them]', says Evelina – echoing her earlier 'amazement' that Mrs Mirvan would have stooped to marry the Captain). Finally, though, Madame Duval's 'stormy passions . . . again roused' by the footman's ridicule, she throws 'the battered curls' in his face. These locutions are unambiguously deflationary, recalling Fielding's mock-epic battles in *Tom Jones*. But the scene is also remarkable for its quieter staging of Evelina's reactions: it is full of physical initiative and oscillating sympathies.

(3) From Vol. II, Letter XXIX (Evelina to her friend Maria Mirvan)

> For some minutes [Villars] was totally silent, and I pretended to employ myself in looking for a book. At last, with a deep sigh, 'I see', said he, 'I see but too plainly, that though Evelina is returned, – I have lost my child!'
>
> 'No, Sir, no', cried I, inexpressibly shocked, 'she is more yours than ever! Without you, the world would be a desert to her, and life a burthen: – forgive her, then, and, – if you can, – condescend to be, once more, the confidant of all her thoughts'.
>
> 'How highly I value, how greatly I wish for her confidence', returned he, 'she cannot but know; – yet to extort, to tear it from her, – my justice, my affection both revolt at the idea. I am sorry that I was so earnest with you; – leave me, my dear, leave me, and compose yourself; we will meet again at tea'.
>
> 'Do you then refuse to hear me?'
>
> 'No, but I abhor to compel you. I have long seen that your mind has been ill at ease, and mine has largely partaken of your concern. . . . But go, my dear, go to your own room; we both want composure, and we will talk of this matter some other time'.
>
> 'Oh, Sir', cried I, penetrated to the soul, 'bid me not leave you! . . .'
>
> * * *
>
> 'My dearest child', cried he, 'I cannot bear to see thy tears; – for my sake dry them: such a sight is too much for me: think of that, Evelina, and take comfort, I charge thee!'
>
> 'Say then', cried I, kneeling at his feet, 'say then that you forgive me! that you pardon my reserve, – that you will again suffer me to tell you my most secret thoughts, and rely upon my promise never more to forfeit your confidence! – my father! – my protector! – my ever-honoured, – ever-loved – my best and only friend! – say you forgive your Evelina, and she will study better to deserve your goodness!'
>
> He raised, he embraced me: he called me his sole joy, his only earthly hope, and the child of his bosom! . . .

Comment

Having earlier compared Evelina to 'a book that both afflicts and perplexes me', Villars easily 'reads' her ill-concealed feelings towards Orville. His tactics recall those of Richardson's Sir Charles Grandison, a hero with a nose for secrets; they also parallel the bait-and-switch moves of the tutor in Rousseau's

Émile (1762).[1] Evelina responds with a shower of tears and filial endearments. Blessings, in Burney's works, are always complex affairs.

The afterglow here is no less complex. Bent on full disclosure from Evelina, Villars is surprised to learn the real problem: a flirtatious (later, we find, forged) letter bearing Orville's name. Villars then turns novelist, reviewing Evelina's emotional vicissitudes. But his account proves incomplete. Even as Evelina assures Maria Mirvan that '[c]oncealment is the foe of tranquillity', she asks her to suppress this blot on Orville's character. Some subversive desires, it seems, really can be kept private.

(4) From Vol. III, Letter IV, and Vol. III, Letter VI (Evelina to Villars; Villars to Evelina)

> Almost insensibly have three days glided on since I wrote last, and so serenely, that, but for your absence, I could not have formed a wish. My residence here is much happier than I had dared expect. The attention with which Lord Orville honours me, is as uniform as it is flattering, and seems to result from a benevolence of heart that proves him as much a stranger to caprice as to pride; for, as his particular civilities arose from a generous resentment at seeing me neglected, so will they, I trust, continue, as long as I shall, in any degree, deserve them. I am now not merely easy, but even gay in his presence: such is the effect of true politeness, that it banishes all restraint and embarrassment. When we walk out, he condescends to be my companion, and keeps by my side all the way we go. When we read, he marks the passages most worthy to be noticed, draws out my sentiments, and favours me with his own. At table, where he always sits next to me, he obliges me by a thousand nameless attentions; while the distinguishing good-breeding with which he treats me, prevents my repining at the visibly-felt superiority of the rest of the company. A thousand occasional meetings could not have brought us to that degree of social freedom, which four days spent under the same roof have, insensibly, been productive of: and, as my only friend in this house, Mrs Selwyn, is too much engrossed in perpetual conversation to attend much to me, Lord Orville seems to regard me as a helpless stranger, and, as such, to think me entitled to his good offices and protection. Indeed, my dear Sir, I have reason to hope, that the depreciating opinion he formerly entertained of me is succeeded by one infinitely more partial. . . .
>
> * * *
>
> Young, animated, entirely off your guard, and thoughtless of consequences, *Imagination* took the reins; and *Reason*, slow-paced, though sure-footed, was unequal to the race of so eccentric and flighty a companion. How rapid was then my Evelina's progress through those

regions of fancy and passion whither her new guide conducted her! – She saw Lord Orville at a ball, – and he was *the most amiable of men!* – She met him again at another, – and *he had every virtue under Heaven*!

Comment

As visitors at neighbouring estates, Evelina and Orville are thrown together under the lax supervision of a bluestocking chaperone. Burney was a fine stylist: the Johnsonian cadences of Evelina's third and fourth statements show the heroine to be quite at ease, unapologetic about her lapse in correspondence. Orville shines forth here as a literary guide, befitting a conduct tradition in which women's aesthetic preferences are shaped and disciplined by men. Alone in the crowd as usual, Evelina glories in Orville's attentions, but injects a quizzical note when she views herself through Orville's eyes as a lost lamb. Such characterization jars with her satisfied sense that Orville is finally, properly, awestruck by her worth. Is Evelina hedging against her mentor's disapproval?

Clearly, the requital of Evelina's infatuation does worry Villars. Sensitive to the risks of unequal marriage, he fears that this nobleman, whatever his virtues, will seduce and abandon Evelina. Further, Orville is now his emotional rival: a triangle has formed. Villars's feverish efforts to bring Evelina home are thwarted. However, his analysis of the situation is essentially accurate. His allegorical warnings (reminiscent of Augustan poetry, and of Fielding) and his turning of Evelina's own words against her (imitative of Richardson) are marks of generational difference, but are wittily deployed. His credibility suffers only when he imputes a peculiarly modern form of depravity to Orville: '[T]his is not an age in which we may trust to appearances', he sputters.

Plot considerations aside, this letter showcases Burney's ventriloquism – her blending of demographics and personality in diction. For an example that does show modern depravity, see the crude gossip of the Branghton siblings, Burney's collective representation of a teenage wasteland in the trading classes.

(5) From Vol. III, Letter XIX (Evelina to Villars on Her Reconciliation with Belmont)

I could restrain myself no longer; I rose and went to him; I did not dare speak; but, with pity and concern unutterable, I wept and hung over him.

Soon after, starting up, he again seized the letter, exclaiming, 'Acknowledge thee, Caroline! – yes, with my heart's best blood would I acknowledge thee! – Oh that thou could'st witness the agony of my soul! – Ten thousand daggers could not have wounded me like this letter!' Then, after again reading it, 'Evelina', he cried, 'she charges me to receive thee; – wilt thou, in obedience to her will, own for thy father the destroyer of thy mother?'

What a dreadful question! – I shuddered, but could not speak.

* * *

Imagine, Sir, – for I can never describe my feelings, when I saw him sink upon his knees before me! 'Oh, dear resemblance of thy murdered mother! – Oh, all that remains of the most injured of women! behold thy father at thy feet! – bending thus lowly to implore you would not hate him. – Oh, then, thou representative of my departed wife, speak to me in her name, and say that the remorse which tears my soul tortures me not in vain!'

'Oh, rise, rise, my beloved father', cried I, attempting to assist him; 'I cannot bear to see you thus; reverse not the law of nature; rise yourself, and bless your kneeling daughter!'

Comment

This scene recalls both Evelina's self-abnegating attitude to Villars and a later, intervening scene in which Orville kneels to Evelina. The novel exults in the idea of three doting fathers who dispense affirmation in several flavours. Paradoxically, this fantasy reinforces all that is strong, autonomous and decisive about Evelina, and notarizes the social education ('A Young Lady's Entrance into the World') that, in real ways, has made her wiser than these men.

Her mother's long-sealed letter affirms Evelina's legitimacy, facilitates her marriage to Orville, and enables a scene of catharsis. As Belmont, increasingly overwrought, begs forgiveness, Evelina keeps her head, remarkably so, given the injuries she has suffered. The logic of Sentiment is to welcome the prodigal son (or father) with open arms, especially when his remorse is so obvious. The physical realities of Evelina and the letter, both proxies for the deceased Caroline, reduce Belmont to a quivering mass. (Cathartic talismans are central to late eighteenth-century fiction.) The early *Lear* reference bears fruit in Belmont's painful recognition of his errors as a father.

The posthumous influence of Caroline Evelyn Belmont resonates biographically with Burney's earliest known work of fiction, whose manuscript she destroyed; titled *Caroline Evelyn*, it is thought to have portrayed the mother Burney lost when just ten years old. *Evelina* considers not only Oedipal tensions, but the power of maternal inheritance and the necessity for women, even those with 'the best' of fathers, to make something of themselves. Burney inserts a series of raucous comic diversions between Belmont's redemption and Evelina's marriage, and closes the novel just before Evelina's long-anticipated homecoming, with the letter she dashes off preparatory to her journey. We sense that she will keep moving.

Note

1 Richardson wrote *The History of Sir Charles Grandison* (1753–4) partly in response to Fielding's *Tom Jones* which had parodied the morals found in Richardson's previous novels, and partly in response to his many female readers who demanded that he create a good male character. The story focuses on Sir Charles after he rescues a woman kidnapped by a rejected suitor. *Émile* or *On Education* (1762) sets out conditions Rousseau thought necessary for the early training of the ideal citizen; sequestration from corrupting social influences; freedom to explore the physical world without strict curricular guidelines; and, paradoxically, autocratic control of all learning situations by the tutor.

5 Case Studies in Reading 2: Key Theoretical and Critical Texts

Steve Newman

Chapter Overview

The 1980s: A 'New Eighteenth Century' Undresses/Redresses *Pamela*

In 1987, a volume of essays appeared edited by Laura Brown and Felicity Nussbaum with the title, *The New Eighteenth Century: Theory, Politics, English Literature*. Its aim was twofold: to show how traditional scholars had resisted the introduction of theory into eighteenth-century studies and to show what contribution theory could make to the field (see p. 134, Chapter 7, Dead Keen on Reason? Changes in Critical Responses and Approaches to the Eighteenth Century).

Students in the twenty-first century may well ask what 'theory' was in 1987 and what it meant for Brown and Nussbaum to claim that eighteenth-century scholarship was 'resisting' it. By the mid-1980s, a wave of Continental theorists, among them Jacques Derrida (1930–2004), Michel Foucault (1926–84), Mikhail Bakhtin (1895–1975), had made their presence strongly felt in the Anglo-American academy and had not only challenged but significantly eclipsed the then-reigning approaches to literary study – the New Criticism and a mode of historicism often referred to as the History of Ideas. The New Criticism, whose eminent practitioners included Cleanth Brooks (1906–94) and W. K. Wimsatt (1907–75), held that the best way to interpret a text was to ignore authorial intent, reader response or historical context and to focus instead on the structure of the text itself.

Their method of looking carefully at the images and ironies of texts came to be known as 'close reading', spawning a pedagogy that many teachers and students still find valuable. Historicism focused on historical contexts as backgrounds that could illuminate literary works; or, alternatively, they considered literary texts as crystallizations of a coherent historical moment, such as 'the Elizabethan World Picture'. Among the important critics in this vein were A. O. Lovejoy, Douglas Bush and Marjorie Hope Nicolson.

So how did the newer forms of theory differ? In contrast to the New Criticism, which emphasized ironies and paradoxes exquisitely balanced in the text, practitioners of newer forms of literary theory were more interested in locating conflicts and gaps in the structure of language and/or society that no text could reconcile. So, for instance, Derrida shows how Rousseau's *Confessions* (1781–88) tries to subordinate writing to speech as a way of producing truth but unwittingly shows how speech in fact relies on writing.

A similar contrast obtained in the case of older forms of historicism, which often emphasized the orderliness of an historical moment or often thought of history as a stable background that literature drew upon. Against this notion, Foucault shows how institutions such as the prison or events like public executions can themselves be read as texts that attest to the techniques of power that make order possible. Or, looking at the work of the French physician, humanist and satirist, François Rabelais (1494–1553), Bakhtin argues that we can see a carnivalesque view of the world that parodies and challenges official discourses of power, suggesting that historical moments never really cohere.

Also crucial to the theory of this time was the rise of feminist criticism. It took a variety of forms, and many books have charted the disputes within feminist theory of the 1970s and 1980s over, for instance, the universal or particular nature of women's experience. But for the purposes of this essay, it is sufficient to note the transformative effect of feminism on literary studies, leading to the recovery of women writers excluded from the canon of English literature and the re-reading of canonical male authors in light of their representation of sexual difference.

By the 1980s, a range of literary fields were increasingly taking their cues from these different theories, including those of class and ethnicity. And so it is with a touch of envy that the editors of *The New Eighteenth Century* note that

> [i]n comparison to current studies of the Renaissance, the Romantic period, or the Victorian novel, work in eighteenth-century literary studies relies more heavily on appreciative formalist readings that seek to describe a stable core of meaning in the text, or on a positivist historicism, unreflective about its theoretical grounds or its political implications. (Brown and Nussbaum, 1987: 4)

The picture of eighteenth-century literature that resulted offered 'an image of equivalent social and cultural coherence [and] a sense of an unchallenged class hierarchy represented and perpetuated in a literary culture where aesthetics, ethics, and politics perfectly mesh' (ibid.: 5). In other words, the beautiful, well-ordered and witty turns of poetic couplets were taken to reflect the beautiful and well-ordered world run by enlightened aristocrats for the good of all that also, somehow, laid the ground for a constitutional democracy. The new eighteenth century that the editors of the volume were calling for would challenge this vision of aesthetic and political order.

Michael McKeon *The Origins of the English Novel, 1660–1740* (1987, Second Edition 2002)

Michael McKeon's chief conceptual tool for challenging the criticism that precedes him is Marxist dialectic, which he uses to explain the emergence of the eighteenth century's heterogeneous genre *par excellence*, the novel (see p. 60, Chapter 3, Literary and Cultural Contexts: Eighteenth-Century Novel; see p. 128, Chapter 6, Key Critical Concepts and Topics: Novel). He does so in *The Origins of the English Novel, 1660–1740*; it was re-issued with a new introduction in 2002, a sign of its influence. Other works on the novel from the 1980s and 1990s, many of them shaped by 'new' versions of literary theory, have also proved influential, among them Nancy Armstrong's *Desire and Domestic Fiction* (1987), John Bender's *Imagining the Penitentiary* (1987), J. Paul Hunter's *Before Novels* (1990), Janet Todd's *The Sign of Angellica* (1989) and William Warner's *Licensing Entertainment* (1998).

The singular advantage of McKeon's work is its breadth; in its five hundred-plus pages, it aims at nothing less than situating the eighteenth-century novel in a history that encompasses everything from 'precursor revolutions' such as those of Classical Greece and twelfth-century Europe to histories of the individual; from saint's lives and criminal biographies to the effect of capitalism on the European absolutism of the sixteenth and seventeenth centuries. More specifically, McKeon argues that the novel emerges out of a twin dialectic: 'questions of truth' (or 'narrative epistemology') and 'questions of virtue' (or 'socio-ethical ideology'), where the movement towards one position engenders a critique, which, in turn, produces a counter-critique:

> At the beginning of the period of our concern, the reigning narrative epistemology involves a dependence on received authorities and a priori traditions; I will call this posture 'romance idealism.' In the seventeenth century it is challenged and refuted by an empirical epistemology that derives from many sources, and this I will call 'naïve empiricism.' But this negation of romance, having embarked on a journey for which it has no maps, at certain points loses its way. And it becomes vulnerable, in turn, to a countercritique that has been generated by its own overenthusiasm. I will call this countercritique 'extreme skepticism.' In refuting its empiricist progenitor, I will argue, extreme skepticism inevitably recapitulates some features of the romance idealism which it is equally committed to opposing. For questions of virtue, the terms alter, but the two-stage pattern of reversal is very much the same as for questions of truth. We begin with a relatively stratified social order supported by a reigning world view that I will call 'aristocratic ideology.' Spurred by social change, this ideology is attacked and subverted by its prime antagonist, 'progressive ideology.' But at a certain point, progressive ideology gives birth to its own critique, which is both more radical than itself, and harks back to the common, aristocratic enemy. I will call this countercritique 'conservative ideology.' (2002: 21)

For McKeon, this model represents a significant advance over Ian Watt's classic *The Rise of the Novel* (1957). While honoring the explanatory force of Watt's work, McKeon follows others in pointing out two flaws in its argument. The first is its claim that what distinguishes the novel is its 'formal realism', which rejects 'traditional plots and figurative eloquence' for 'the particularization of character and background, of naming, temporality, causation, and physical environment' (McKeon, 2002: 2). The problem, according to McKeon, is not that this claim is false but that it is partial, overlooking the degree to which Daniel Defoe (1660–1731), Samuel Richardson (1689–1761) and Henry Fielding (1707–54) all draw heavily on 'the idea and ethos of romance' even as they subvert it. McKeon sets out to remedy this problem by showing how romance and its cognate, 'idealism', persists, even in ironized form, in the prose fiction of the eighteenth century.

The second weakness of Watt's argument is that he ties the rise of the novel to the rise of the middle class. Many scholars have struggled with identifying just who or what made up the middle class in the eighteenth century or, indeed, whether the middle class can be said to exist at all at this time. After all, the aristocracy hardly melts away during this era, and those we might be tempted to call middle class do not exhibit the sort of self-conscious sense of group identity evident in the Victorian era but, instead, aim to be assimilated into the gentry or the aristocracy.

McKeon presents class not in terms of a consciousness shared by a particular group of people determined by their relationship to a mode of production, or even particular attitudes and behaviours. Rather, class emerges, for McKeon at the point at which a social order based on land ownership gets destabilized by, among other factors, a new economy based on credit and thus more freely-circulating capital (2002: 166). Thus, while the aristocracy certainly remains firmly ensconced in the eighteenth century, it must mount a defence against this alternative mode of value, and the stridency of the aristocracy's response registers the dynamic that will *later* produce a middle class (ibid.: 169).

That we might see an analogy between the persistence of romance and the persistence of the aristocracy is not a coincidence according to McKeon. For one of the advantages of his two-track model of 'truth' and 'virtue' is to see that the novel has its foundations in this very analogy:

> [T]he coherence of the analogy can be seen in the correlative logic by which, in a movement that only culminates with Richardson and Fielding, the formal posture of naïve empiricism tends to accompany a substantive stance of progressive ideology, and extreme skepticism is reflected in an analogous, conservative ideology. This insight – the deep and fruitful analogy between questions of truth and questions of virtue – is the enabling foundation of the novel. (2002: 22)

McKeon's claim here speaks to a final way he departs from Watt and many other theorists of the novel. Rather than looking for a singular cause that necessarily led to the 'rise' of the novel, McKeon looks for many. Here, again, he takes his cue from Marx, working backward from the moment when the novel becomes a 'simple abstraction'; predicated upon 'a long history of "novelistic usage" – the moment when this usage has become sufficiently complex to permit a generalizing "indifference" to the specificity of usages and an abstraction of the category whose integrity is supposed by that indifference' (ibid.: 19).

To give this 'simple abstraction' some concreteness, I would like to consider McKeon's reading of Richardson's *Pamela* (1740–41), which, along with

Fielding's novels, marks the arrival of the genre *as* a 'simple abstraction'. In McKeon's novelistic dialectic, *Pamela* presents the conjunction of 'naïve empiricism' and 'progressive ideology'. We can see the former in Richardson's celebrated and controversial use of letters to tell Pamela's story. The great bulk of the letters in this epistolary novel come from Pamela herself, and their intimate relationship to her mind and body is crucial to the truth her letters purport to tell:

> Epistolary method permits Richardson's characters, unlike Cervantes', to engage in self-reflexive discourse, an advantage Richardson fully exploits in order to insinuate the documentary objecthood of his material. If the claim to historicity consists in the assertion that the story one is telling really happened, the apotheosis of the convention in Richardson's hands depends upon his creation of the sense that it is really happening at this very moment. And the celebrated Richardsonian technique of 'writing to the moment' . . . is closely related to the self-reflexive effect by which the narrative incorporates, as its subject matter, the process of its own production and consumption. The gaps in the text where Pamela 'breaks off' in apprehension, the tears and the trembling lines that we are told deface the calm surface of the original manuscript – these constitute highly emotional 'evidence of the senses' that comes very close to the presentational and objective power of the drama while escaping its vulnerability to disconfirmation. . . . So the epistemological status of *Pamela* is difficult to disentangle from that of Pamela – from her claims to, and her capacity for, credibility. And questions of truth provide one medium for much of the social and sexual conflict in Richardson's narrative. Needless to say, Mr. B. is not always so content to take Pamela's word as authoritative, since what it subserves is a plot of typically progressive ideology (to which I will return). Early on he persistently accuses her of 'romancing,' of inventing absurdly distorted and fantastic fictions about the absolute moral gulf between her persecuted innocence and his own black intentions. . . . B. works hard to reverse the spell of Pamela's progressive plotting with his own inventions, which are characteristically aristocratic in ideology and often even take written form. (2002: 358–9)

It turns out that Richardson himself encourages us to agree with Mr B. that Pamela has something of the 'romancer' in her (McKeon, 2002: 363), as when she aborts her attempt to flee from her confinement upon mistaking a harmless cow in a field she has to cross for a terrifying bull. This might seem, then, to question Richardson's commitment both to 'naïve empiricism' and 'progressive ideology', with Mr B. occupying a position akin to that of Richardson's great antagonist Fielding, who spoofs Pamela's and Richardson's 'naïve empiricism' and social climbing in *Shamela* (1741). But it turns out that this evidences the very dialectic that McKeon sees at the origins of the novel:

> In truth, this epistemological reversal has been potential from the start, in an authorial dedication to naïve empiricism so intense and uncompromising that it extends the claim to historicity to the extreme frontier of writing to the moment, to the notion of an objectivity so minutely responsive to the very process of recording the truth that it must come to disclose the radically subjective bases of all cognition. (2002: 363)

That Richardson anticipates the critique of Pamela/*Pamela* shows that he is part of the same dialectic that forces Mr B. to defend his aristocratic status, which should be beyond question, through writing letters of his own. And Richardson's 'primary commitment' in matters of truth and virtue remains firm (McKeon, 2002: 363); through her letters, Pamela proves the more persuasive storyteller, convincing Mr B. to abandon his attempt at seduction and to marry her instead, elevating her socially and thus realizing the fantasy of 'progressive ideology'.

In achieving this aim, letters are important not only for their documentary function (questions of truth) but also for their position in a social network (questions of virtue). For in her written defence of her own innocence and her condemnation of her master's ungentlemanly behaviour, Pamela subverts the genre of the 'character reference', which employers depended upon in hiring servants (McKeon, 2002: 369–70). This is but one aspect of Pamela's volatile position as a servant who seems to have gone as high as a servant can go, the favorite of her now-departed mistress, educated in various domestic tasks that would seem more proper to a lady (ibid.: 371). To actually become a lady, she needs Mr B. to marry her, but for this to happen, she must no longer see herself or be seen as a servant, and this transformation ironically depends upon the imprisonment that would seem to epitomize her status as a mere servant, for it gives her the leisure time to write in the letters that sway her would-be seducer onto a virtuous path.

The transformative power of Pamela's writing, then, implies a radical commitment to meritocracy that would value people in terms of their in-born virtue rather than their birth. But this social volatility is contained by Mr. B's claim to an exclusively-male right to elevate a spouse – a king can elevate his wife to a queen, but a queen cannot do the same for her husband. This takes us back to the dialectic:

> Just as Richardson's 'objective' claim to historicity is driven so far that it seems at times to unearth its dialectical antithesis, the subjectivity of

> perception, so the progressive empowerment of individual merit leads in the end to the crucial case of women, a condition of social injustice so deeply rooted its very disclosure marks the limits of progressive ideology. (McKeon, 2002: 380)

This claim leads to some parting questions we might ask of McKeon, which he anticipates to some degree in his introduction to the 2002 edition. The first has to do with dialectic itself. If, as McKeon claims in his later introduction, that dialectic makes explicit the duality that inheres in historical existence, does history *always* move in a dialectical fashion? Or, to limit ourselves to eighteenth-century literature, if these dialectical questions of truth and virtue figure so importantly in this era, should we be able to chart other genres in relationship to them? The other set of questions has to do with gender. The case studies that constitute the third part of the volume are all of men (Cervantes, Bunyan, Defoe, Swift, Richardson and Fielding), which may be a bit embarrassing given the number of studies during the 1980s and 1990s of the central role played by Aphra Behn (1640–89), Eliza Haywood (1693–1756), and other women in the emergence of the novel. McKeon does not address this objection directly; he prefers to shift the ground from the gender of the authors in question to what he takes to be the more important issue subtending it, the importance of gender in the social structure as a whole.

According to McKeon, it is not that gender is unimportant; we can see this in his reading of *Pamela*. But gender, he asserts, *is* less important than status and class prior to the 1740s, when the novel becomes a 'simple abstraction': 'It's as though during the first half of the century, gender difference has not yet been sufficiently separated out from status difference to receive direct attention' (2002: xxv). Eighteenth-century scholars might quarrel with his claims, but it is clear that his account of the eighteenth-century novel has supplanted Watt's as the one that others most frequently think with and against.

Terry Castle, *Masquerade and Civilization: The Carnivalesque in Eighteenth-Century English Culture and Fiction* (1986)

Although Terry Castle's *Masquerade and Civilization: The Carnivalesque in Eighteenth-century English Culture and Fiction* (1986) is not cited quite as frequently as McKeon's volume, it has often been looked to and may be more prophetic of recent trends in eighteenth-century criticism. Where McKeon sees the novel at the meeting point of philosophical and ideological 'questions', Castle reads literary texts by way of the broader cultural phenomenon of the masquerade, 'an established and ubiquitous feature of urban public life in England from the 1720's to the end of the century (1986: 2). Thus, her work might be seen as an early example of the cultural studies approach that currently dominates eighteenth-century scholarship. For Castle, there is a 'basic homology' at work, and in describing it she gives a summary of her thesis about the masquerade itself:

> [T]he literary fascination with the masquerade, displayed most intricately in fictional works of the period, mirrors the generalized interest the carnivalesque held in English society. It may seem an obvious enough point to make, but the way that the masquerade functions in contemporary narrative (as an episode diverting and yet threatening to the implicit taxonomies of the fictional world) is roughly analogous to the way it functioned in eighteenth-century culture (as a discontinuous, estranging, even hallucinatory event), yet one that carried with it an intense cognitive and cathartic éclat. (ibid.: 129)

The spectacle of the masquerade thus embodies something crucial about eighteenth-century England as a whole, including its literature.

To pursue the elusive phenomenon of the masquerade, Castle analyses a range of periodicals and pamphlets. She also focuses on a series of novels where masquerades appear, including two by women, Fanny Burney's *Cecilia* (1782) and Elizabeth Inchbald's *A Simple Story* (1791) since '[t]his realm of dream, dismay, and laughter is also, par excellence, the realm of women' (1986: 253). By embracing the more plastic possibilities for identity offered, if only for a fleeting moment at the masquerade, women authors could imagine a utopian moment where the repression they suffered at the hands of a patriarchal system could be defied (ibid.: 256–59).

As may already be clear, Castle's model for how culture relates to ideology differs from McKeon's dialectic. Instead, she draws most heavily on Bakhtin's idea of 'the carnivalesque':

> Bakhtin used the term mainly to indicate a thematic – that traditional body of festive imagery preserved in European literature in various forms from the Middle Ages through the Romantic period. But it can also suggest a process of generic destabilization. The carnivalized work, he argues, resists formal classification, and instead, like Rabelais's *Pantagruel*, combines a multiplicity of literary modes in an increasingly mixed or 'polyphonic' form. It is worth noting finally that eighteenth-century novels containing masquerade scenes often display a notable generic instability. At times the masquerade scene may even prompt a formal shift in the work in which it occurs. In *Amelia* the scene coincides with a general shift from the satiric to the mimetic mode. In Richardson's sequel to *Pamela* there is even more generic instability. After the masquerade scene the text becomes a true

> hodgepodge of discourses – a mixture of embedded exempla, 'table talk' (the symposia of the B. and Darnford households), and miscellaneous non-narrative items, such as Pamela's lengthy commentary on Locke's *Education*. (1986: 35–6)

The carnivalesque is a theme in eighteenth-century novels but it is also an indicator of formal hybridization (the joining together of two or more discourses to make a new one that contains elements of all), as the novels in question register the masquerade's disturbing force by bringing in a range of discourses in an attempt to represent and contain its energies. We might say, then, that the masquerade is what helps to underline the hybridity inherent in the novel, the polyphony that Bakhtin opposes to the monolithic discourse of the epic poem. The model of culture that underlies this account of the carnivalesque and the novel has a different dynamic to McKeon's dialectic The masquerade serves to express the impulses 'repressed by the "institutionalized oppositions" ' (Castle, 1986: 78) of eighteenth-century English culture.

Castle makes use of psychoanalytic criticism to illustrate the instabilities at the heart of society as it is seen by Bakhtin as well as anthropologists like Victor Turner (1920–83) and Clifford Geertz (1926–2006).[1] By allowing people to dress as who they were not, the masquerade unwittingly allows people of the lower classes to penetrate surreptitiously spaces normally reserved for the polite (1986: 28), and women to swear, initiate conversations and speak bawdily (ibid.: 34–5). The effect is not the necessary movement of the dialectic or a clash of contradictions papered over by ideological imperatives but rather the unleashing of an unpredictable, perverse and transformative energy, though Castle is quick to point out that the decline of the masquerade at the century's end suggests a grim triumph of rationalism and fixed identities.

The pay-off of her approach for literary analysis can be seen in her analysis of the often-overlooked *Pamela, Part 2* (1741). To justify writing *Part 2* Richardson pointed to the 'spurious sequels . . . that attempted to cash in on *Pamela*'s success', but Castle argues that Richardson's deeper reason was to respond to Fielding's accusation that *Pamela* 'was a book with revolutionary moral and social implications' (1986: 135). Richardson's aim, then, in *Pamela* was '*de*carnivalization', to erase the first novel's implication that 'serving girls became ladies simply, it seemed at times, by donning ladies' clothes' (ibid.: 137). It turns out, however, that Richardson's attempt to erase the implications of his own prior novel proves impossible:

> *Pamela*, Part 2, is analogous to an act of repression: it attempts to cover over, without ever really revoking, the very story on which it relies for its raison

> d'être. . . . The various patterns of mystification at work in the sequel inevitably fail, since it is clearly impossible for Richardson to have and yet not have his original story. Because only repressed – never done away with – the plot of metamorphosis retains a subterranean hold over this supposedly purified text. It breeds contradictions and tensions, disturbing an otherwise becalmed narrative surface. And finally, it behaves as repressed material is wont to do. At the enigmatic heart of the fiction, the forgotten story of Pamela's gratifying transfiguration makes an abrupt reappearance. (ibid.: 139)

These contradictions are set into motion not by Marxian dialectic, as in McKeon, but by an analogy to 'repression'. In this particular passage, the workings of the text are *analogized* to that of a mind subject to repression. The space of analogy leaves unsettled the degree to which texts really are like minds, but there is no doubt that Castle believes that the repressed returns, and it does so, not surprisingly, in Pamela's visit to the masquerade.

Although Pamela expresses her resistance to accompanying her well-born husband to the event in the terms of 'conventional anti-masquerade rhetoric (1986: 158), she is forced to go. Unlike with a trip to the theater or opera, she must become a participant as well as a spectator. Deep into her pregnancy, Pamela is dressed like a Quaker, a costume chosen for her by her husband. This contradiction between a full body testifying to a consummated sexuality and the primness of her garb is part of a re-carnivalization that calls attention to the very social instability Richardson is trying to erase in his sequel, her elevation from serving girl to Lady of the Manor. The masquerade also activates a plot in which Pamela must again call attention to her social elevation.

During a visit by a Countess Dowager, who was misleadingly dressed as a nun during the masquerade and who is a rival for Mr B's affections, Pamela 'symbolically humbles herself . . . wear[ing] a plain white damask gown, like that of a servant, so as not to 'vie' with her aristocratic tormentor' (1986: 165). In the end, the threat posed by the Countess is contained after Pamela actually offers to withdraw from the field, to pretend that Mr B's socially embarrassing marriage to her never existed. In response, Mr B. embraces her once again and professes not to care a whit for anybody's opinion of her, but this happy ending is belied by what has occurred before it: 'Whatever the other intentions of its teller, each embedded retelling of the masquerade affair thus serves ironically to spotlight the B. couple, and to bring to mind again their indecorous, incorrigible, unforgettable history' (ibid.: 173). The masquerade thus acts both to picture and defy the 'institutionalized' orders of eighteenth-century elite culture.

The 1990s: Empire and Affect

During the 1980s and 1990s, a new trend emerged in scholarship on English literature that addressed how the texts of the time were informed by the rise of England as a colonial power (see p. 187, Chapter 10, Mapping the Current Critical Landscape). This mode of criticism, which came to be known as 'postcolonial' – coming after the colonization of the East by the West and the South by the North but also aiming to envision alternatives to it – seeks to interrogate the way that texts, other cultural artifacts, and various practices are complicit in and/or resist European imperialism. While post-colonial theory and criticism is too complex to be traced back to one text, the publication of Edward Said's *Orientalism* in 1978 can safely be posited as 'foundational' to this 'anti-foundational' discourse, though we might also look back even further to works such as Frantz Fanon's *White Skin, Black Masks* (1952). For Said, the representations of 'the Orient' and especially the Middle East by European authors are not finally about unearthing knowledge about these 'foreign lands' but rather a way of dominating them by creating the Orient as an 'Other' – exotic, titillating, even wise in its mystical, non-Western ways but also inscrutable, oppressive, effeminate and, in any case, inferior.

Not surprisingly, Victorian and modernist literature offered itself as a key locus for these inquiries, since it was witness to the consolidation of the British Empire. But eighteenth-century literary studies did not lag behind by much. For instance, Mary Louise Pratt's important *Imperial Eyes* (1992) begins one of its chapters with an epigraph from Defoe, and the 1990s saw the release of Moira Ferguson's *Subject to Others: British Women Writers and Colonial Slavery, 1670–1834* (1992), Laura Brown's *Ends of Empire: Women and Ideology in Early Eighteenth-Century Literature* (1993) and other works, which, like this pair, showed how issues of gender, race, class and empire were interwoven in the texts of the time.

Srinivas Aravamudan, *Tropicopolitans: Colonialism and Agency, 1688–1804*

The fruitfulness of this approach can be seen in a more recent text, Srinivas Aravamudan's *Tropicopolitans: Colonialism and Agency 1688–1804* (1999). The title tips the reader off to the orientation and difficulty of the text. What is a 'tropicopolitan'? The term joins 'the tropics' with a resident of a particular 'polis' and thus someone who should have political agency, with the echo of 'cosmopolitan' thrown in. The more fluid identity and world-views associated with the cosmopolitan point to another term woven into 'tropicopolitan', which is 'trope'. Trope came into prominence in the post-structuralist criticism of the 1970s, and it refers to a 'turn' in language away from the literal and towards figures like metaphor, metonymy, symbol and allegory. By paying attention to tropes, then, the critic can show how all signs depend for their meaning on other signs; language that we think literally represents something 'out there' in fact depends upon its relationship to other words, and it often turns out that literal words have dead metaphors inscribed within them.

Recognizing the mutability of language through attending to tropes is often a first step in criticizing the political status quo that language often seeks to enforce, especially when it represents people subject to outside powers. Bringing these two aspects of 'tropicopolitan' together, the linguistic and the political, Aravamudan accordingly defines a tropicopolitan as a 'name for a colonized subject who exists both as fictive construct of colonial tropology *and* actual resident of tropical space, object of representation *and* agent of resistance' (1999: 4). This definition also points to the both/and logic that obtains throughout the text. Aravamudan rejects any account that insists on text and persons as either wholly resisting or wholly assimilating to imperialism, wholly authentic or compromised (ibid.: 14–15)

Aravamudan organizes his book around three modes of 'tropicalization', the process by which 'colonialist tropologies', the signs at the heart of the imperial enterprise, are revised by 'tropicopolitans' themselves and other authors and readers (1999: 4–5). The first, 'virtualization', involves an ideological freeing-up that is effected by unpredictable subtractions of textual detail, 'a process that enables readier identification and manipulation by readers, thus putting the trope of the tropicopolitan into motion toward an open-ended future' (ibid.: 17). Texts that exemplify 'virtualization' include *Oroonoko* (1688), *Robinson Crusoe* (1719) and *Gulliver's Travels* (1726), not to mention many less-canonical texts such as Defoe's *Captain Singleton* (1720) and Gordon and Trenchard's *Cato's Letters* (1720–3).

The second, 'levantinization', brings us back to the territory of Said, 'a creative response to orientalisms as a plural rather than singular category and the specifically dynamic interactions of European culture with Islamic ones that go back at least to the Crusades' (ibid.: 19). Among the texts considered here are Mary Wortley Montagu's *Turkish Embassy Letters* (1763), Edmund Burke's *A Philosophical Enquiry into the Origin of our Ideas of Sublime and the Beautiful* (1757) and Samuel Johnson's *Rasselas* (1759). Finally, we have 'nationalization', which most resembles the postcolonial practice of 'writing back' against the empire but which also spurs Aravamudan to question the postcolonial tendency to celebrate uncritically the agency claimed by such authors as Olaudah Equiano and Toussaint L'Ouverture, as if these figures were not themselves bound up in the imperial enterprise (Aravamudan, 1986: 21–3).

Aravamudan is not the first postcolonial critic to wed a deconstructive attention to language with an attention to the complexities of colonial politics;

he follows in the steps of Gayatri Spivak, Homi Bhabha and others. But he is among the first to bring these modes of reading to such a broad range of eighteenth-century texts, and his work is marked by a sophisticated reflection *on* postcolonial criticism itself.

This is apparent in his reading of *Oroonoko*, which takes up the imposing bulk of recent criticism on Aphra Behn's novella and stage adaptations of it. Of all the Restoration and eighteenth-century texts that have been happily recovered in the past few decades of criticism, *Oroonoko* is perhaps the most representative of recent trends.[2] It relates the tale ('a true history') of a noble African prince ('the royal slave') taken captive by a treacherous European ship-captain, shipped to the English colony of Surinam where he is reunited with his love, Imoinda. After the slave rebellion he leads proves unsuccessful, he kills the now-pregnant Imoinda with her consent to save her and his heir-to-be from falling back into captivity. Then he himself is captured, tortured horribly and dies. This story is told by a narrator who identifies herself as a woman and seems to be Behn herself – or, at least, Behn as she would have been some 25 years earlier. So, in addition to its formal interest as one of the earliest texts that might be classified a novel, it provocatively represents the interlocking axes of gender, race and empire.

Aravamudan cleverly frames this intense critical interest by first dividing the texts' recent critics into two camps. On one side are those who adhere to 'oroonokoism', using Oroonoko to celebrate the text as a precursor of any one of a number of phenomena, from American fiction to abolitionism (1999: 29–31). On the other are the adherents of 'imoindaism', who use Imoinda to highlight the text's complicities with the structures the oroonokoists say that it critiques – for instance, in its fetishization of a black, male body by the white, female narrator and the violence visited on her competitor, Imoinda (ibid.: 31–2).

Arvamudan's next move is to show how both of these positions unwittingly partake of what he calls the logic of 'pethood'. He cites various textual and visual sources that illustrate the growing fashion for pets, in which animals are treated like people as well as the fashion for treating Africans as if they were domestic animals. He then makes the case that Oroonoko is treated like a 'royal pet' by the narrator/Behn, sympathized with but also denied full human agency: 'If *Oroonoko* initiates antislavery discourse, as . . . successive readers have argued, it does so by building on the fantasized project of the aristocratic subordination of the royal slave as pet. The literature of empathy, which creates antislavery discourse, is itself a vicarious replacement for the more personalized dramas of pethood, seen here as the culture of the caress' (1999: 49) and thus for oroonokoism. But the only alternative imoindaism offers by reclaiming the butchered princess is merely 'a pious wish, an analogue of liberal desires of affirmative action' (ibid.: 59).

The alternative that Aravamudan advocates, paying attention to the neglected 'logic of parodic subversion', returns us to 'virtualization' and also may remind us of the parodic energies of Bakhtinian masquerade:

> Parody in Behn's novella is present in subtle but widespread fashion. Oroonoko's chivalric heroism consists of a quixotic belief in the inviolability of promises, ensuring his failure on many occasions . . . Oroonoko simplemindedly confuses honor with wit: 'for it was one of his Maxims, *A Man of Wit cou'd not be a Knave or a Villain.*' If the narrator's tone here patronizes Oroonoko, it also criticizes, implicitly, the hypocrisy of the Restoration rakes . . . There are many such moments of parody, of inadvertent pastiche at the very least, moments that are invested with satirical potential if read imaginatively. For instance, at the high point of Oroonoko's and Imoinda's suicide pact, a telltale rhyme undercuts the moment of overkill, when Oroonoko 'drew his Knife to kill this Treasure of his Soul, this Pleasure of his Eyes.' Does the rhyme enhance the melodrama or undercut it? . . . The pet romance, as it is elaborated here, parodies martyrology, and is therefore maudlin *and* burlesque. These random instances represent an exercise in Restoration simulation, where parodic counterfeiting can conceal as well as expose its own task of critical refunctioning. Parody in the novella follows a comedy-of-errors pattern: the African prince who is a slave trader is himself sold as slave (smirk), only to be himself resuscitated as pet-king for the English colonists (smirk), only to rebel against that very construction as feminizing him (smirk), only to be put to death as the real king himself was not so long ago (smirk). However, the more conventional interpretive sentence passed on Behn's *Oroonoko* would be formally identical to the one above, given that the pattern of sentimental melodrama prevails. If parody creates the parenthetical negative reaction (the smirk), it is in place of an affirmative one (the sigh). It is this structural, indeed, structuralist, identity of sentimentalism at the heart of *Oroonoko* that most clearly explains the logic of virtualization. (1999: 60–1)

So, in the complementarity of 'smirk' and 'sigh', of the supposedly-sincere response of the sentimental reader and the knowing wink of the parodist, we see the malleability that accompanies 'tropicalization' and 'virtualization'.

While *Oroonoko* may deny its title character full agency by making him a pet (however much it may stroke him), there are traces in the text that lead us to consider the more successful resistances and revolts of 'real-world tropicopolitans' like Toussaint L'Ouverture,[3] traces that also promise agency for the post-colonial reader who can find them. Aravamudan's dual commitment to the history of the tropics and the slipperiness of tropes offers the possibility of rewriting the past rather than being dominated by its contradictions.

Passion and Emotion

Aravamudan's interest in 'sentimentalism' points towards a final strain in recent eighteenth-century criticism – an interest in the history and structure of affect. In *The Long Revolution* (1961), Raymond Williams, whose work inspired many changes in eighteenth-century studies during the last few decades, first put forth his idea of a 'structure of feeling'. He held that a particular historical moment could be grasped in both its continuities and discontinuities by looking towards a kind of *gestalt* of impulses and attitudes that could be divined not only from texts but also social practices and records of 'lived experience', thereby acknowledging both the effects and the limits of domination.

We might say, then, that many scholars of the eighteenth century have of late been coming to the conclusion that the structure of feeling in that era *is* feeling, to judge by the upsurge in texts, from lyric poems to philosophical treatises to medical guides, that concern themselves with how people do and should feel. Out of these texts and practices emerge a pair of terms often applied to the literature and culture of the eighteenth century, especially the latter half – sympathy and sensibility (see p. 132, Chapter 6, Key Critical Concepts and Topics: Sensibility).

That feeling should have taken an increasingly central role in eighteenth-century scholarship is not surprising. Questions of feeling in the eighteenth century (and today) are intimately bound up with gender, sexuality, race and class. Beyond these categories of identity, the nature of affect raises questions about the very notion of identity. Because 'the culture of sensibility' (Barker-Benfield) in the eighteenth century tended to presume the centrality of the social world, it offers a notion that happily agrees with a key claim in the social constructionist bent of recent criticism – namely, that the self is the effect rather than the source of feeling, and that the source of feelings themselves is encounters with other people.

Adela Pinch's *Strange Fits of Passion: Epistemologies of Emotion from Hume to Austen*

There have been many recent studies of these topics, and among the subtlest and supplest is Adela Pinch's *Strange Fits of Passion: Epistemologies of Emotion from Hume to Austen* (1996). I repeat the full title to suggest how her study extends the boundaries of eighteenth-century studies in at least two ways. First, by including David Hume (1711–76), she undoes the separation of literature from philosophy that was a fundamental move in establishing the modern literary canon. Indeed, 'literature', as many critics have pointed out, referred in the eighteenth century to 'polite writing'[4] more generally, including philosophy and history, not the more restrictive notion of it as poems, novels and other forms of 'imaginative writing'. Pinch challenges this separation from both directions. She reads Hume's *Treatise on Human Nature* (1739) in a literary way, illustrating how his claims about how we come to know things are bound up in his use of narrative and metaphor. Conversely, she shows how the poems and novels of Charlotte Smith (1749–1806), William Wordsworth (1770–1850) and Jane Austen (1775–1817) make claims about knowledge as deep as those made by any philosophical treatise.

She also expands the scope of eighteenth-century criticism by tracing a line from Hume to authors normally considered as belonging to the Romantic era. This is in keeping with a move towards conceptualizing a 'long eighteenth century' that stretches from 1660–1832. The reasons for this shift are complex. It has something to do with the historical dependence of British Romanticism on a group of six white male poets in an age when criticism has challenged the linking of canonicity to masculinity and whiteness. It also has something to do with the decline of history that depends on punctual national events – such as the French Revolution (1789–99) – as an informing paradigm for literary criticism. Instead, broader historical changes that speak more directly to the role of women and other marginalized groups, such as the rise of a commercial society, have become of greater interest, parallel to a turn in cultural studies. Shifts like this have made 'the long eighteenth century' more available as an organizing rubric.

Pinch's readings of Hume and Smith illustrate how she bridges genres and eras. She focuses on two peculiar elements in Hume's understanding of sympathy. One is that sympathy has the unique power to reverse the normal direction of empiricist epistemology. Empiricism understands the ideas in our minds as fainter versions of the impressions we receive from the world. But sympathy can take our idea of someone else's feeling, as signaled by 'external signs in the countenance and conversation', and make us feel '*the very passion itself*' (Hume cited in Pinch, 1996: 34). Sympathy does more than tie us to other people; it is what makes us conscious of ourselves, since the force of feeling someone else's passion as if it were one's own exemplifies the 'force' that makes the mind aware of its own workings (Pinch, 1996: 36).

The power of sympathy here is analogous to the power Hume accords to the passions that sympathy helps to circulate. Rather than understanding the passions as produced by a subject, he posits that the subject is produced by the passions. Following an analysis of how Hume's notion of pride as a feeling that lets us know who we are by reflection on the objects attached to us, Pinch concludes, 'What passion does in Hume's *Treatise*, as exemplified by pride, is enact a kind of person-ification. It ties the "bundle of perceptions" into a recognizable human form we can claim as our own, just as Hume's prose 'turns impressions and ideas – the basic particles of empiricist philosophy – into recognizable, personified agents' (ibid.: 24).' Attending closely to the relationship between tropes and subjectivity, Pinch draws upon the elements of post-structuralism, but her aim here is not the 'reading against the grain' typical of earlier instances of this approach. Rather than critiquing Hume for relying on a suspect metaphysics, Pinch uses the techniques of deconstruction to situate him historically as post-structuralist *avant la lettre*, making the self posterior rather than prior to feeling and the signs that indicate it.

Our sense of Hume as our precursor (without mere anachronism) is heightened as Pinch digs more deeply into his writing. When Hume expresses his melancholy at the world's rejection of his views and his own internal weakness, readers have historically refused to sympathize with *him*, viewing these passions as either a sign of the proper wages of his atheistic skepticism or as merely staged. This reaction, however, merely confirms two paradoxes. First, we feel the feelings of others more than we feel the passions that seem to originate from us. Second, we feel the feelings of others more acutely when they are oblivious of our fellow-feeling, such as 'men of good families, but narrow circumstances' who exile themselves in order to avoid the disagreeable pity of those who know their situations:

> Readers' response to the figure of Hume confessing his vertigo and distress in the conclusion are thus quite different from our responses to the men who flee sympathy . . . Readers seem not to have fallen into Hume's despair, catching disagreeable sensations of pain and harm; nor have they commiserated with his plight. Rather, they have cast the feelings expressed as false – as either strategically ironic or unwisely melodramatic and exaggerated. Perhaps Hume's lesson about emotion is indeed that to be found in the example of the fleeing men or in his comments about our sympathy for those murdered in their sleep: sympathy is most forthcoming when the object in question seems most oblivious, when the feelings in question are the imaginary feelings that we – or a narrator – attribute to the object. The difference between the conclusion and the story of the men who flee is the difference between a text that confronts the reader with an authorial figure who directly expresses his feelings and a text in which both reader and author together are involved in speculation about another figure in the text. This speculation, I argued earlier, consists of sympathetically attributing feeling to a figure to whom we have special access, a figure

> who is unaware of our sympathy. The lesson about the relationship between persons and passions in the *Treatise* is that feeling may always be vicarious, something we generate in attributing to another figure. Our sense that the fleeing men may indeed be blood relatives of the figure in the conclusion – that the fleeing men's story is Hume's story – would only strengthen our sense of the overlapping identities between reader, writer, and characters. . . . For Hume, persons feel most the feelings they catch from others, as if by contagion. Their ability to do so is the basis of all social relations. The force of this process – called 'sympathy' – by which another's feeling is converted into something we feel, is the force that links impressions and ideas, mind and world. (1996: 43–4)

Having shown how the truth claims of philosophy are imbricated with elements normally thought of as literary, Pinch then proceeds to explain how the poetry of Charlotte Smith signifies within philosophical debates over feeling. Smith's *Elegiac Sonnets* (1784) reveals the peculiar situation of women poets within 'the culture of sensibility' that Hume helped to delineate. Hume was not alone in seeing women as particularly susceptible to feeling, a susceptibility that at once made them valuable teachers of how to appreciate feeling and artworks and yet also vulnerable to seduction and accusations of emotional volatility (1996: 53). To think about Smith's representation of feeling in her poems, then, is to 'clarify our understanding of the relationship between sensibility and feminism by focusing on what women's sentimental literature has to say about the expression of feeling. . . . What does it mean for women to write about their own feelings? What exactly does it mean to say that feelings are personal? And what does it mean to call women's poetry "sentimental"?' (ibid.: 55).

In Smith's case, her relationship to sentimental expression is complicated by her practice of quoting from other poets, thus 'borrowing' the feelings of the speakers of her poems from other poems. For Pinch, this intertextuality is Smith's way to claim a space in a masculinist literary tradition while working to revive the genre of the sonnet:

> [T]he sonnet that opens each edition of the collection may be read as a revealing declaration of how Smith's poetry links gender and genre, quotation and feeling. She begins by claiming that the muse of poetry has 'smiled on the rugged path' she's been 'doom'd to tread,' accompanying her in her unhappiness and weaving 'fantastic garlands' that decorate her in her misery. . . . But the final couplet reinforces the claim that writing itself can make one miserable:

> Ah! then, how dear the Muse's favours cost,
> *If these paint sorrow best – who feel it most!*

> The final line – as a note in the text directs us – virtually quotes the final couplet of Pope's *Eloisa to Abelard*. There, Eloisa looks forward to a time when a poet may put her sorrows into verse:
>
> > The well-sung woes shall soothe my pensive ghost;
> > He best can paint them who shall feel them most.
>
> Eloisa is making a relatively conventional claim about the relationship between affect and language: feeling precedes writing; the capacity to feel someone's feelings sympathetically is the condition for persuasively and accurately writing about them. But if feeling precedes writing in Pope's couplet, Smith's sonnet leads precisely to a reversal of that claim. Following the preceding line – 'Ah! then how dear the Muse's favours cost,' – her final line – even though its syntax is almost the same as the original – asserts rather that those who paint sorrow best feel it most. Here writing precedes feelings. Smith recontextualizes Eloisa's claim to shift into its opposite, suggesting that the price you pay for the Muse's favor is feeling, and therefore that writing, according to this reversal, makes one miserable.
>
> It seems crucial that this reversal of our understanding of the relationship between feeling and poetic language takes the form of a repetition and reversal of a quotation from another poem: asserting that writing makes one miserable takes the form of quoting someone else. If quotation involves incorporation of someone else's expression, perhaps writing makes one miserable because writing always involves taking in, reproducing, other people's expressions of feelings. However, I do not think we should take the affective dimension of this formulation, this misery, as the sign of a woman poet's defeat at the hands of a patriarchal literary tradition, her depression at being always already written: rather, this gloominess is a sign and medium . . . of a successful literary transmission. (1996: 62–3)

So, Smith is able to clear a space for herself even in the act of expressing misery – indeed, by expressing the misery she excerpts from Pope. The literary origins of the textualization of these feelings opened Smith up to a charge like the one leveled at Hume, that the dismal tone that pervades her sonnets is not really hers. She defends herself by pointing to the truly awful conditions of her existence, having been married off young to an unfaithful and spendthrift husband, supporting herself and her family through her writing while fighting a long legal battle to obtain the trust due to her children from their paternal grandfather. But Pinch is less interested in Smith's defense, which feminist critics of a prior generation would be tempted to use as an indubitable claim for women's difficult experience. Rather, she wants to press into service the very doubling of the conventional and the personal, for this opens up a possibility for feminist inquiry. She warns that

> [w]e cannot assert a simple continuity between the expression of misery in women's sentimental literature and the expression of political grievance in late eighteenth-century feminist writing. [Nevertheless] the formal and epistemological dimensions of a literature of feelings must be taken into account. But doing so may in fact make it possible to see sentimental poetry as *enabling* a political discussion about personal feelings. That is, we might view Smith's poetry as an occasion for seeing 'experience' as a strategic, explanatory political category, being constituted within late eighteenth-century women's discourse in dialectical relationship to the wandering feelings of poetry, which know no person (71).

The 2000s: Looking Ahead

(See p. 134, Chapter 7, 'Dead Keen on Reason?' Changes in Critical Responses to the Eighteenth Century; see p. 187, Chapter 10, Mapping the Current Critical Landscape)

The revisionary energy of *Tropicoplitans* and *Strange Fits of Passion* strongly suggests that 'the new eighteenth century' heralded two decades ago has largely come to pass. Most of the scholarship being published and most of the classes being taught in the field today take it for granted that 'theory' (however tacitly drawn upon in a time now said to be 'after theory') and 'politics' will play a central role in understanding 'English literature'. The success of what was 'new' in 1987 is indicated by Aravamudan's and Pinch's need to reframe and complicate the suppositions of recent criticism – arguing in Aravmudan's case against the reductiveness of 'Imoindaism' or 'Oroonokoism' and in Pinch's case against taking women's poetry as an expression of women's experience in any simple way. The triumph of the 'new' is also indicated by the fact that three of the contributors to *The New Eighteenth Century* have served or are serving as presidents of the American Society for Eighteenth-Century Studies (ASECS), an organization roundly criticized for its conservatism in the introduction to the volume.

Of course, we might also wonder whether the Young Turks have once again been transformed into the Old Guard, betokening a shift in the future. As Swift's *Bickerstaff Papers* (1708) reminds us, making predictions about the future, especially something as changeable as literary criticism, is a tricky business. If the eminent close reader Cleanth Brooks had been asked in 1970 to say what the field would look like in twenty years, it is highly unlikely he would have been able to envision what happened. Nonetheless, I feel some confidence in predicting that many of the strains in the criticism I have discussed in this essay will continue to lead productive lives. Important feminist revisions of the canon and eighteenth-century culture continue to appear; see Paula Backscheider's *Eighteenth-Century Women Poets and their Poetry* (2005) and Melissa Mowry's *The Bawdy Politic in Stuart England, 1660–1714* (2004). The canon also looks as if it will expand in other directions, as in the multi-volume edition *Eighteenth-Century English Labouring-Class Poets* (2003) under the general editorship of John Goodridge. Also likely to be in the mix are further studies of the literary marketplace itself, exemplified by recent works such as Jody Greene's *The Trouble with Ownership* (2005). Empire continues to be a key topic, as is evident in Clement Hawes's *The British Eighteenth Century and Global Critique* (2005) or Betty Joseph's *Reading the East India Company, 1720–1840* (2004); with it, we see a growing interest in the idea of a 'trans-Atlantic' eighteenth century, as in Tim Fulford's *Romantic Indians* (2006).

But we can also see signs of a more fundamental shift in critical attention away from the ideology critique that has been the hallmark of recent historicism. Concomitant with a wider turn towards ethics in literary theory, there seems to be a return to some basic questions about the legacy of the Enlightenment, with more credit perhaps being given to how the eighteenth century itself understood these issues. I have in mind here texts like Lisa Zunshine's *Why We Read Fiction* (2006), which includes *Clarissa* among its examples of how literature speaks to the cognitive theory of the present. There is also Blakey Vermeule's *The Party of Humanity* (2000), which re-reads Pope and others as offering the basis for a self-interested ethics that anticipates the position of evolutionary psychologists. In a more sociable vein, we have Adam Potkay's *The Passion for Happiness* (2000), which focuses on Hume and Johnson, and *The Story of Joy* (2007), which ranges more broadly but also includes the eighteenth century's views on the 'history of the good pursued by affective means'.

Finally, we have affect of another and more self-reflexive and yet also unabashedly uncritical kind – 'author love' – at the center of Helen Deutsch's *Loving Dr. Johnson* (2005). Employing the insights of recent criticism on the body, on figurative language and on canonization, it weaves together an account of how Dr Johnson became so central to our vision of the eighteenth-century English with Deutsch's own affection for him. If 'The Age of Johnson' has largely passed as an organizing term for the eighteenth century, Deutsch shows us that, however much he has been wreathed in Englishness, masculinity and other *passé* honorifics, the Great Cham still has the power to move us.

I do not foresee a spate of similar books forthcoming; Deutsch is too brilliant and idiosyncratic a reader to allow for much imitation. But I hope that others pick up in a general way on her conjunction of 'theory, politics, English Literature', which does not banish but rather re-modulates the hermeneutics of suspicion that has ruled literary criticism for the last few decades in a way that seems to me truer to our animating desires as readers of eighteenth-century literature in English. In addition to struggling with these texts, we love them (we love the struggle) and want to enter into conversations with others about what we have found. This might be the root of another new eighteenth century in the twenty-first.

Notes

1 Both men were champions of symbolic anthropology, whose basic assumption is that symbols are the means by which we perceive, perpetuate, communicate and develop our understanding of the world. Turner worked on the role of symbols in conflict resolution but he was also interested in the how symbols were used in ceremonies marking the right of passage from, for example, girlhood to womanhood. Geertz worked on religion and, particularly towards the end of his life, on Islam. Geertz's attempt to define the guiding symbols of a culture influenced Stephen Greenblatt, one of the key theorists of American new historicism.

2 Among important studies of *Oroonoko*: Laura Brown, 'The Romance of Empire: Oroonoko and the Trade in Slaves' in *The New Eighteenth Century*, 41–61; Catherine Gallagher, *Nobody's Story: The Vanishing Acts of Women Writers in the Marketplace, 1670–1820* (Berkeley: University of California Press, 1994), 49–87; and Susan Z. Andrade, 'White Skin, Black Masks: Colonialism and the Sexual Politics of Oroonoko', *Cultural Critique 27* (Spring 1994): 189–214. For a measure of the text's sky-rocketing critical fortunes, the MLA International Bibliography lists 14 hits for Oroonoko from 1900–79; from 1980–89, 14; from 1990–99, 59; from 2000 to the present, 58.

3 L'Ouverture was the leader of the slave revolt, which transformed the French colony of St Domingue into the independent country of Haiti.

4 The term 'politeness' was placed in opposition to political divisions and religious bigotry. It was the means by which one improved one's mind and refined one's taste. (see Glossary)

6 Key Critical Concepts and Topics

Richard Terry

Richard Terry

Chapter Overview

Aesthetics: We now take for granted the enjoyment afforded by a panoramic view from the top of a mountain: people walk up hills precisely in order to experience the view. But why does gazing at a panorama induce sensations of pleasure? Children, after all, seem totally indifferent to looking at picturesque views, and it is not clear that human beings have always been receptive to such pleasures. The eighteenth century is the first age in which scholars and critics tried to analyse pleasures of this kind: the first age, that is, in which people became preoccupied with the subject of aesthetics. One such critic is Joseph Addison who wrote a group of essays devoted to the 'Pleasures of the Imagination'. Addison distinguishes between what he calls 'primary' and 'secondary' imagination, the first relating to the sensation of viewing a particular spectacle and the second to the experience of recollecting it, seeing it again through the mind's eye. As the century progresses, critics and philosophers such as Edmund Burke try to categorize the various types of sensory pleasure to which people are susceptible. Beautiful objects are unsurprisingly deemed pleasurable to look at, but so also are ones belonging to a slightly different category: the sublime. Sublime spectacles were seen as ones that inspired awe or even a degree of fear, such as craggy mountaintops or plunging waterfalls. Another category sometimes invoked was novelty, where we are surprised at the unpredictability of a spectacle, the quality of novelty tending to be related to comedy. It should be noted that aesthetics concerned itself with the properties of both nature and art.

Biography: Biography is one of the most prolific and popular genres in the eighteenth century. Biographies of statesmen, racy tales of the lives of actresses and of other scandalous ladies, and lives of notable criminals were all avidly consumed. Biography, though, is important not just for its own sake but for the contribution it makes to the development of the English novel. Most early eighteenth-century novels are biographical or autobiographical in nature, concerned with narrating the life history of the principal character. Where a novel addresses only a fleeting episode, the author will sometimes add a sort of addendum, as happens in Richardson's *Pamela* (1740–1), quickly running through his or her character's subsequent life-narrative. Such a technique testifies to a belief that a novel that did not span the central character's full life would be unsatisfying. We can also see the centrality of biography in the fact that so many titles of novels take the name of the main character, like Laurence Sterne's *Tristram Shandy* (1760–7) and Fanny Burney's *Evelina* (1778). Johnson's *Lives of the Poets* (1779–81) constitute the first true critical biographies of English authors, and Johnson himself was memorialized after his death in James Boswell's *Life of Johnson* (1791).

Comedy of manners: 'Comedy of manners' is a rather elusive term applied to certain plays of the Restoration era and, to a lesser extent, the eighteenth century. Dramatists whose work is associated with the label include Wycherley, Etherege, Congreve and Sheridan. What seems fundamental to these plays is the idea of provoking humour through depicting characters behaving badly or at least foolishly. Some plays seem to offer a censorious view of such behaviour, with the worst offenders seeing their activities curbed at the end of the play, whereas others, such as Wycherley's *Country Wife* (1675), remain more non-committal about it. From the 1690s onwards, comedies of manners were challenged by the rise of sentimental comedies, which tended to take a more charitable view of human nature, and which sought to reconcile laughter with the spectacle of people actually behaving well. As well as depicting outright immorality, comedies of manners also satirize the cultivated insincerity and artificial social rituals that were seen as belonging to the genteel, leisured classes. Some plays, often termed comedies of wit, contain rapier-like verbal exchanges between characters. A popular dramatic convention was the 'witty couple', epitomized by Millamant and Mirabell in Congreve's *The Way of the World* (1700), whose brilliant intellectual sparring eventually leads them into marriage.

Consumption: Historians associate the early eighteenth century with the rapid development of a modern consumer economy. What allowed for this was a combination of factors: a less aggressive foreign policy that emphasized the advantages of peaceful co-existence and trade with other nations; the economic exploitation of Britain's colonies; and an increase in the spending power of the middle classes. Increased consumption by the better-off sections of society did have the virtuous effect of spreading opportunities for employment and subsistence to poorer people. However, many social commentators were exercised by what they saw as the inherently immoral nature of the new patterns of consumption. For the first time, it was observed, consumers were purchasing large numbers of non-necessary commodities; repeat-purchasing items that might previously have only been bought once; and buying items purely for reasons of competitive fashionableness. These consumption habits became branded as examples of 'luxury', a word that acquired a strongly negative connotation at this time. Many literary works in the early eighteenth century comment on the increase in trade and the inward flood from abroad of fashionable commodities. Many also address luxury as an issue of social concern, often associating it, as Pope does in the *Rape of the Lock* (1712), with the frippery of women. It should be noted that culture itself becomes much more commodified at this time. The growth of galleries, concert halls and circulating libraries all diversified the opportunities for educated people to consume high culture.

Copyright and censorship: The historical moment when literary works become seen as the intellectual copyright of their authors is hard to pinpoint. Shakespeare certainly showed little interest in publishing his plays or exercising public ownership over them, and in the theatrical culture of the post-1660 era the recycling or plagiarizing of older playscripts was rife. The world of eighteenth-century publishing was notoriously unruly. Literary piracy, the printing and sale of a work without the permission of its author or agreed publisher, was commonplace, and many writers can be found protesting, or even pursuing legal action, against unscrupulous publishers. An attempt was made to crack down on such abuses in the Copyright Act passed in 1709, but this only had limited success in deterring malefactors. At the same time that authors risked loss of revenue through the pirating of their works, they also faced the threat of retribution if their writings offended the government. After the theatres reopened in 1660, all newly performed plays were required to be licensed, though the administration of censorship remained quite lax. Originally conceived for moral purposes, censorship however was revived for political ones under the government of Robert Walpole. Having been offended by personal allusions in John Gay's *Beggar's Opera* (1728) Walpole ensured that the play's sequel, *Polly* (1729), was banned from performance; and, as a direct consequence of two politically satiric plays written by Henry Fielding, he introduced the Licensing Act of 1737, further extending state regulation of the theatre. This act, some of the stipulations of which were only abolished in 1968, has had a greater effect on the course of English literature than any other single piece of legislation. It dismayed aspiring dramatists of the day, and redirected Fielding in particular to an alternative literary career as a novelist. It also accounts for why eighteenth-century drama on the whole pales alongside the great achievements of the Renaissance and Restoration playwrights.

Criticism: Nowadays we are habituated to the idea of literary criticism. Indeed, students pursuing a degree in English literature will spend most of their time actually practising criticism: that is, producing pieces of writing that reflect on literary works. Yet criticism as a textual phenomenon only comes into existence after 1660, when writers like John Dryden and Thomas Rymer first start producing examples of the form. Early criticism often seems to us to be very aggressive and hectoring in its tone, and it is hardly surprising that original authors and critics often found themselves at loggerheads. The most poisonous feud of all was perhaps between Alexander Pope and the critic John Dennis who routinely harangued Pope's new works as they were published. In his *Essay on Criticism* (1711), Pope complains about the proliferation of critics whom he tends to view as failed literary authors. What perhaps exacerbated the fractiousness existing between creative authors and critics was that criticism at this time tended to be more directly evaluative than nowadays. The rise of criticism, and also the expanding market for book reviews, contributes to the making of the larger cultural-economic system within which literature figures, one that also includes publishers, libraries and bookshops.

English language: Nowadays our relation to the language of everyday usage is largely unquestioning: we do not ask whether it is getting better or worse or how it compares in quality to other past or current languages. Yet these questions seemed unavoidable to eighteenth-century writers and grammarians. Moreover, it was widely believed that the state of the language went a long way to determine the possibilities for literary excellence. If the language was not up to scratch, how could poets produce works of timeless standing composed in it? Views about when the English language had been at its height differed from one commentator to another. Some thought the language used in the eighteenth century represented English in its most refined form, whereas others believed that it represented a deterioration from the more pure and vigorous language of the pre-Restoration era, which Dr Johnson called the 'wells of English undefiled'. Whatever the case, it was seen almost universally as desirable for the language to be fixed, and so not subject to the flux and obsolescence to which it had been prone since as far back as could be traced. Both Swift and Johnson were interested in 'ascertaining the English tongue' as they expressed it: that is, fixing the language to some agreed standard. Anxiety about the quality of the language manifests itself also in linguistic nostalgia. Many poets, including Thomson and Gray, wrote poems that use antiquated diction or 'archaism', and Gray asserted that 'the language of the age is never the language of poetry'.

Enlightenment: The Enlightenment is generally seen as a broadly European movement that flourished in eighteenth-century Scottish universities if not especially in England. Up until the eighteenth century, the cultural horizon of most educated people was dominated by two sources of authority: the Bible and the classics. The Enlightenment can be seen as a process of casting aside these authorities, and an attempt to understand mankind in more emancipated terms. The German philosopher Kant, for example, in 1784 described the Enlightenment as being concerned with 'the liberation of man from his self-caused state of minority' and the achievement of intellectual maturity through trust in our innate powers of understanding. Crucial to the intellectual adventure of Enlightenment thinking was a trust in reason to dispel accumulated dogma and superstition. This manifested itself in religious terms in deism, the belief that religious convictions should be defensible on rational grounds rather than purely through faith. Elsewhere, the Enlightenment spirit can be seen in David Hume's attempt to understand mankind in strictly empirical terms in his *Treatise of Human Nature* (1739–40). Consistent with Enlightenment thinking was a belief in the possibility of improving the human lot through progress.

Epic: Eighteenth-century poets and critics agreed that the epic poem was the most prestigious of all literary genres. Epics were poems that dealt with human trial, either through military conflict or through an heroic quest or journey. The genre is unusual in that exalted examples of it are so few in number, and those that do exist express strong connections with each other. The Greek poet Homer's *Iliad* and *Odyssey* comprise the fountainhead of the epic tradition, with the latter strongly influencing Virgil's Roman epic, the *Aeneid*. In the eighteenth century, there was a growing recognition that an English epic, Milton's *Paradise Lost* (1667), demanded a place alongside the august company of the three classical epics, while Spenser's romance-epic *The Faerie Queene* (1590–96), though based on a different, non-classical aesthetic, was also championed as a supreme achievement in its own right. Critics of the time tried to establish the true properties of epic, including the extent to which such poems illustrated a moral and deliberately sought to achieve sublime effects. Despite such interest in the subject, very few epic poems were actually written in the century, and none that was distinguished. Instead, the leading poets channelled their interest into translations of the great epics (as carried out by Dryden and Pope) and also mock-heroic poems, ones that used epic conventions for comic purposes.

Feminism: Most women in the eighteenth century faced lives of unenviable toil and impaired freedoms. Working-class women often had to combine childminding with the performance of arduous jobs, a predicament described vividly in Mary Collier's poem 'The Woman's Labour' (1739). Women of higher social rank were of course much more comfortable, but many still felt unfulfilled by a life largely immured in the home. University education remained unavailable to women throughout the century, and access to rewarding employment was limited for gentlewomen. At higher social levels, arranged marriages, contracted for familial enrichment, remained common, and women were expected to develop themselves intellectually only with a view to becoming helpful and amiable companions for their husbands. They were instructed to this end by numerous conduct books legislating on women's proper role. While the hardships facing working-class women were generally accepted as a natural state of affairs, protests against the plight of other sorts of women were increasingly voiced. Mary Astell, often mentioned as the first English feminist, attacked the limited educational opportunities for women, and advocated the creation of female academies where single women could be admitted for study before going into society to teach and perform charitable works. In her later *Some Reflections on Marriage* (1700), she conducts the first critique of marriage as an institution intrinsically opposed to the true interests of women. This sceptical view of marriage is evident in later female writers such as Sarah Fielding. At the end of the century, Mary Wollstonecraft, in her *Vindication of the Rights of Woman* (1792), urges women to resist the subjection imposed on them by the cult of femininity. Women's prominence as literary figures rises during the century, a fact that is reflected by the so-called Bluestocking club, initiated by Elizabeth Montagu, which fostered intellectual conversation involving both sexes.

Gothic: The appearance of gothic fiction in England was preceded by the vogue for graveyard poetry in the first half of the eighteenth century. Such poems included Thomas Parnell's 'Night-Piece on Death' (1721) and Robert Blair's 'The Grave' (1743) as well Thomas Gray's more celebrated 'Elegy Written in a Country Churchyard' (1751). Poems of this kind were interested in exploiting the grisly frisson that comes with hanging around graveyards at night, but they also meditate on human mortality and, in Gray's case, on issues of social equality and justice. Moreover, the graveyard setting provides in general an opportunity for a self-induced creative gloom. The word 'gothic' referred literally to the Middle Ages, and many of the Gothic novels that flourished in the wake of Horace Walpole's pioneering *The Castle of Otranto* (1765) would make use of a loosely medieval setting. Gothic plots are characteristically set in gloomy castles or other ruined edifices. The stories draw upon legends and superstitions, and abound with supernatural occurrences, with a common plot motif involving an innocent heroine falling into the power of a cruel and lustful suitor. Successful fictions of the general kind include William Beckford's *Vathek* (1786), Ann Radcliffe's *The Mysteries of Udolpho* (1794) and Matthew Lewis's *The Monk* (1796). Gothic fictions aimed to generate powerful emotional effects in their readership, including voyeuristic pleasure as well as shock and terror.

Journalism: The relation between journalism and literature is a complex one: literature can be journalistic in nature, and journalism in its turn can have literary merit. One useful distinction, however, is that journalism is usually intent on acquiring only an immediate, fleeting significance whereas literary works aspire to permanence. Historians have traced the beginnings of a journalistic culture to the 1690s, a decade which saw an explosion of periodicals and news pamphlets. The aim of journalism has always been to capitalize on the newsworthy and journalistic effusions poured out on a wide range of topics. The great storm of 1703 led to a number of documentary accounts, including one by Defoe, and there were numerous journalistic narratives of supernatural events, notorious crimes and deathbed conversions. The early eighteenth century sees the rise of polite periodicals such as *The Tatler* (1709) and *The Spectator* (1711), which contained essays on moral and social issues as well as literary criticism. The *Gentleman's Magazine* appeared in 1731 and the *Monthly Review* in 1749, in time becoming the leading journal for literary reviews. Numerous authors devoted some of their time to penning ephemeral pamphlets (as Defoe did in great number) or composing essays for the periodicals. Addison, Fielding and Johnson were all exponents of the latter form of writing. In his *Journal of the Plague Year* (1722), Defoe achieved a form of writing that is both journalistic and novelistic at the same time.

Labouring-class poets: Most of the authors who traditionally feature on eighteenth-century literature syllabuses are highly educated, belonging to the small cultural elite who benefited from a university education. While Pope never attended university and Johnson never actually graduated, both had opportunities to become widely read in classical literature. Not all authors, though, shared this privileged background. Many men and women from the uneducated classes also valued poetry and tried to make a name for themselves as practitioners of it. Stephen Duck, author of *The Thresher's Labour* (1730), was perhaps the most hailed in his own time of these self-taught poets, becoming celebrated by members of elite culture as a sort of prodigy of his social class. Duck writes about the annual toil of a rural worker: he experiences the countryside as someone who laboured in it, not as a country gentleman contemplating it from the window of his country seat. Yet we should not assume that working-class poets were unlearned by definition. Duck's style is quite literary in nature, as is that of Mary Leapor, a kitchen maid whose writing was encouraged by her employer amongst others. However, with other poets, such as the washerwoman Mary Collier, we are aware of a direct rendering of their experience that seems largely unmediated by the conventions of high literature. Issues of valuation are often unavoidable when we confront such poetic voices. Do we value the vivid honesty with which someone like Collier records her working experience, or do we attach more significance to a poem like Gray's 'Elegy Written in a Country Churchyard' (1751), full of beautifully phrased but also highly inexperienced reflections on the plight of the rural poor?

Letter writing: Most eighteenth-century authors were also voluminous letter writers. Literary correspondence was made easier by the improved efficiency after 1700 of the postal service but it was also encouraged by the changing social status of authors. The eighteenth century is the first period in which some authors were viewed as celebrities and the preservation of their possessions and effects (including letters) as a valuable undertaking. Pope appears to be the first English author to have published his own correspondence. Letters were also to prove crucial to the development of the novel. Richardson, Smollett and other influential novelists practised a technique called epistolary fiction in which the story is rendered entirely through the interchange of letters between characters. The method can support a multiplicity of points of view and also permits a greater degree of intimacy with characters than is often the case with a third-person narrator.

London: In the eighteenth century, London, as well as being by far the largest city in England, was the only one in which aspiring writers could hope to forge a career. It exerted a massive attractive force on young literary talent. Some writers whose upbringing was in the English provinces (such as John Gay and Samuel Johnson) relocated to London to find literary work, and numerous others flooded in from Scotland and Ireland. What attracted them was participation in a fully developed literary economy in which they could reasonably expect to make a living from selling their wares. Many literary works of the age are set in London and exploit the scenes and topography of the city for literary effect: such works include Defoe's novel *Moll Flanders* (1722) and Pope's poem *The Dunciad* (1728). One particularly important social institution was the coffee house, of which there were a great number in London. They provided a venue where cultured gentlemen could meet and debate the topics of the moment. In the later eighteenth century, poets start to react against the city. Wordsworth and Coleridge both see themselves as making an ethical statement when they choose to live in the country.

Mock-heroic: Mock-heroic poems work by telling a story through a series of orchestrated parallels with epic poems, either the classical epics of Homer or Virgil or the celebrated English epic, Milton's *Paradise Lost* (1667). The weighty allusions to the world of epic invariably throw into ironic relief the underlying pettiness of the incidents being depicted. Pope's celebrated mock-heroic poem *The Rape of the Lock* (1712), for example, concerns the trifling lifestyle of a society lady and in particular her vexation when a suitor cuts off a lock of her hair. It was modelled on a real-life incident, and the portentous references to epic incidents were intended by Pope to contrast with the silliness displayed by all the parties involved in the squabble. In a looser sense, mock-heroic effects arise when an author represents lowly or unimportant events in a deliberately 'high' style. Henry Fielding frequently does this in his novels. In *Joseph Andrews* (1742), for example, he describes in grandiloquent mock-Homeric style an incident in which Joseph and his friend Parson Adams find themselves attacked by a pack of dogs.

Neo-classicism: In the eighteenth century, being educated meant being able to read Latin and knowing something about the nature of classical culture. Most children attended school for only a short time, but those who were able to continue with their studies would attend grammar schools, specifically so-named because they taught Latin grammar. It should come as no surprise that authors, being mainly drawn from this educated elite, should be heavily influenced by classical models. For many people, acquaintance with classical literature was accompanied by an attitude of deep reverence towards it and a despondent conviction that modern authors could never rival the achievements of their ancient predecessors. Others, however, maintained that contemporary writers should adopt a much more competitive relation towards what the classical authors had achieved. When scholars describe the early eighteenth century as a neo-classical age, they mean that it was a period in which authors routinely looked towards the classics, using classical genres, alluding to classical works, and trying to uphold classical literary values. The main English literary genre that, to some extent, bucks the trend and shuns neo-classicism is the novel. The early novelists Defoe and Richardson both lacked a classical education and seem in their writings to be indifferent to classical culture.

Novel: Many of the literary genres practised in the eighteenth century derived from the classical period, but one that is in many respects the eighteenth century's own invention is the novel. The novel has turned out to be literature's greatest success story: nowadays many more people read novels, in any of the different guises the form now presents, than delve into either poetry or drama. The development of the novel in the eighteenth century has often been associated with the advent of a new literary concept: realism. Early novels, especially of the kind written by Daniel Defoe, depict recognizable types of people trying to weather misfortunes that are for the most part of a familiar kind. Novels are also the first literary kind in which the plausibility of the action mattered to the reader's rewarding engagement with the text. Why and exactly when the novel began has been a source of considerable debate among critics. An influential theory is that its growth is closely related to the rise of the entrepreneurial middle classes. While Daniel Defoe has often been hailed as the 'father' of the English novel, critics now appreciate how the novel constitutes a coalescence of numerous earlier strands of prose writing.

These include popular journalism, biography, travel writing, the Puritan tradition of spiritual biography represented by Bunyan's *Life and Death of Mr Badman* (1680), and the amatory or scandalous fiction of Delarivière Manley and Eliza Haywood. It is hard to differentiate in practice between novels and pre-novels.

Ode: The ode is a form of lyric poem, that is, a poem of relatively short length that normally represents the thoughts and words of a single person. In the eighteenth-century, odes written in the style of the Greek poet Pindar enjoyed a marked poetic vogue. Pindar, a Theban, wrote a series of ceremonious odes in honour of victors in the Greek Olympics. They were composed in an elaborate structure, consisting of sequences of lines termed the strophe, anti-strophe and epode. Pindaric odes become a speciality of several poets in the mid-eighteenth century including Thomas Gray and William Collins.

Originality: For many writers in the early eighteenth century, originality was not such a paramount literary virtue as it is today. For poets such as Pope, the imitation and emulation of classical models was more important than the pursuit of the authentically new. Pope would almost certainly have considered his greatest literary imitation to be, not an original work at all, but his applauded translation of Homer's *Iliad*. Similarly, in the fable of the bee and the spider in his *A Tale of a Tub* (1704), Swift condemns modern authors as being like spiders, spinning their literary works entirely out of themselves rather than gladly drawing nutrition from the writings of others. In the middle of the eighteenth century, however, a notable change of attitude occurs, sometimes associated with the appearance of Edward Young's *Conjectures on Original Composition* (1759). Young believed that while it might be no bad thing for writers to model themselves on their predecessors, they should not be slavish in doing so. They should always be striving to surpass, rather than be contained by, what earlier writer had done. In the wake of Young's essay, other critics start more openly extolling the virtues of originality and exploring its characteristic psychology, which they increasingly associate with 'genius'. This new climate was unsettling for authors whose poetic technique made use of extensive borrowing from others. Both Thomas Gray and Charlotte Smith added footnotes to later editions of their works in which they identified references expressly so as to avoid the charge of plagiarism. One of the casualties of the new attitude is Pope. His poetic reputation drops significantly in the second half of the century because of the perceived lack of originality of his poetry. At the same time, Shakespeare becomes increasingly venerated as a paragon of literary genius and originality.

Patronage: For all that the literary marketplace was expanding rapidly, many writers still had to scrimp to make ends meet. Many lived on, or in the vicinity of, Grub Street, a notably insalubrious part of the city, and stories of genuine hardship suffered by writers are grimly common at this time. One source of financial support might come from a patron, normally of aristocratic station, who would provide an author with the means of subsistence. In reciprocation, authors would provide flattering dedications, publicly extolling the merits of their patron, and use their writing to promote his or her interests. Writers who were supported by patronage had to put up with having their freedom curtailed but this was seen as a necessary compromise if the arrangement brought financial security. Some authors, however, expressed resentment at the patronage system and felt let down by the indifference of patrons. Dr Johnson wrote a famous letter to Lord Chesterfield, sometimes described as sounding the 'death-knell of patronage', admonishing the nobleman for broken promises of support over Johnson's project for an English dictionary. Yet few writers who themselves lacked aristocratic connections could make ends meet without patronage. One who could, though, was Pope, the first financially successful poet in the history of English literature. Because of his wealth, Pope never required the services of a patron and prided himself on his creative and intellectual independence.

Poetic diction: What should the proper relation be between the language of poetry and the language of everyday usage? In the eighteenth century, most writers subscribed to the view that poetry was different from normal language: poems had to be composed of a language that was consciously refined and perfected. This is indeed one of the obvious distinctions between the aesthetic of poetry and that of the emerging novel. One way that poets distanced their poetic language from ordinary language was through archaism, through using words that had already become old-fashioned. One such poet is Thomas Gray whose poems are full of examples of linguistic quaintness as when he addresses his old school, Eton College, with the line 'Ye distant spires, ye antique towers'. One linguistic technique that seems particularly instrumental in eighteenth-century poetic diction is periphrasis or circumlocution. Poets seem to have delighted in roundabout, sometimes teasingly cryptic ways of expressing concepts. Gray, for example, in the same poem on Eton College refers to a careering hoop as the 'rolling circle's speed', and James Thomson routinely uses such expressions about animals, referring for example to farmyard hens as 'household, feathery People'. It was the artificiality of Augustan poetic diction that Romantic poets like Wordsworth felt a particular need to repudiate. For Wordsworth, the poet's true vocation rested in plain communication, as 'a man speaking to men'.

Political writing: The early eighteenth century is the first period in which literary culture is significantly influenced by party politics. The two main political parties were the Tories and Whigs: the Tories supported the absolute hereditary right of the monarchy, tended to support the cause of the landed aristocracy, and were seen as the High Church party; Whigs, on the other hand, believed in the curtailment of monarchical power, backed the interests of the commercial classes, and were Low Church and anti-Catholic. It should be noted that neither party in any way supported the interests of lower-class people since these were denied the vote and accordingly had no political representation. Though members of parliament could increasingly be identified as either Whigs or Tories, their respective numbers did not determine the complexion of the executive. The government of the country was determined simply by the nature of the advisers chosen by the monarch. It cannot be emphasized too much that eighteenth-century writers are much politicized: there exist few who cannot be identified with allegiance to a particular political persuasion. Alexander Pope, a Tory, is a good example of a poet whose writing expresses strong political leanings, and whose vocation as a satirist owes a lot to the fact that his party was in political opposition during almost the entirety of his literary career. For many writers, including Pope, a particularly hated figure was Sir Robert Walpole who as a Whig held the post of prime minister (the first to occupy such a role) between 1721 and 1742.

Pre-Romanticism: The eighteenth century has always proved a difficult period to categorize, resisting trite labels. While the early eighteenth century has tended to be seen as a period in which neo-classical principles are particularly dominant, literary neo-classicism is already on the wane by the time of Pope's death (1744). Indeed, even as early as 1730, we can see new forms of poetry emerging that seem to swerve away from neo-classical tenets and point forward to a Romantic aesthetic: such poetry is often called 'pre-Romantic'. The poetry we associate with neo-classicism tends to take the heroic couplet as its main expressive form; tends to be committed to depicting and often satirizing an exterior world, essentially that of English society; tends to use the city of London as its principal venue or backdrop; and views poetry as an inherently moralistic art. However, in poetry written by the likes of James Thomson, Thomas Gray and William Collins, these characteristics are notably absent. These poets show a greater interest in the natural world, and often depict the poet as a remote outsider, producing poetry out of a rapt process of self-communion. They are also more likely to exalt the imagination as the essence of poetic creativity. Their poems also tend to be emotional in tone, and intent on inducing pathos in the reader. When later Romantic poets like Wordsworth look back at their earlier eighteenth-century predecessors, it is works such as Thomson's nature poem *The Seasons* (1730) that they characteristically admire most.

Romanticism: Romanticism is a broadly European movement from about 1789 to 1830, affecting literature, music and painting. Its English dimension has come to be associated with the six major poets: Wordsworth, Coleridge, Blake, Shelley, Keats and Byron. Wordsworth's 'Preface' (1800) to the *Lyrical Ballads* has sometimes been viewed as a manifesto for the movement in England. Recent study of English Romanticism, however, has been particularly vexed by problems of definition. For one thing, concentration on the six canonical male poets has drawn attention away from female writers such as Charlotte Smith, who were significant in their own time, as well as from a range of non-poetic voices that could loosely be called Romantic. Although it is accepted that common themes can be traced across Romantic authors, such as an interest in nature and in the transcendence of the imagination, these similarities are perhaps outweighed by differences. The sense of common cause remains limited. Some critics now argue that all that truly binds such authors together are shared historical circumstances. They all lived in a period of revolution, and participated in the hopes and anxieties of the age. In this sense Romanticism can be dated quite precisely from the outbreak in 1789 of the French Revolution, which sent shockwaves across Europe and led to a protracted state of war between England and France.

Satire: The eighteenth century has often been viewed as a satiric age, and there is perhaps no other literary period in which so many of the leading poets practised forms of satire. Satire was a mode that eighteenth-century authors had inherited from classical poets, especially Horace and Juvenal: Horace being associated with a gentler tone and Juvenal with a rougher, more aggressive one. Satire was less a genre as such than an attitude that could be expressed in many different kinds of literary work. John Gay's *The Beggar's Opera* (1728), for example, is a notable satiric play. Satirists like Pope tend to justify their attacks on individuals and society in general by claiming their purpose to be that of moral reform. In one of his best satiric poems, the *Epistle to Arbuthnot* (1735), Pope draws attention to his own personal morality and professional impartiality as a means of establishing the probity of his attacks on his enemies. However, readers nowadays are not obliged to accept eighteenth-century satire at its word. Even Pope, the most brilliant satiric wit of his day, resorts regularly to bludgeoning defamation of his enemies. Many satiric poems of the early eighteenth century employ insults that are so abusive and foul-minded that they would be unprintable in the modern day.

Sensibility: The word 'sensibility', little used before the mid-eighteenth century, denoted a rarefied susceptibility to feeling, very often expressed as a sympathetic concern for the anguish of another person. Sensibility, as a way of responding to the world, is evident in a wide range of literary writings between 1740 and the end of the century. Novels of sensibility (or sentimental novels) often show how feelings of distress or sympathetic concern imprint themselves on the body, with characters blushing, crying or swooning as a response to nerve-wracking situations. In novels such as Sarah Fielding's *The Adventures of David Simple* (1744), a generous-spirited and openly emotional response towards other people and their problems is seen as morally superior to a more analytical and dispassionate reaction. Sensibility is an ingredient in the work of several major poets of the period including Thomas Gray and Charlotte Smith. A characteristic motif in Smith's poetry is a sort of optical recession in which the narrator watches and sympathizes with the emotions experienced by another character at some affecting spectacle: take, for example, her elegy 'addressed to a young lady, who was affected at seeing the funeral of a nameless pauper'. In Laurence Sterne's *A Sentimental Journey* (1768), the self-indulgent and comically precious nature of sensibility is treated in an ironic way.

Versification: Eighteenth-century poets use a set of verse forms that have long passed out of vogue and can seem rather alienating for modern readers. The most common is the heroic couplet, consisting of ten-syllable lines in which alternating lines rhyme with each other. This is the verse form we associate with Pope, its finest exponent. Pope's preference for the heroic couplet reflects many of his larger convictions about culture and society. The exterior form is orderly and disciplined (we might say regimented) though Pope is able to achieve many subtle, modulating effects in individual lines and across couplets. The form chimes with Pope's general sense that all art forms should aim to achieve a principle of harmony. Though the dominant verse form in the early century, the heroic couplet quickly falls out of favour after about 1750. Other important verse forms you might come across are the eight-syllable (octosyllabic) rhyming couplets preferred by Swift, which often accompany a comic and ribald tone of writing, and Miltonic blank verse, a non-rhyming form based on sprawling verse paragraphs. It should be noted that all three verse forms mentioned here are continuous or non-stanzaic. Though many eighteenth-century poems do employ stanzas, a higher proportion of non-stanzaic poetry is probably written in this era than in any other.

7 'Dead Keen on Reason?' Changes in Critical Responses and Approaches to the Eighteenth Century

Philip Smallwood

Chapter Overview

The elder of us were bred up in the critical conviction that the eighteenth century was one century we need not worry about: we knew precisely where it stood, and what it stood for. It was fixed in its appointed place, and there it would always be when we cared to look again. We understood its values, and they bored us. The interesting thing was to see how the

> human spirit struggled out of that straightjacket into new life. (Anderson and Shea 1967: 15)

> If the 'Eighteenth century' ever could be defined in and as itself, it would quite simply become unreadable to us, and . . . its continued readability and availability for discussion depend on our not quite knowing what it is and in general on its failure to be quite itself. (Bennington 2007: 392)

Change and Continuity in 'Eighteenth-Century Studies'

'Smug men' with their 'tight little couplets', and 'so dead keen on reason', was how the American poet Sylvia Plath (1932–63) styled her loathing of the eighteenth century when in *The Bell Jar* she relates how she decided to 'skip' the period as part of her undergraduate literary studies (Plath 2005 [1963]:120). From the time of Plath to the present age of easy electronic access to eighteenth-century texts that is afforded by Literature on Line (LION), and, more specifically, by the indispensable online Eighteenth-Century Collections (ECCO), much has changed, and much has gone unchanged. The following section of this volume is devoted to ways of seeing the literature and culture of the eighteenth century that have accompanied transitions in scholarship and tastes over the last thirty or so years. And because methodological shifts in 'Eighteenth-Century Studies' are bound up with why and how we construe the period's lasting achievements today, the argument I am about to advance is a prologue to the next chapter of this volume which focuses on the so-called literary 'canon', and is preparatory to later discussions of present critical attitudes, to history and to definition, to gender and sexuality and to some key theoretical concepts. The present chapter does not attempt to replicate the detailed *resumés* of scholarly production from past individual years; these are best encountered in the qualitative-narrative overviews that can be found in the volumes of the *Year's Work in English Studies* (1919–), published by The English Association.

The first change (significant of one most imposing development) is the surge in popularity of the eighteenth century over the last three or four decades amongst scholars and students. A swing in affections since the time of Plath is striking, and is a reversal that has taken place despite the dire observation of a few years ago to the effect that more graduate students of literature in the United Kingdom had enrolled to conduct new research into the 'magic realist' fiction of Angela Carter (1940–92) than were recruited to investigate the entire eighteenth century. The number of scholarly books published upon the period offers an approximate guide to the present state of public opinion and undergraduate taste, and predicates a substantial market of purchasers, borrowers and readers. Strong attendance at major conferences can suggest that the eighteenth century is now arguably one of the most active of the chronologically-defined academic literary fields.

Any survey of critical and scholarly change is bound, however, to focus mainly on developments in the British and North American study of the eighteenth century, and I am leaving out of the account, arbitrarily no doubt, scholarly research into the eighteenth century by *dix-huitièmistes* in France, Spain, Italy or Germany, or even in India or Japan, where eighteenth-century literature is taught at university level, and where original research on English writing of the period is pursued. I have therefore made no attempt to provide an accurate conspectus of the 'globalization' of 'Eighteenth-Century Studies' in this essay. The influence of national histories on scholarly and critical perspectives cannot, however, be left entirely out of the account. Most significantly perhaps (and for example), American readers did not enjoy the reign of a Queen Victoria, and much American political and cultural life has its roots in the world of the eighteenth century. This is in virtue of the work of the Founding Fathers, a written constitution based on Enlightenment values, and the prestige of such Enlightenment figures as Thomas Jefferson (1743–1826) and Benjamin Franklin (1706–90). Such factors encourage a more unbroken continuity of historical and cultural contact with the period than has been possible in the British Isles, while the sheer magnitude of the North American academy, when set beside the minuter business of British university life, has always ensured that nothing of much importance has been too completely ignored for very long.

Two major characteristics in the expansion of 'Eighteenth-Century Studies' over the last three decades can be discerned on both sides of the Atlantic. The first is that it is now called just that – 'Eighteenth-Century *Studies*' (and not specifically the study of literature, history, politics, law, art or philosophy, etc.); the second is that the period which constitutes the scope of 'Eighteenth-Century Studies' requires its inverted commas, in that it has been stretched to some extent at both ends, but mainly in the early part of its range, it having hitherto traditionally been thought to begin forty years before the chronological eighteenth century with the restoration of a Stuart monarch (Charles II) to the English throne. In company with this widening out, the coverage and identity of the eighteenth century has slid back and forth between newly extended limits (DeMaria 1997, 2001; Zwicker 1998; Fairer and Gerrard 1999), and at the latter end of the scale, the concept of the 'Long Eighteenth Century' vies with the so-called 'Romantic Century' for ownership of the age of Johnson (1709–84), Wordsworth (1770–1850), Blake (1757–1827), Cowper (1731–1800), Jane Austen (1775–1817), Peacock (1785–1866) and Crabbe (1754–1832). At the earlier end it merges with the recently coined but very pliable category of the so-called 'Early Modern'.

The Culturalization of 'Eighteenth-Century Studies'

To take first, however, what is, 'Eighteenth-Century Studies' studies, and to ask why, hand in hand with the advance in its popularity, such a period of years should now deserve more of our time. It is a truism that all history, including the history of literature and its cognate cultural expressions, requires to be broken up if it is to be understood. At the same time our sense of the past is as an unfragmented story, a narrative related (it is often said) to explain the present. But a narrative of what? Of literature? Of the visual arts? Of philosophical enquiry? Of political events? All these domains still separately attract their specialist students, but one prominent feature of the last thirty years has been the extent to which it has seemed possible to embrace these histories as a homogenized entity or synthesis called simply 'culture'.

One might meaningfully speak, I therefore suggest, of the *culturalization* of 'Eighteenth-Century Studies'. By this I observe that it is *de rigueur* in scholarly circles of late to require that any individual cultural expression (such as literature) should be conceptually opened to question, and that scholars should interpret the expressive value of such literature in its intimacy with other disciplinary forms. Such a development might be understood as a tilt in the direction of the 'interdisciplinary' which has found general institutional favour, and is widely encouraged by conference agendas and the syllabi of undergraduate and postgraduate programmes. This is not to deny that English Departments and English Studies – in which literature plays an important role – stand at the heart of such studies; but the inclusiveness of interdisciplinary studies has without doubt helped give 'Eighteenth-Century Studies' its newly advantageous critical mass.

One of the most important motives for change that has impelled the 'culturalization' of 'Eighteenth-Century Studies' has been the growing suspicion that the moral focus of such study ignores everyday social realities or fails sufficiently to take them into account; that literature is of itself objectionally elitist or class-burdened in some way. Such anxieties have surfaced through courses in popular literature, or popular forms of cultural expression that are not 'literature' (in one sense) but susceptible, nevertheless, to analysis by tools of textual interpretation. The concern is that the time has come to re-balance the scales in favour of more proletarian forms.

Great impetus has therefore been given to this movement by the development – alongside, out of, and to some extent *against* the study of literature – of academic Cultural Studies. The work of such British pioneers as Richard Hoggart (1918–) and Raymond Williams (1921–88) (neither of whom are scholars of the eighteenth century as such) is significant here, while the institution which Stefan Collini has characterized somewhat disparagingly as 'grievance studies' (Collini 1999: 252–68) has been given a simultaneous boost by celebrated French 'literary' theorists of recent years. The philosophical, psychological and political thinkers of a mingled Marxist, semiotic and Freudian persuasion – critics, in the broadest sense of the term, such as Roland Barthes (1915–80), Jacques Derrida (1930–2004), Michel Foucault (1926–84) or Jacques Lacan (1901–81) – came to international prominence in the 1970s, were widely translated into English, and still resonate. Their writings have had a compelling influence on critical manners in the North American academy, mainly, and almost always in translation, by mediation through 'theory guides', 'readers' and anthologies, where they have underpinned debates about identity politics, minority representation, and the unjust oppression of women, religious groups, homosexuals and the plight of people whose skin colouring happens to be black.

Again, we see, the study of literature as an autonomous category becomes merged, or submerged, in the formal and deeper examination of society in all its dimensions – moral, political, sexual, racial and so forth. 'Scholars interested in historical phenomena', writes Ruth Perry representatively, 'stand to learn a good deal from literary texts once they recognize that texts do not record behaviours but structures of feeling about social practices' (Perry 1999: 168).

Such has been the intensity of this interest in the eighteenth-century 'social practice', signified or disclosed by literature's 'structures of feeling', that the field once judged unappealingly narrow, boring, traditional, tight-shut and smugly elite (in Plath's sense of the eighteenth century), is now regarded as opened out, democratized, even revolutionized, and that as Perry exhorts, the study of the social *through* the literary cannot be contained within the limits of the present, but must fold attention back chronologically to engage with preceding societies. The *culturalization* of 'Eighteenth-Century Studies' can thus be seen as a consequence in part of important shifts in contemporary modes of studying humanity; most especially an affirmation of the belief that disciplinary distinctions are no longer enduring necessities marking off the intellectual habits of one subject from another, but provisional signs of the hidebound, of the traditional, of the academically (and therefore culturally) obsolete.

But before looking more closely at some of the reservations that must be entered in the face of this optimistic account of 'advance' and 'progress' in 'Eighteenth-Century Studies' over the last thirty years, let us consider some general consequences of the present dispensation. We see that while other categories have grown up to replace the ones that are now judged redundant or wrongly divided or defined, earlier structures remain as undegradable deposits within the complex of the present.

Politics and Society

The major forms that now characterize 'Eighteenth-Century Studies' have broadly the orientations established by the present modes of modern critical radicalism in its debt to nineteenth-century revolt against the eighteenth century: they are social and political, and they entail an acquaintance with society and politics as their *end*. We can thus speak of the reception of the eighteenth century as having acquired a cutting edge from, for example, Feminist and Gender Studies, where literary historians who were hitherto exclusively committed to charting the development of literature through the writings of men, have turned to the literary history of women. Numerous eighteenth-century women poets once overlooked by such historians while patriarchy held fast, are now presented in distinguished modern selections, editions and anthologies, are taught and examined with the same devoted attention once given (it is said) to a Dryden (1631–1700), a Swift (1667–1745), or a Samuel Johnson (see p. 41, Chapter 2, Contexts, Identities and Consumption: Gender; see p. 170, Chapter 9, Gender, Sexuality and Ethnicity).

So, therefore, while the 1973 Penguin Classics edition of *Eighteenth-Century English Verse* by Dennis Davison contains material by three female poets only, the new Fairer and Gerrard *Anthology* of 1999 includes work by an impressively wide array, and at a time when the desirability or existence of a literary canon is itself in question, the simultaneous canonization of female poets is a major development in eighteenth-century scholarship's *au courant* forms. In the Romantic narrative of freedom from oppression reinforced by critics of the New Left, the 'marginal' (or rather – undeservedly – 'marginalized') writer is newly centralized, and the role of the author, when female creativity replaces male authority, may still count for much.

Study of the novel in the eighteenth century is similarly made new by the challenge to an ideologically selective, and thereby reductive, literary history dominated by such male fictional writers as Samuel Richardson (1689–1761), Henry Fielding (1707–54), Daniel Defoe (1659–1731), Tobias Smollett (1721–71) and Laurence Sterne (1713–68) (Watt 1957; Turner 1992), while attention to the seventeenth- and eighteenth-century drama has been overwhelmed by the scholarly popularity of Aphra Behn's Restoration plays (1640–89), the dramatic works of a female author who possibly generates more discussion than all the male dramatists of the Restoration together. Memoirs, autobiographies, modes of life-writing (all forms thought to be especially congenial to women) have also come to prominence (Connolly 1993; Clarke 2004), while alongside this elevation of writers who were themselves women, there have arisen complementary feminist *readings* of writings composed by both sexes.

One speaks here of the 'gendering' of the eighteenth-century literary text, and the role of gender (as method on the one hand and as logical subject of literary scholarship on the other) has more than any other single influence attracted new admirers to the period's literary work. This is at various levels, so that traditional devotion to the canonical signature of Jane Austen's novels, for example, has been enhanced in latter years by liaison with the popular phenomenon of post-feminist 'Chick-Lit' (so-called) (Rumbold 1989; Clarke 2000). We want to know more about how women figured in the great male writers' lives. But mainly we want to see women asserting independent influence in the literary and cultural world and shaping on their own account a distinct tradition that foreshadows the great female emancipation and liberation movements of more recent times, within literature and (more importantly) without it.

From the question of 'gender' naturally arises the question of sexuality, including its homosexual and lesbian forms: the century, we say, has been 'queered' (see Chapter 9). Again, the rehabilitation of the eighteenth century over the last thirty years has been greatly assisted by heated debates over human sexual proclivities, deviations or rights. The role of feminized masculinity has here provided a point of reference for examination of eighteenth-century fashion, voyeurism and desire, casting new light on the courtly, poetic and dramatic culture of the famously licentious Restoration world (Webster 2005). The express obscenity of certain poems by the Earl of Rochester, the notorious John ('c'-word) Wilmot (1647–80), or the prostitution narratives of Cleland's *Memoirs of a Woman of Pleasure*, or *Fanny Hill* (1748–9), can now be examined with present sexual-ideological crises in mind. This intellectualization of Restoration erotica appropriates old literary works for today's debates, and brings the content of obscene poems and novels into the historical mainstream, even if the role of neo-puritan reaction to such writings (by feminist, political or religious moralists and fundamentalists for example) must qualify and complicate the narrative of liberalization.

The politics of sexuality arises from a wider sense of the political, and one of the most significant developments (again, not as new as it may at first appear) has been the harnessing of literary study to the objectives of the period's political-historical research. One powerful motive in this conjunction has once more been the imperative to read political history *through* literature; to see literary texts as having value as historical source material on the grounds that history is 'encoded' by literature, and to suggest that literature exists as a means to an exterior or ulterior end, just as historical events, conversely, provide an explanatory and reflective context for the de-codification of literary works.

The number of books and articles which take literary texts or figures as their *focus*, but are historical in their *objectives*, has correspondingly grown (Erskine-Hill, 1996: 5; Hudson, 2003). Such an approach aims to enhance sensitivity to the play of historical allusion within literary texts, even as it redefines literature's *raison d' être* as the medium for historical enquiry. Again, a logical corollary has been the working out of present-day intellectual, moral, political and aesthetic topicalities through eighteenth-century texts, such as the ethical issue of literary forgery represented by Macpherson's 'Ossian' (1761), or by Thomas Chatterton's poems. This class of phenomena is the focus of much new scholarship on the period having origins outside the world of 'Eighteenth-Century Studies', and may take place independently of the detailed textual analysis of literature, as does the study of fashion, dress, war, slavery, race, luxury, prostitution, medicine, gender, sex (or recent interest in the fact and figure of 'the body'). Once more, a pressing present moral and aesthetic agenda is extended back in time to texts of the eighteenth century which must be accorded a more significant historical role than they might have had. Probing of 'material culture' has under the same rubric prompted a return to the history of the book, as distinct from the literary quality of its contents, and conceived with more awareness of the economic dimension of its production, as a commodity that might be consumed (Rivers 2001).

Preoccupation with forms of the postmodernist novel, appreciative engagement with its narrative fragmentation, its 'carnival' and play, has promoted, in turn, a creative recurrence to aspects of the writing of Laurence Sterne, Jonathan Swift and Daniel Defoe, to re-imaginings of the eighteenth century by novelists such as John Coetzee (1986), Jeannette Winterson (1990) and Peter Ackroyd (1987), and has re-united the literature of the period with moral and social priorities of the critical present. The same eighteenth-century writers have also re-focused historical interest in the literature of travel (second only perhaps to the study of gender in effecting a wholesale revival of 'Eighteenth-Century Studies'), in a literature shaped through the discovery of new worlds by explorers such as Captain Cook (1728–79), and in the project of colonial expansion under the aspect of the 'postcolonial'. Expressed in slightly more sceptical terms, the linkage has overlayed the template of the present's social, economic and cultural order upon the materials of the eighteenth-century texts.

The Canon Displaced?

Two kinds of evidence enable us to plot this advance in 'Eighteenth-Century Studies', and – just as importantly – to see how over the last few decades the advance may be attributed less to a change of taste involving fully-argued revaluations of the period's authors, than to an adjustment in methods of thinking about them, this underpinned by an ideological shift having implications for taste that are not necessarily confronted or declared (see p. 155,

Chapter 8, Questioning Canonicity). One kind of evidence is the formation, contents, orientation and categories of the best standard histories of literature of the period; the other – more ephemeral – is an evolving emphasis on the major international conference agendas.

Thus, the Thirty-Eighth Annual Meeting of the American Society for Eighteenth-Century Studies (2007) held in Atlanta, Georgia, marshals papers on canonical British authors and such topics as the creative relations between William Cowper and Alexander Pope (1688–1744). But the meeting also prominently mounts presentations that are by turns intercultural, international and interdisciplinary: such, for example, as the matter of 'Pleasures and Female Desire in *Clarissa*', 'Punishment Fantasies in Eighteenth-Century Germany', 'Negotiating Maternal Femininity within the Professional Lives of Late Eighteenth-Century Actresses', 'Balloonomania in the French Periodical Press, 1783–1784', 'Austen on the Web, in Your Home, and in a Theatre Near You', 'Aborted Signification: Pregnancy and the Exiled Body in Behn's Love-Letters' and (combining in a single title two very popular themes) 'Dressing the British: The Habits of Nationalism in Eighteenth-Century Costume Books'.

From titles of this form one infers how far major writers of both sexes, such as Austen and Richardson, are still valued by the current population of scholars, though they are most often recruited for the purposes of cultural-historical analysis in new, surprising and sometimes delightful, sometimes eccentric or consciously eye-catching ways. Even within the community of specialist scholarship, a more popularized and even sensationalized study of the eighteenth century has successfully gained ground. At the same time, the de-canonization is real enough, and the programme for the 2007 meeting of the International Society for Eighteenth-Century Studies held at Montpelier in France contains – perhaps not surprisingly – very little on the century's most important English poet: Alexander Pope. Significant of the critical atmosphere of the times is that there are few signs to the effect that this absence constitutes a crisis of perspective in 'Eighteenth-Century Studies'.

In the recently published *Cambridge History of English Literature, 1660–1780* (2005), the volume editor has correspondingly reduced the role played in the older, grander historical narrative by authors who once seemed 'Major', and in their place sought to represent various kinds of current social and political commitment whose value is manifest in the production of eighteenth-century literature – most especially by women and writers of the 'labouring class' (Richetti 2005, 1–9). There is the confidence of having made an ungainsayable judgement in the comments of one contributor to this volume (Paula Backschieder) who wrote that 'We know that literary movements are not made by single great poets' (Richetti 2005: 234), while in the Introduction it is stated as fact (and without complicating engagement in the controversies) that 'there has been a disorientating succession of intellectual revolutions' which has served to challenge the notion that 'literature is a privileged artistic and cultural institution' (Richetti 2005:1). For the purposes of re-writing the literary history of the eighteenth century, such a challenge is assumed to be real and its consequences desirable.

This assurance, to be taken largely on trust, that we are now passing through a phase in eighteenth-century scholarship when the period's literary eminences have been brought low, is reflected in the contents of the volume – a series of specialized essays by diverse hands – where the stress falls on various general categories and themes (such as the book history mentioned above) rather than single authors. In such a way, then, and in response to an increasingly culturalized literary study characteristic of the present day, has the narrative of eighteenth-century literary history also evolved. New units of significance have emerged, but without always a high degree of contestation on the desirability of whether they should.

One could, on this foundation, conclude that the study of the eighteenth century has now been democratized, though the essays in the volume remain unashamedly specialized contributions to knowledge. One could deduce that eighteenth-century literature had been de-canonized, except that areas held in high esteem by eighteenth-century readers, but neglected by scholars of later generations – such as verse translation – are not always acknowledged; nor, for that matter are certain non-canonical but historically influential authors – such as Abraham Cowley (1618–67) – hitherto considered as 'minor', but who, not being women, or sufficiently of the labouring classes, lack sufficient credentials for a wholesale revival (Mason and Hopkins, 1994).

The reluctance of such prominent literary histories to foreground fully the role of translated verse is balanced out, however, by other evidence suggesting that a post-Victorian cultural aversion to translation has now been shed (Mason 1972; Hammond 1999; Hopkins and Gillespie 1995–2005). Once an 'Age of Satire' in which two quite early satirical poems, *MacFlecknoe* (1682) and *Absalom and Achitophel* (1681), were given almost exclusive attention by university teachers of Dryden, the period can now be seen as a phase of profound cultural transmission inspired by Dryden's later (translated) work – his versions of Ovid (from 1680), of Horace and Lucretius (of 1685), Juvenal (1692), Virgil (1697), and in 1700 Homer, Ovid, Boccaccio and 'our old English poet' Geoffrey Chaucer. Thus can the mediation of Dryden's poetry begin to move beyond an imbalanced attention to contexts of poetical origin, such as compulsory study of the so-called 'Popish Plot'[1] (the indispensable political and religious background to Dryden's *Absalom*), to the texts themselves and to the foreground of their intrinsic poetical qualities. Renewed attention has been given to a pedagogy based on the plays of Dryden, but with the disadvantage of a focus that is not always or often the best of his work, as his contemporaries were the first to admit.

The Role of Scholarly Editions

This re-discovery of the *range* of Dryden's poetic achievement over the last thirty years is due in part, I suggest, to the fresh editorial efforts devoted to the long eighteenth century, whereby verse translation has begun to encroach on satire as the period's signature genre, and where satire can be enjoyed *in* translations as well as in original poems. The final volumes of the 'Twickenham' Pope were published at about the beginning of the scholarly era we are concerned with here (the verse translations of Homer appeared in the 1980s) while sustained energies have also been devoted to the editing of Samuel Johnson. Since the appearance of its earliest volume in 1958, the standard Johnson has been *The Yale Edition of the Works*, an editorial joint effort for the most part, and involving teams of scholars working on individual volumes or volume groups. This project has proceeded in order over the years to include important reprintings of the *Poems* (1964), the *Rambler* essays (over three volumes in 1969), the *Idler and Adventurer* (in a single volume in 1963) and the Shakespeare criticism (over two volumes in 1968).

More recently there has appeared an edition of *Rasselas* (1990), and a volume of Johnson's reflections on language (2005). A 'Yale' edition of Johnson's critical and biographical masterpiece of 1779–81, *The Lives of the Poets*, hitherto available in the standard three-volume edition of George Birkbeck Hill (published in 1905), is at the time of writing in press. Roger Lonsdale's impressive four-volume Clarendon *Lives* published in 2006 (and running to over 2,000 pages with copious commentary) offers in the meantime a highly authoritative alternative, a comprehensive critical and textual introduction and extremely learned and generous notes.

Other standard editions recently published, or under construction, include the Cambridge University Press printing of Jane Austen's *Works*, and a fresh edition, from the same press, of the *Works* of Jonathan Swift. Both bring, or will bring, an enhanced professional expertise to the editing of major eighteenth-century authors and they come with the methodological imprimatur of new editorial schools. As in the major editions of North American origin – such as the multi-volume 'California' Dryden or the 'Yale' Johnson – there is again a team approach. We see the expertise of the wider corporate environment informing the elucidation of eighteenth-century literary texts.

In addition to these important new primary texts, critical and scholarly monographs of a specialized nature have at the same time rarely seemed more abundant, with dedicated eighteenth-century series augmenting the lists of such publishing houses as Cambridge, Delaware, Georgia and Bucknell University Press. Publishers such as Macmillan, AMS and Ashgate have built impressive eighteenth-century series, and seem keen to expand them apace. For all the success of the move to de-canonize literature, prominent critical studies of Dryden, Pope and Johnson have appeared from Oxford University Press, from Harvard, and from Chicago during the period under review. Major critical biographies, volumes such James Winn's study of Dryden (1987), Maynard Mack on Pope (1985) and John Wain (1974), W. J. Bate (1977) or Robert DeMaria Jr (1993) on Johnson, have likewise strengthened awareness of such major figures.

Scholarly Journals and Literary Criticism

Journal publication on the eighteenth century observes the orthodoxy that the most respectable advanced-level scholarship should ideally mingle disciplines and approaches. This is an explicit policy, for example, in the case of *Eighteenth-Century Studies* itself, of *Eighteenth-Century Life*, which is 'committed to interdisciplinary exchange', of *Studies in Eighteenth-Century Culture*, and of the British Society's equivalent of these publications, *The British Journal for Eighteenth-Century Studies*, now re-born as *The Journal for Eighteenth-Century Studies*. There is presently no journal, on either side of the Atlantic, exclusively devoted to publishing articles and essays on eighteenth-century literature (as distinct, say, from the narrower category of 'eighteenth-century fiction' which is specifically served).

The relationship of literature to theory motivates two periodicals (both American): *The Eighteenth Century: Theory and Interpretation* and *1650–1850: Ideas, Aesthetics and Inquiries in the Early Modern Era*, while the annual *Age of Johnson* caters for a literary and a cultural interest alike under the rubric of 'Johnson Studies'. Other critical essays on eighteenth-century authors can be found in a wide variety of locations: *Studies in English Literature: 1500–1900*, *English: the Journal of the English Association*, *The Review of English Studies* and *Essays in Criticism* amongst several. None of these channels of scholarly communication would claim an exclusive focus in the literature of the eighteenth century.

At the same time, aiming at a readership somewhat beyond the limits of a purely academic reception, the essays and reviews in the *Times Literary Supplement* (*TLS*), and in the *London Review of Books* (*LRB*), have made a steady contribution to the body of general criticism on the period, which again implies a more general audience. And if the distinction between scholarly writing and criticism can be sustained, much good critical comment on long-eighteenth-century topics can be extracted from *The Cambridge Quarterly*, a British periodical that 'was established on, and remains committed to, the principle that literature is an art, and that the purpose of art is to give pleasure and enlightenment'. A recent number of this journal (37 [3]), the latest published at the time of writing, appeals to a Johnsonian test of time as a principle for the construction of modern literary anthologies. Of this the intended effect is concertedly anti-historicist and suggests the currency of Johnson's ideas as they manifest a practical pertinence to problems in literary studies of the present day (Hopkins 2008).

There is, then, evidence that the study of eighteenth-century literature can still draw upon twentieth-century traditions of close reading of literary texts, can be driven by evaluation as distinct from interpretation, and can prioritize critical practice as it differs from literary history or theory. The most active voices in the British criticism of the 1940s and 50s did not notably reinforce the positive claims made for English eighteenth-century work, and the critic F. R. Leavis (1895–1978), in his essays on Johnson and on Pope, could be both respectful and disparaging by turns, celebrating the most powerful satires of Pope (as also Swift's) on some occasions, and on others re-invigorating a Plath-like sense of the period's narrowness, conventionality, and rigidity compared with the revolutionary achievements of, say, a Donne, a Dickens or a Blake. 'The thoughts that the Augustan poet, like any other Augustan writer, sets himself to express', wrote Leavis (in an essay on 'Johnson and Augustanism'), 'are amply provided for by the ready-minted concepts of the common currency' (Leavis 1952: 109).

Some of the best essays on Dryden, Cowley, Johnson and Pope in *The Cambridge Quarterly* at the same time successfully recall the spirit that Leavis extends to other parts of the poetical past, in that they assume that eighteenth-century authors have something of immediate value – and something of intrinsic pleasure – to contribute to the life of the present time. We read them, in Leavis's phrase, 'as we read the living'. There is, in this, a significant departure from the historical, cultural or political-ideological orientation of the bulk of historically-minded journal scholarship, and behind such a project stands the remains of an educated general readership for literary production; one that goes beyond university departments, and connects professional commentary with the teaching of English in schools, and with the enjoyment of literature in the population at large. Such critical writing appeals to a global, democratized, *espace public* in a different sense from that defined by the academy's *culturalization*, and affirms the enduring continuities of intra- and extra-mural communities of reading.

Controlling Concepts and Categories

That being said, it remains the period's historical categories, in their cultural dimension, that have been most generally significant in attracting new scholarly writing to the field. Thus, in its widest application, the term 'Augustan' is still credibly employed to describe literature as a component part of culture in the period from Milton to Wordsworth, the time when, in creating original work, writers turned for inspiration to Latin authors contemporary with the

Emperor Augustus – and in particular to Virgil (born 70 BC), to Ovid (43 BC–AD 17), and to Horace (65 BC–AD 5). In its most limited extension, this 'Augustan' designation may represent little more than the early maturity of Alexander Pope, and one of the first recorded uses of the term was that of Joseph Warton (1722–1800), writing in the middle of the period, who refers to the latter years of King William and the reign of Queen Anne (Warton 1756: 154).

But when and where, within the period, we ourselves find this Augustan spirit operative, applicable, and at large is always subject to critical interpretation, and confidence in the use of the term is often correlative with a low (homogenizing) estimate imposed on the major literary achievements of the eighteenth century – an evaluation, I would suggest, unconsciously derived from the estimates of the rebellious Romantic sons and daughters of the Augustans. In any event, there is no unifying formula to capture the variety of ways that creative contact was established with Roman works. One may talk of 'classical models', and English and French writers did, in some explicit respects, 'model' their work on the classics of the ancient Roman world, not least in their translations and imitations; but the range and intimacy of relationships between model and modeller is largely lost in the phrase (see p. 128, Chapter 6, Key Critical Concepts and Topics: Neo-classicism).

A more capacious term is 'Enlightenment', a classification necessary to cultural history which links the British (including the Scottish) 'Augustan' literary scene with its philosophers and thinkers (especially Adam Smith [1723–90], David Hume [1711–76], Edmund Burke [1729–97] and Edward Gibbon [1737–94]) and embraces contemporary continental movements, such as the work of Voltaire (1694–1778), Montesquieu (1689–1755), Diderot (1713–84), and others of the French *philosophes*. Such a vision is especially congenial to an interdisciplinary conception of the eighteenth century, while at the same time it is able to suggest a substantial ideological target for late-twentieth-century Foucauldian questionings of the culture of reason, this seen as epitomizing the corrupted bourgeois world against which the ideology of radical 'Theory' has defined its revolutionary purpose (see p. 123, Chapter 6, Key Critical Concepts and Topics: Enlightenment).

Others have asked – correctly in my opinion – whether the Enlightenment (or *Aufklärung*, or *Illuminismo*, or *Illustración*) is really a coherent category; whether we should in preference speak of 'Enlightenments' (as the French speak of *lumières*), or whether, as in the case of the Left's assault on Enlightenment rationality, 'humanism', and 'common sense', its insights have been reasonably repelled. For John M. Ellis, in *Literature Lost: Social Agendas and the Corruption of the Humanities* (1997), recent theorists of race, of class and of gender have both extended and distorted the Enlightenment ideals, born in the seventeenth and eighteenth centuries, of equality and humanity:

> The idea of a common humanity was the Enlightenment's precious gift to humanity. . . . The central Enlightenment idea that all peoples share a common humanity, and that their allegiance to that commonality transcends any allegiance to their national or racial group, brings with it a set of related ideas. Words like *racism, genocide,* and *imperialism* belong in this new context but would be out of place in an environment not imbued with Enlightenment attitudes. In fact [in the present context], all these words signal various ways the Enlightenment's philosophy of common humanity is violated. (Ellis 1997: 93–4)

But while not ceasing to serve as conceptual vehicles of literary history, 'Enlightenment' and 'Augustan', as we shall now see, have also provided an explanatory framework for understanding the terms of the period's *own* tradition of literary criticism, and have defined its historical, and largely historicist, relation to our own.

Eighteenth-Century Critical History

Though the historical dimension of literary criticism is not at the heart of the most active recent controversy in literary studies, the period when the light of modern criticism (as we now know it) seems first to have dawned, was the eighteenth century. This verdict is supported by Samuel Johnson's contemporary description of Dryden, who died in 1700, as the 'father of English criticism . . . the writer who first taught us to determine on principles the merit of composition' (Johnson [1779] 2006: 1: 118). Pope, at the end of the century's first decade, wrote that '*Critick* Learning flourished most in France' (Pope [1711] 1963: 167: l. 712) (see p. 122, Chapter 6, Key Critical Concepts and Topics: Criticism).

As it has developed from this point of chronological departure, the major form of critical history as realized in concept and genre, has proved, however, relatively static, and has reinforced conceptual stereotypes of the period at large. So, for example, in the relevant volume of the *Cambridge History of Literary Criticism* published in 1998, we find in effect the plot of 'classic to romantic' prominent many decades ago in the work of W. J. Bate (1946), and a reconstruction of the narrative of progress described by René Wellek's *History of Modern Criticism* begun, once again, over half a century earlier (Wellek 1955–92). The constituents of literary criticism (critics' responses to emotional qualities and the activation of their own emotions by literary texts) bring the best critical writing of the world of Johnson and Pope closer to literature, and enable us to imagine a world outside the conceptual. And yet in the writing about it published over the last thirty years, eighteenth-century criticism is most often thinkable as a branch of the history of *thought*, and as a subdivision of the history of ideas.

It is not that past criticism is ignored by students of the 'Enlightenment', but that we remain again (without advancement) within the range of a largely nineteenth-century, more specifically Romantic, historiography by which its importance is explained as a precursor to the superior critical present from which it is viewed. Eighteenth-century critical writers are in consequence typically excluded from a *dialectical* liaison (between equals as it were) with this present. As David Womersley has argued in the Introduction to his anthology of *Augustan Critical Writing* (1997):

> The end result of the scholarly tradition dealing with critical writing between the Restoration and the French Revolution is . . . a complicated misrepresentation, arising from both the selection of which works to foreground and the approach to selected works. . . . [T]he discussion of some included works has been skewed by the need to fit them into a narrative which was committed to depicting their authors struggling blindly towards positions of which they had no knowledge, and which they might have rejected with a frown or a laugh had they been proposed to them. (Womersley 1997: xiii)

The persistence of such 'scholarly tradition' has led, I suggest, to a present-day undervaluing of the most important seventeenth- and eighteenth-century critics.

The challenge of telling a different kind of literary and critical story – one that is more truthful because it is more observant of the *range* of the evidence we now have at our disposal, and is best understood by the scholar's and historian's recognition of an extensive literary and critical *continuity* – thus offers new scholarly opportunities for an immanent history of criticism and of literature, by which I mean that rather than place literary works in the context of politics or society, as 'context' has been often understood, literary works are explained historically in the company of other literary works and via critical and creative reactions to them, often by major authors. One might begin with Lord Byron's love of Pope, Sir Walter Scott's devoted editorial and critical attention to the poetry of Dryden and the prose of Swift, Wordsworth's borrowings from Abraham Cowley, from Pope and from Johnson, Stendhal's plagiary of Johnson in the name of Romanticism, or the classicism of Keats (1795–1821) and of Shelley (1792–1822).

Such lines of enquiry need not be predicated on change for the *better*, but rather suggest the cyclical rhythms of literary and critical revolution, or may relate the authors of the eighteenth century to their classical originals in Greek and Roman poetry, and to such Renaissance texts as the *Essais* of Michel de Montaigne (1533–92), widely admired in the eighteenth century itself.

New Categories for Old: the 'Global Eighteenth Century' and the 'Age of Reason'

In histories of both literature and of criticism of the late nineteenth and early twentieth century, the eighteenth century is often referred to as an 'Age of Reason', a tribute, in its way, to the many advances in rationalistic and scientific procedures that provided an external context for literary production. But, over the years, this label came to signify the intellectual, emotional and spiritual poverty of the period. Much of what has occurred in 'Eighteenth-Century Studies' over the last three decades has further degraded this image: an interest in the sub-cultural life of Grub Street, for example, in the scatological Swiftian mess beneath the rationalistic skin, in the study of appetite, horror, extremity and chaos that has accompanied a growing taste for the period's brilliant satirical caricatures by William Hogarth (1697–1764), Thomas Rowlandson (1756–1827) and especially James Gillray (1757–1815). The moral shamefulness of the period's imperial and commercial expansionism, viewed with the superiority of hindsight, has been mercilessly exposed. This fragmentation of the 'Age of Reason', or the 'Neoclassic' or 'Augustan Age', or the 'Enlightenment', is coherent with a populist disrespect for the subtler meanings of 'decorum', of 'manners' and of 'propriety' valued at the time.

A turn from the 'Age of Reason' towards a study of the 'Global Eighteenth Century' (Nussbaum 2003) is one more novel expression of modern resistance to an eighteenth century understood on its own terms. Here commitments to identity politics beyond the literary have done much to displace the central criteria of both Johnson and Pope. Such 'imperialist' values as 'Eternal' and 'General' Nature, it is objected, elide differences between different racial groups whose cultural diversity demands our discrimination and respect. But the argument that such critics as Nussbaum have spelt out appears to pass over the egalitarian implications of these terms, whereby all human beings, regardless of race, caste, class or colour, are in their deepest and most significant respects the same: the Enlightenment's 'most precious gift' to humanity according to Ellis. Couched in the language of the eighteenth-century's own distinctions, the appeal to a universal humanity recalls the difference between the depth of 'nature' and the surface 'manners' of contemporary polished life, and through this distinction the dissolution of custom, language and social hierarchy within the unity of the human. As far as the idealism of Johnson and of Pope has been deemed obsolete, the 'development' we see here in

'Eighteenth-Century Studies' most usually entails a present that claims more enlightenment for itself than the Enlightenment.

Literature and Society

One concomitant of the eighteenth century's recent reinterpretation that follows from this anti-universalism is the thought, which rarely runs the gauntlet of wide comparison with conditions in other periods, that literature and society are in this period *exceptionally* close. The evidence for such a suggestion appears variously in the *Cambridge History* (Richetti 2005) and elsewhere in guides intended for a student readership (Zwicker 1998). The hypothesis at issue is that poetry in this period was more pervaded by, and connected to, political life than at any other time. The observation that writers formed themselves into clubs and cabals (the 'Scriblerians', the 'Kit-Kats', the 'Literary Club' of Johnson), or that they interacted with the ruling political classes in an especially intimate way that is not our way and was not the way hitherto, supports this suggestion, as does the contents of such imposing volumes of political verses as *Poems on Affairs of State* (1963–75).

Such a defining emphasis has been developed in detail in recent years by attention to the category of 'Whig poetry' (Williams 2005), and by approaches that identify literature's explicit and implicit political affiliations at the level of party, revealing, it is again suggested, an awareness supposed not duplicated in other ages and at other times. In fact, a more concerted attention to the translated verse of the period, which looks beyond the present of its own composition, would exhibit the period's uniqueness in a different, more comprehensive, light, and would call into question the sense that scholarship has advanced overall significantly beyond Leslie Stephen's *English Literature and Society in the Eighteenth Century*. In his Ford Lectures of 1904, Stephen writes that 'The relation between the political and the literary class was at this time closer than it had ever been' (21), a view that students of the literature and politics of the fifteenth and sixteenth centuries might feel obliged to contest.

Culturalization and Some Futures for 'Eighteenth-Century Studies'

To conclude with a suggestion on where the future of 'Eighteenth-Century Studies' might now lead (see p. 116, Chapter 5, Case Studies in Reading 2: Key Theoretical and Critical Texts: Looking Ahead; see p. 187, Chapter 10, Mapping the Current Critical Landscape). We have seen that there are issues of literary and cultural theory and that there are issues of literary and cultural history; that despite a consensual air, these matters remain unresolved, and that they are part of a larger set of untended problems within the field of literary and cultural studies. We have asked, for example, whether students and scholars of the eighteenth century still think of the literature of the literary past as historically special, worthy of consideration in distinct disciplinary forms.

The answer seems to be 'yes' in one sense and 'no' in another. Literary works have a special status amongst students and scholars of literature (as works of philosophy might matter to philosophers, historical works to historians, works written in German to Germanists, etc.). At the same time scholars may study literary works as literary means to ends not primarily connected with their literary value. Denied all other access to historical sources, doubtless, one would still learn something true about the early years of the eighteenth century from a reading of the poems of Pope that any historian of the period would value. But the developments in question have also implied that there is no special status accorded to literary works that corresponds with the special attention that philosophers are entitled to give to philosophical works, historians to historical documents, or Germanists to texts in German.

This more fundamental disruption of literature's disciplinary bounds has given rise to changes in critical responses and approaches to the eighteenth century that I attempt to outline here. The belief that literature differs as a privileged, bourgeois, or purely ideological construct which needs to be knocked off its elitist high horse I have suggested as a source of the current optimistic state of scholarship upon the period. The most intense versions of this conviction have originated within literary studies itself, and it has been well observed that scholars are often most abhorrent of literary 'privileged discourse' when they are initiates in literary studies who have then abandoned literature in favour of a broader postdisciplinary terrain (Collini 1999: 253–4). The 'Studies' of 'Eighteenth-Century Studies' are significant of this broadened view, but as we also see, with concomitant limitations. I conclude with a summary of these.

Culturalization and the Logic of Cultural Self-Limitation

We have observed that the thriving professional organizations that serve the eighteenth century, ASECS in the USA and BSECS in the UK, embrace a flexible pair of dates but do not fix the disciplinary distinctions within it, and I have suggested that the emphases of these scholarly societies over the last ten or so years clearly portray the newly institutionalized classifications. I have also argued that the editorial policies of the journal *Eighteenth-Century Studies* and its British equivalent have produced in recent years many contributions which seem to suggest an end for literary evidence, as distinct from literary experience and enjoyment, beyond the narrow confines of literary study. In the editorial matter of the American journal we read accordingly that 'essays employing interdisciplinary perspectives or methodologies, or addressing contemporary theoretical and cultural concerns relating to the eighteenth century, are especially encouraged'.

Various recent guides to the eighteenth century, or anthologies intended for purchase by students studying literature, have likewise made eighteenth-century 'culture' their *end* and the study of literature their *means*. Augustan England, in Zwicker's view, was 'a world in which social relations and the life of the state were inextricably bound to the imagination of writers' (Zwicker 1998: xi). The editor of the relevant volume of the new *Cambridge History of English Literature* expresses related convictions: 'In an obvious and important sense', he writes, 'British eighteenth-century writing was deeply embedded in and overtly addressed to social, political and moral issues, and literary historians have always stressed the essentially occasional and often specifically political or didactic and pragmatic purposes of even the most classic texts . . .' (Richetti 2005: 8).

My counter-suggestion, in seeking an eighteenth century defined, according to Bennington's epigraph to the present essay, 'in and as itself', has been that significant works of translation and allusion now undergoing revival look beyond their immediate context in politics, society and the material universe, to classical literature or to posterity – to 'Eternal Nature' and to 'General Nature', and to the sense of a common humanity viewed as a timeless good. And that correspondingly, what is appreciated and valued in an eighteenth-century relationship between the social, the political and the literary cannot be denied to other periods when it is looked for there.

While, therefore, the modest pieties of 'contemporary cultural studies' have extended their logic to the literary past of the eighteenth century, if we happen to be interested in literature, and wish to know what literature of the eighteenth century can 'say', as *only* literature can 'say' anything – not primarily as a means of access to cultural history but as a purpose that is distinct from its function ('What Ever Happened to Pleasure?', asks Susan Manning [Manning, 2001: 215–32]) – then the development I have described has subtractive consequences for literature's cultural role. Among the negative effects, I would suggest, has been a narrative whose limits are too simply chronological. In garnering the requisite social and political evidence from representative literary texts, stylistic qualities, imaginative distinctions, and the sometimes vast difference between literary merit and literary mediocrity or failure, may be overlooked. But these are the very distinctions by which canons are formed and by which they fall. To this extent, the developments we have discussed may take away from the varied richness and immediacy of the interdisciplinary 'culture' we have set out to 'know'.

The task, then, is to restore the distinctive value of literary value to 'Eighteenth-Century Studies'. In the present case, the practice of especially prizing what falls outside the imagined literary canon has two other consequences its advocacy may not have intended. One is to harden up the canonical and the traditional to the point where they are preserved as unassailable foils to the more desirable marginality. (In the socio-political model that prevails in 'Eighteenth-Century Studies', the critic or scholar must implicitly hold – but need not independently judge – that poetry by women, for example, is necessarily inferior to the poetry of Pope.) The second consequence is to encourage the belief that the value judgements themselves are unique to literary study.

These attitudes have proved difficult to dislodge in the current climate, if only because they accommodate the practice of criticizing eighteenth-century literature to present socio-political norms. In so doing they encourage the assumption (not very logical in an interdisciplinary age) that the concept of the canonical and the traditional are bugbears only literary scholars need worry about.

Note

1 The term refers to an alleged conspiracy to murder Charles II and replace him with his Catholic brother James, Duke of York, later James II. The fraud, which led to the execution of 15 supposed plotters, was eventually exposed and its chief architect, Titus Oates (1649–1705), was thrown into prison.

8 Questioning Canonicity

Bridget Keegan and
Amber Haschenburger

Chapter Overview

. . . What we have loved,
Others will love and we will teach them how.
– William Wordsworth, *The Prelude* (1850) 14.446–7

Since the publication of the first of its seven volumes in 1997, J. K. Rowling's Harry Potter series has invited critical disagreement in both popular and academic circles. A recent search of the MLA bibliography supplied the titles of over 200 scholarly articles, chapters and books devoted to the novels and debating their literary merits. Some condemn their less than elegant language or their derivativeness, but for others the series has inspired a wealth of more serious analyses from Freudian, Marxist and feminist perspectives. Among the non-academic reading public, some have descried the novels as promoting the occult, corrupting young readers with images of sorcery and implicit Satanism. Christian schools have banned the books from their libraries, and no less than Pope Benedict has stated that the books 'distort Christianity in the soul before it can grow properly'.[1] Others are suspicious of the books only for the very simple reason that they are popular. Surely, something that millions of children are wild about must be the aesthetic equivalent of sugared cereal. Nonetheless, the books have simultaneously delighted some educators, who are hopeful that the novels are fostering a love of reading – and of reading long, complex books – that other evidence has indicated has been declining in an age of television and video games. Teachers of the eighteenth century in particular (that century well known for the doorstop novel) may be optimistic that a generation who cut their literary teeth on 700-page stories might slow the decline in popularity of this more 'remote' literary historical period.

The Harry Potter phenomenon raises issues related to the question of the literary canon in general and, as we hope to show, to the eighteenth-century canon in particular. Rowlings' novels are undeniably one of the best-selling book series of all times, but the jury remains out as to whether they are truly 'any good'. While the novels are popular now, will they be read in 25 or 50 or even 200 years – and not as just a curious cultural artefact of the past? Will the works still even be in print (or even more relevantly, will print still be in print)? Will they become part of the curriculum of the college English class of the future? Will they be looked to by English teachers and students in the twenty-third century as especially representative of the key values of Western society in the early twenty-first century and thus included in literature surveys two or three centuries hence? In short, will Harry Potter become 'canonical'?

The History of the Canon in the Eighteenth Century

(See p. 141, Chapter 7, '"Dead Keen On Reason": The Canon Displaced?')

How we answer the questions posed above, indeed the very terms and methods by which we attempt to form our answers, owes much to the eighteenth-century. As Douglas Lane Patey has argued, in the eighteenth century the word 'canon' first comes to 'designate a selective list of literary writers or literary work' and the modern idea of literature itself is born (1998: 17). But as soon as the concept came into being so too did the debates about it. Indeed, the idea of 'canon' is inseparable from parallel critical dispute, as is evident from the early eighteenth-century English version of the *querelle des anciens et modernes* or in the efforts on the part of a cohort of powerful literary critics to establish Shakespeare, Spenser and Milton as a triumvirate of literary virtue over and against shoddy modern productions.

The eighteenth century set the terms for a discussion that has been carried out in different settings and by different opponents ever since. The role of authors and critics in these disagreements has most recently been thoroughly examined in recent issues of the journal *Eighteenth-Century Life*, and in monographs by Jonathan Brody Kramnick (1999) and Trevor Ross (2000), who disputes the question of a purely eighteenth-century origin. Thomas Bonnell (1989 & 1997) and William St Clair (2004) have each also persuasively demonstrated the importance of the role of powerful London publishers in shaping how the reading nation was formed more by copyright legislation than by any values or ideologies inherent in the texts they printed and anthologized.

In terms of the current version of this long-standing argument, it is useful to remember that the earliest uses of the word 'canon' were primarily religious in context, as the concept dates back long before the twenty-first or the eighteenth century. In the second century AD, Jewish rabbis established the texts of the Hebrew Bible that they believed, after much study and debate, to represent the authentic word of God and to which they granted full doctrinal authority. In the next century, the Catholic Church followed suit with similar determinations about the New Testament. The Gospel of Peter, for example, was deemed apocryphal – false, inauthentic, not bearing transcendent truth. In its classical etymology *canon* means a standard or rule, something against which another thing is measured (Richter, 2000). The sticking point during the past three centuries has been what is being measured against what.

The eighteenth century opened with important debates on literary value by two authors who have since attained what might be called 'hyper-canonical' status in eighteenth-century British literature: Jonathan Swift (1667–1745) and Alexander Pope (1688–1744). Swift's 'The Battle of the Books' (1704) is his contribution to the larger dispute, initiated by Swift's former employer Sir William Temple, in his *Of Ancient and Modern Learning* (1690). Although the question was more broadly whether ancient or modern authors and learning were superior, the place of what we would today call literary writers in this argument was central. Swift's satire cleverly avoids telling us whether the classical or contemporary writers were victorious. Significantly, in Swift's text, not only are the ancient and modern authors at war, but the authors and the critics as well. The rise of the professional critic in the eighteenth century, and the growth of reviews and periodicals, are also essential threads in the genealogy of the concept of canon, as is the institutionalization of literature in the university. As Patey observes:

> because every canon requires the existence of some authoritative group of *canonizers*, radical changes in canons are usually accompanied by rearrangements in the social structure of such authority. In the eighteenth century, academic specialties change, as there begin to appear the first university chairs of 'poetry', 'belles letters' and 'fine arts'. Literature itself becomes a profession distinct from any previous system of academic or social affiliations. (1988: 23)

Concern over the critic's qualifications to determine literary value (over and against the poet's qualifications to produce it) is elaborated in Alexander Pope's *Essay on Criticism* (1711), often selectively taught (if the eighteenth century is taught at all in modern survey courses) as a prescriptive statement – and enactment – of Augustan poetic values full stop. But as anyone who has grappled with this poem knows, its prescriptions are more elusive than might seem at first glance, particularly in so far as they are directed to critics, not poets. Pope appears to come down squarely in favour of the value of the Ancient writers who 'follow Nature' (though what precisely 'Nature' means has been subject to equally great dispute). His advice to modern critics is to steep themselves in the works of the classical authors and observe the rules they follow as the standard (or canon, in the Greco-Roman sense of the word) by which any other work ought to be evaluated.

Pope made it easier for his contemporaries to study the works of classical writers such as Homer through his translations, helping to ensure their continued canonical status in the age often labelled neo-classical. But Pope was not entirely averse to promoting more 'modern' writers as is evidenced by his edition of Shakespeare (1725) and his generous patronage of his contemporaries – including those from less refined backgrounds such as the footman turned poet Robert Dodsley (1703–64), about whom more below.

Pope was not the only important writer during the eighteenth century to promote the 'canonization' of Shakespeare. A generation later, Samuel Johnson (1709–84) would bring out his own edition of the Bard. Like Pope, Johnson is a figure many twenty-first-century commentators love to hate in the debates about the canon. His work producing the *Dictionary* (which drew exemplary quotations from only certain authors) and his efforts with his *Lives of the Poets* (which privileged only certain poets for these prestigious editions) are often held up as evidence of his efforts to cut women writers and other lesser worthies out of literary history. But the choices for who would be reprinted in the *Lives* series were his publisher's not Johnson's. And as anyone who has studied Johnson's biography knows, he supported all kinds of struggling writers, both men and women, including one of the more intriguing women novelists of mid-century (and herself a critic of Shakespeare), Charlotte Lennox (?1729–1804).

Johnson's publishers were not alone, nor the first to try to exert an influence on the reception of poetry in their own age. The vital role that publishers have played in fashioning the canon of eighteenth-century literature is only recently coming to be fully understood at an empirical level. The story behind how footman turned publisher Robert Dodsley's *A Collection of Poems by Several Hands* (first published in 1748) came to attain the status of a canonical text is more complex than twentieth-century critics have acknowledged. Michael Suarez, S. J. asserts that studying how this collection was compiled, marketed and read has much to reveal 'about the relationship between the book trade and the process of canonization' (1996: 229). Suarez unearths several (sometimes surprising) factors in the *Collection*'s status and success.

One key reason for its triumph was its association with the recently deceased

Pope and Pope's aesthetic agenda, as many of the contributors were affiliated in some way with Pope (who had also been Dodsley's patron): 'the very nature of the literary project that Dodsley was effecting in the *Collection* had strong ties indeed to Pope's beliefs about the need to preserve poetry in its proper sphere and to protect it from defilement by "Smithfield Muses", "Grub Street", sycophantic laureates, and other compromising, pretentious, or low-born influences' (Suarez, 1996: 305). The work's success was also determined by how Dodsley marshalled elite editors (predominantly the Lord Lyttelton [1709–73]) to give the work an aristocratic cachet. Suarez observes, 'some ninety-five of the 226 poems in these volumes, no less than 47 per cent, are either written by peers or are dedicated or addressed to peers' (ibid.: 306).

Suarez further observes that

> The fact that nearly 50 percent of the poems in Dodsley's *Collection* are so closely associated with the aristocracy almost inescapably leads one to recall that the term *classicus* originally denoted the wealthiest of the five Roman propertied classes before Aulus Gellius first used the word to signify a 'first-class' and taxpaying author, not a proletariat. (1996: 307)

The modern equation of having read certain texts (the 'classics') as a mark of membership in an elite social class will be discussed in more detail below, as this equation may no longer hold in our own era, where money alone (and not any kind of 'culture') has become an end in itself and not necessarily the means to an end.

What Suarez demonstrates is that the choices determining who was included in Dodsley's *Collection* was driven less by ideology than by economy. Dodsley drew from those authors who published with him or for his periodicals, making use of the 'stock' of poems he had ready to hand in his backlist. Suarez productively counters the errors of 'bibliographic Darwinism' by which

> literary historians and teachers of English letters have routinely assumed that what was often reproduced – and so transmitted to subsequent generations – must have been what was most worthy of survival . . . The canonical status of a text or group of texts is not exclusively a property of the work itself; the question of canonicity is inseparable from the question of transmission. (1996: 312)

Making that case at a macro level, beyond the history of a single work or a single genre, is William St Clair, whose monumental materialist history, *The Reading Nation in the Romantic Period* (2004) builds on arguments such as Bonnell's and Suarez's to change the terms of the debate according to which we understand how and why particular literary canons – whether they are canons of literary historical period or of genres – are formed. Taking a systems theory approach, St Clair challenges the two previous models of literary history (and thereby of canonicity), which he identifies as the 'parade' and the 'parliament' models.

According to the first 'The printed writings of the past have been presented as a parade of great names described from a commentator's box set high above the marching column' which points out those texts which the commentator believes capture 'some of the essence, of the historical situation from which they emanated' (St Clair, 2004: 2). More recently, the 'parliament' model shows 'the printed texts of a particular historical period as debating and negotiating with each other in a kind of open parliament with all members participating and listening' (ibid.). St Clair believes that neither of these text-based models satisfactorily accounts for how exactly reading shapes the way that people think, as neither adequately represents what books were actually read at any given historical period. Moreover, both models assume a chronology of actual reading which is idealized at best. Actual (as opposed to implied) readers do not limit themselves only to contemporary literature nor do they read works 'in the chronological order in which they were first published' (ibid.: 3).

For St Clair, intellectual property laws and the economics and politics of the book trade are the base from which to understand what was read and why, both in the eighteenth century and beyond (see p. 65, Chapter 3, Literary and Cultural Contexts: Eighteenth Century Print Culture). Working from empirical data gathered from industry records, data that has heretofore only been considered in a fragmentary and anecdotal way, St Clair makes a compelling case for why particular poets were republished and anthologized, particularly at the start of the Romantic period. As he demonstrates with a raft of factual data, the brief relaxation of copyright regulations between 1774 and 1808 opened the way to the publication of anthologies and editions such as Johnson's *Live of the Poets*, texts that have come to shape our modern understanding of what constituted the eighteenth century's notion of the English canon and which continue to have influence today.

As noted above, it was not Johnson but his publishers who chose the authors included in that series, but St Clair argues that even the publishers' choices were controlled more by commercial than by ideological factors. St Clair is able to support empirically the claim that 'In the canonising process, literary historians, critics and editors had played only a small part. The old canon of poetry owed its long life more to the vagaries of the intellectual property regime than to any carefully considered judgments' (2004: 128). This is not to say that an ideological component was absent from those texts that were first primarily selected because of their copyright status. St Clair observes that the works that were reprinted (and not just in anthologies of poetry, but in series and collections of novels, essays and conduct literature as well) did share some features, namely an emphasis on English rural life.

The ideological dimension of publishers' choices is unsurprisingly most clearly seen in the anthologies developed for the schools at the end of the eighteenth century, as literary selections replaced collections of explicitly moral maxims (or *sententiae*) as the cornerstone of English education. The role of the teaching anthology as a key artefact in discussions of what the canon is or should be continues today, and in our own age, the teaching anthology has been one of the main arenas for battle of the modern Canon or Culture wars that flared with renewed vigour in the 1980s and have been smouldering ever since.

The Canon and the Curriculum

To many students it may seem (to paraphrase the annual Beloit College Mind-set List[2]) as if Stephen Duck and Aphra Behn have always been included in the *Norton Anthology of English Literature*. But this is not so. Those committed to women's rights and civil rights struggled to get them on the syllabus, to ensure that students' understanding of what constituted Romantic literature, for example, meant more than the work of 'five or six dead white guys'. As women and minorities were gaining greater political representation in the present, academics looked to ensure that they had adequate literary representation in the past.

The questioning of the canonical status of certain authors and/or the extension of canonical status to more authors has led to a physical expansion of the teaching anthology. The *Norton Anthology of English Literature*, for example, is now in six volumes when it had previously been able to limit itself to merely two. Furthermore, there are now specific anthologies dedicated to literature by women and minorities (such as the *Norton Anthology of Literature by Women* which first appeared in 1986). Yet the semester is still no longer than 15 or so weeks, and choices must be made, even if there are more texts to choose from. Practical as much as ideological determinants affect what can be taught and why.

The question of canon, then and now, must also contend not simply with ideological content but with form. As Alistair Fowler (1979) argued cogently almost 30 years ago, issues of what we understand to be canonical are inseparable from issues of genre. The eighteenth century is rightly identified as giving birth to that now-dominant genre, the novel. Many of the most celebrated novels of the eighteenth century made their own marginalized and counter-canonical status part of their subject matter. Fielding's satirical efforts, in a novel like *Joseph Andrews* (1742), to offer 'metafictional' commentary alongside a quixotic plot make it useful to include in a programme that foregrounds questions of literary value and debates about the canon.

Yet the ability to teach novels such as Fielding's is likely more affected by 'practical' rather than ideological issues. To fully appreciate *Joseph Andrews*, one must also have read the equally long *Pamela* (1740–1). Put another way, in a 15-week survey class, Aphra Behn's *Oronooko* (1688) may get taught more frequently than *Robinson Crusoe* (1719) simply because of its more manageable length (although it certainly helps that its non-white characters have a bit more personality than Friday).

The temporal limit of the academic term is not mere minor logistical detail. Despite Harold Bloom's best efforts, a full and definitive literary canon does not exist anywhere. No great master list resides in the recesses of the Bodleian or the British Library. Where the canon exists – if it exists at all today – is only in partial, ephemeral form, instantiated in college curricula and in course syllabi. As was so often rehearsed in the contentious debates of the 1980s, precisely because of its association with the institution of the school canonicity has become so hotly politicized. It is widely (and probably accurately) believed that schooling inculcates particular cultural values and ideals. Since large, complex institutions are by nature conservative, the generally liberal modern professoriate assume that whatever is sanctioned to be taught by the 'establishment' must be being taught only because it promotes a conservative political agenda. Hence the need to identify (even at the risk of anachronism) more liberal literary forces.

While a cursory reading of Pope's *Essay on Man* (1711) might worry those concerned with promoting democracy, and someone dedicated to promoting respect for women might blanch at some of the scenes in *Gulliver's Travels* (1726), only the most reductive of interpreters could flatten Pope's poetry or Swift's satire to a unified and explicitly political message. Pope's argument in favour of a hierarchical order encompasses a cosmic scale, and Swift is as misanthropic as he is misogynistic. Positing that Pope's or Swift's writing is meant to reproduce in its reader a two-dimensional ideology presumes that these texts would be read and taught as unproblematic vessels of such ideas.

If we have moved away from the idea that white male authors are automatically purveyors of repression so we may need to reconsider the notion, widespread in the 1970s and 1980s, that the value and interest in studying women and minority writers derives from their 'counter-cultural' status. We may teach Eliza Haywood (?1693–1756), for instance, because she represents a rebellion of one kind or another against the values espoused by Henry Fielding, or privilege broadside ballads because they exhibit a more authentic political voice than the one found in Joseph Addison's essays.

Leaving aside for the moment the question of the truth value of such propositions (indeed, a case could be made that Haywood might actually do damage to the feminist principles modern readers anachronistically wish to derive from her work), the strategy of teaching these works as 'counter-cultural' assumes that students have already read Fielding and Addison, and are ready to see them subverted. That is almost guaranteed not to have happened, given that most undergraduates are unlikely to have been exposed to eighteenth-century literature during the course of their education. Surveying the current state of teaching eighteenth-century literature in the secondary schools, at least in the USA, a college professor cannot depend on students having read a novel of any kind, let alone one from the eighteenth century. Making a virtue of teaching 'non-canonical' writers implies that somewhere, at some time, a canon, whatever it might consist of, has already been delivered and digested. What is the value of studying particular writers as contra-canonical if students have only the most notional sense of what such writers are presumably writing against?

All of this again presumes that literary texts are transparent and uncomplicated vessels of unambiguous ideas, and that dominant cultural institutions, like the university, intentionally and systematically employ them as such. In *Cultural Capital* (1993), the most interesting and sophisticated assessment of the 1980s canon wars, John Guillory argues that reading previously neglected writers exemplifies the contradictions inherent in a pluralist identity politics: 'The typical valorization of the non-canonical author's experience as a marginalized social identity necessarily reasserts the transparency of the text to the experience it represents' (1993: 10). How does this work?

Self-taught labouring class poets such as Stephen Duck (1705–56), Mary Collier (?1690–c.1762), Mary Leapor (1722–46) and John Clare (1793–1864) use their experience as something their poetry works as much against as from (see p. 126, Chapter 6, Key Critical Concepts and Topics: Labouring-Class Poets). Because they are reluctant to affirmatively claim the situations their texts describe, it is difficult to hold up their lack of education or destitution as a positive value to be celebrated and reclaimed, as one might be more likely to do in the case of an author's gender or racial background. If a plebeian poet did not necessarily wish to be identified with others of his class (and most wrote poetry precisely to distinguish themselves from their socio-economic peers), then a simple assertion of the justice of identity politics will not suffice.

Moreover, at the level of style, poets like Duck and Leapor do not represent in their writing a more authentic plebeian or 'low' style. Both writers aspired unabashedly to emulate Pope in their language, and Leapor was largely successful in this endeavour, thus writing 'against' rather than 'for' her particular discursive identity as a member of the labouring classes. Studying Duck and Leapor, then, a student reader is more likely to come away with an increased admiration for the style of Pope than with a sense of two authors pitting themselves in ideological and stylistic opposition to Pope and the values he may or may not represent.

Historically social groups tended to privilege texts which represented their best ideas of themselves, but today's scholars must guard against that. Even as the canon expands to include more minority authors, any canon (or any anthology that purports to materialize it) can only represent a minute fraction of all of the texts created within any given period, and thus cannot be truly representative of that era's literary or moral values. Guillory argues that, too often, scholars fall into the trap of believing that a selection of an age's literature can be representative of the values and culture of a certain time period. Non-canonical texts, within today's study, occupy a space that is different from total absence, one which sets them up as a counterpart or perhaps even as opponents to canonical texts. This means that they are often made out to be intrinsically subversive or progressive. Canonical texts then are also seen to possess some sort of unifying ideology with which the non-canonical texts (also uniformly) contend.

This unity, for Guillory, simply does not exist on either side. For instance, women's writing, a category often equated de facto with the non-canonical, demonstrates varieties of tone and theme that would be overlooked if women writers are studied only in terms of their exclusion and opposition. Moreover, religion is one of the most popular topics for women's writing. But, because such a subject generally lacks a potentially revolutionary protofeminist agenda (which is often the entry point for women writers into a syllabus), women's religious writing is almost never taught. As Bridget Keegan (2005) has observed, Susannah Harrison was one of the most widely republished female poets of the late eighteenth century. Yet even though she was a woman *and* a servant, because she composed only pious verse, few scholars and even fewer teachers have bothered to examine her work.

As Guillory writes, 'The "open" canon can lay claim to representational validity in the experience not of "women" or "blacks" but of women or blacks in the university – which is not itself a *representative* place' (1993: 37). American or British culture (or our systems of higher education) will not become a representative place, as Guillory puts it, simply due to an expansion of the canon. Minority students are still under-represented in ways that will take more efforts than adding to or changing a reading list will cure, (even if it is still a significant symbolic gesture). Guillory thus warns against perceiving changes in the canon as changes in society.

By including more female writers, we do not make society more gender inclusive, either in the era being studied or in our own. In America, for instance, even if Lady Mary Wortley Montagu (1720–1800) and Frances Burney (1752–1840) have found comfortable niches in the Norton Anthology, American women still earn 70 cents for every dollar a man earns (the figures are comparable for the UK). As Guillory and others have observed, the motivations for such wishful misprisions derive from a concern among academics about their own 'relevance'. Given the status of literary studies in the twenty-first-century university, debates about who is in or out of favour in any literary canon – especially the one from what is now a more 'remote' historical period – may amount to the proverbial rearranging of deck chairs on the *Titanic*.

The Eighteenth-Century Canon and Twenty-First-Century Culture

Extending Guillory's argument to apply to the condition of the liberal arts education in general, James Engell and Anthony Dangerfield (both of whom happen to be English professors) argue, in *Saving Higher Education in the Age of Money* (2005), that at least in the United States (and arguably in similar ways in the UK), 'The fastest-expanding and often strongest motivation in American higher education is now money. While other aims and functions certainly persist, they are increasingly eclipsed by the ultimate goal of wealth accumulation' (2000: 2). In short, money has become an end in itself in education, and not simply a means to an end.

As Engell and Dangerfield claim, only those disciplines that study money, promise a career making money, or bring in extensive grant money have shown growth in the twenty-first-century university. As the annual data collected by the ADE (Associated Departments of English) bear out, the number of students electing to focus on the humanities is small and appears to be getting smaller. According to ADE statistics, in 2000, out of every 100 Bachelors degrees awarded, only 4 were given to English majors (down from a 50-year high of 7 per 100 in the mid-1960s).[3] Reviewing the most recent statistics published by the American *Chronicle of Higher Education* in 2004, 13.2% of all college freshmen indicated an interest in majoring in the broader collective fields of 'Arts and Humanities'. This is fewer than those whose chosen fields were in Business (19.9%) or the Health Professions (16.4%). In the UK, according to the Higher Education Statistics Agency's most recent data on full-time undergraduates for 2000–01, there were 24,655 students pursuing degrees in English in comparison with 122,095 pursuing areas related to Business and 145,810 interested in Health Professions degrees.[4]

To a certain extent, one could observe almost ironically that this outcome is predicted and prepared for by the eighteenth-century novel. Despite how they may masquerade as fables of conversions celebrated or virtue rewarded, novels such as *Robinson Crusoe* (1719), *Tom Jones* (1749) and *Pamela* (1740–1) are unambiguous about the real rewards that their protagonists reap. A happy ending always has a dollar (or pound) sign attached to it. Yes, the protagonists gain an education (moral or otherwise) in the course of their narratives, but the fruits of that education are always made manifest in money.

The myth of social ascendancy, the objective correlative of which is newly found or newly rediscovered wealth, is the recurrent plot line of almost any of the 'great books' of the eighteenth century. Perhaps the ranks of English students (and students studying the eighteenth century) might grow if professors did a better job of outlining how so many of these books show that a certain degree of literacy is essential to that social ascendancy and wealth. Robinson Crusoe's learning how to read the Bible properly is critical to his conversion, which appears to be the precondition for the fabulous riches he ends up taking home at the end of the novel. Pamela's skills with her pen are enough to convince Mr B to make an honest and wealthy woman of her. These facts aside, one might almost wonder why the eighteenth century is not faring better in the curriculum given how its stories support the dominant financial ideology of today. Indeed, the answer in some schools to help carve out a zone of relevance for literature is to create courses devoted to 'Entrepreneurs in Fiction' (here *Moll Flanders* [1722] might make an interesting case study) or 'The Literature of Health Care' (Matthew Bramble's battle with gout in *Humphry Clinker* [1771] could be a topic).

The possibilities for specialist or 'boutique' courses such as these aside, the study of the eighteenth century is in perilous straits. In universities that are trying to run themselves like businesses, academic departments are increasingly being asked to pay for themselves via enrolments. Courses in Creative Writing are more likely to generate revenue than courses devoted to 'The Age of Johnson' or early modern popular women novelists. A brief survey of a variety of institutions across the USA and the UK confirms that it is now entirely possible for a student to obtain an undergraduate degree in English without having encountered James Thomson (1700–48), Thomas Gray (1716–71), Fielding and certainly not Tobias Smollett (1721–71) who produced works that are arguably the most 'representative' of many of the broadest and most interesting values of the age. Nor are they likely to have had the chance to encounter the former slave and campaigner against slavery Olaudah Equiano (?1745–c.1797), the novelist Eliza Haywood or the shoemaker turned poet James Woodhouse (1735–1820). Students pursuing degrees in Creative Writing might not have to take a single course engaging literary history per se, or any writing done before that semester. The wisdom that to be a great writer one must study writers of earlier generations is no longer conventional.

How did it come to this? Those on both sides of the debate over what is worth reading certainly had good intentions. Have teachers and scholars of literature done themselves more harm than good with their in-fighting over the canon? Can we really take advantage of the Harry Potter phenomenon to help turn the ship around? Literary critics stereotypically have eschewed involving themselves with anything 'commercial', seeing commercial success as unilaterally associated with the low and vulgar discourse that, in the eighteenth century, was associated with the 'hacks' excoriated in works like Pope's *Dunciad* (1729 and 1743). Such anti-commercialism is a luxury we may no longer be able to afford, and works like St Clair's offer one way to use a materialist analysis to our advantage. We cannot and should not give up a discussion of literary value, which is what the question of canon is really about. But how can we frame it in ways that are less divisive and more productive, and that understand the many forms in which 'value' can be measured?

Both the Harry Potter series and *Pamela* represent various 'ideologies' and both were hugely successful works financially. They are both simple and complex, both ideological and material, products of their respective historical moments. Both had behind them individuals well informed about how the publishing industry works and with a strong sense of the market possibility. They are both stories about the power of love and how love can empower people to do things previously thought impossible. Lily Potter's love for Harry allows him to defeat Voldemort. Mr B's love for Pamela – a love fuelled by his reading of her letters – enables the rake to be reformed and the servant-girl to be ennobled through marriage (something which, at least in the early eighteenth-century, was perhaps as rare as Invisibility Cloaks).

In *Why Read?* Mark Edmundson makes the compelling case that perhaps the best response to the crisis of canonicity is for teachers to teach works that they love, and that perhaps this love, shared and honestly expressed, will encourage the next generation of students to read those works.[5] As we all know, love does not always operate by logic. We do not always love the people or things we should, and some of those choices might be condemned as politically incorrect. But love still remains the one thing that may just be more powerful than money. For those of us, as faculty and students who love the eighteenth century, an acknowledgement of that shared passion may help us frame a more productive politics surrounding our discussion of the canon.

Notes

1 'Pope criticises Harry Potter', *Times Online* 13 July 2005, available at http://www.timesonline.co.uk/article/0,,1-1692541,00.html
2 The Beloit College Mindset List is published every fall to help identify the world-view of the 18 year old, the typical age of the first year university student. See http://www.beloit.edu/publicaffairs/mindset/
3 See 'Report of the 2001–2 ADE Ad Hoc Committee on the English Major' available at www.ade.org
4 The data is available on the agency's website: http://www.hesa.ac.uk/
5 Edmundson, Mark (2004). *Why Read?* New York: Bloomsbury.

9 Gender, Sexuality and Ethnicity

Chris Mounsey

Chapter Overview

Introduction

Until the late twentieth century, the three areas to be discussed in this section have, typically, been related to each other under the banner of literary theory and many books have been written about these topics from a theoretical perspective. This is largely due to the fact that the eighteenth century was a period which saw, as part of the rise of the scientific method, a great many taxonomic studies of all aspects of natural history (Henrey, 1975). To undertake classification and nomenclature one must begin by listing characteristics which define a type: does the new plant you have just found growing in China bear the characteristics which would enable you to call it a 'rose', or do its characteristics mean that the name 'daisy' would be more appropriate, or maybe it looks like a completely new species. But it was not just plants which were to be described and named, but men and women, and their types and behaviours.

In 1711, Anthony Ashley Cooper, Lord Shaftesbury (1671–1713) wrote extensively on the *Characteristicks of Men, Manners, Opinions, Times*, and in so doing gave, in effect, a list of features which defined what he thought of as a moral man typical of other contemporary lists of characteristics of other natural phenomena in more general taxonomies. By so doing, Cooper intended to set up an opposition which would distinguish moral men from immoral men, for example, explaining ignorance thus:

> . . . the greatest of Fools is he who imposes on himself, and in his greatest Concern, thinks certainly he *knows* that which he has least study'd, and of which he is most profoundly *ignorant*. He who is ignorant, but knows his Ignorance, is far wiser (1999: 252).

Cooper's use of 'he' in this passage is supposed to include all 'mankind', that is, all men and women. However, when we note that Cooper wrote telling his brother of his infatuation with a young man, and delayed his conventional dynastic marriage as long as possible, preferring the company of men, the inclusiveness the word 'man' becomes even less certain.

A theoretical approach to Cooper's *Characteristicks*, however, would focus not on Cooper's inclusive use of the term 'man' to describe moral men and women, but on the unintentional binary oppositions set up between worthy men and women, between worthy men and men who though worthy enjoyed sexual relations with their own sex, and between worthy men and men who though worthy were ethnically different. Such binary oppositions were fuel for the deconstructionist theorists of the 1980s and 1990s, and gave rise to studies such as Terry Castle's *Masquerade and Civilization* (1986) which inverted the binary opposition between men and women and brought the excluded woman into the centre of the debate. Likewise, Michel Foucault's *History of Sexuality* (1979) inverted the binary opposition between heterosexuals and homosexuals and in his study of sodomy, brought homosexuals into the centre of the debate. Likewise too, Homi K. Bhabha's *Nation and Narration* (1990) inverted the binary opposition between white and black people, and brought ethnicity to the centre of the debate.

While literary theory must be praised for ensuring that women, sexuality and ethnicity were no longer excluded from academic study, it also fell prey to navel-gazing, to being more interested in its own inner workings than in its political, in the broadest sense, applications. Theoretical analyses could also be criticized for bringing twentieth-century philosophical perspectives to bear on eighteenth-century phenomena. Since the beginning of this century there has been a growing dissatisfaction with theoretical analysis, and interest has shifted from theory to the subject matter itself. Being careful not to return to Shaftesbury's inclusive term 'man', academic study has returned to taxonomic facts. Therefore, the history of women is no longer studied simply as feminist history, nor is the history of sexuality the history of oppression of an excluded minority, nor is the study of ethnicity now focussed on hybridization of cultures. In each case, study now centres on how eighteenth-century men and women, heterosexuals and homosexuals, and people of non-white races were perceived, and perceived themselves.

With the recent availability of eighteenth-century full-text database resources such as *Eighteenth-Century Collections Online* studies of gender, sexuality and ethnicity have turned to primary texts, looking for the diverse range of viewpoints that were expressed by eighteenth-century writers. The white heterosexual male behind the term 'man', whom Shaftesbury has long been thought to describe, who was once believed to be the given of eighteenth-century thought, is now seen to have been challenged in his own time by women, homosexuals and non-whites. And it is these types of study which will concern us here.

Gender

(See p. 41, Chapter 2, 'Contexts, Identities, and Consumption: Gender')

It is probably best to begin with how white masculinity was seen in the eighteenth century. Alexander Pope's Moral Epistle *To Cobham* (1733) gives us the ground-rules for how white males regarded themselves. Pope (1688–1744) starts with the taxonomic observation that there are 'as many sorts of Mind as Moss', and footnotes the fact that 'There are above 300 sorts of Moss observed by Naturalists' (1993: 320. 18 and note). In this we can see that Pope believed observation was the key to knowledge, taking his stance from the pre-eminent British empiricist philosophers of his age, Isaac Newton (1643–1727) and John Locke (1632–1704) who can be described as believers in observation as the sole source of knowledge. It may seem strange therefore, that a little later on in the poem, Pope muses that although he observes many types of men, perhaps there is a characteristic common to many, which though hidden, accounts for variety: 'Something, as dim to our internal view, / Is thus perhaps the cause of all we do' (1993: 32 l. 49–50).

Pope's reasoning that 'Something' lies behind his observations comes directly from Isaac Newton's *Philosophiae Naturalis Principia Mathematica* (1687), where Newton (1642–1727) argues that although observation is the source of knowledge, the measurement of observations is so inaccurate that in order to find out the truth it is necessary to imagine a perfect situation where the inaccuracies are ironed out. Newton describes this double move of empiricism in terms of practical Mechanics, where we make imperfect measurements, and Geometry, which is the ideal world where all measurements are perfect.

> The ancients considered Mechanics in a twofold respect; as rational, which proceeds accurately by demonstration, and practical. To practical Mechanics all the manual arts belong, from which Mechanics took its name. But as artificers do not work with perfect accuracy, it comes to pass that Mechanics is so distinguished from geometry, that what is perfectly accurate is called Geometrical, what is less so is called Mechanical. But the errors are not in the art, but in the artificers. He that works with less accuracy, is an imperfect Mechanic, and if any could work with perfect accuracy, he would be the most perfect Mechanic of all. (1968 [unpaged])

In this way, Pope is following Newton's scientific method to search the varied observations of men's behaviour in order to find 'Something' which underlies it. The 'Something' by which to characterize men must account for the apparent differences in behaviour between them but, by beginning with Newton's method, his answer is already secure: the 'Something' (singular) that he will find is a unifying principle. After a long discussion, Pope argues that although we observe the various Natures, Actions, Passions and Affections of men, it is in the '. . . ruling Passion: there alone, / The wild are constant and the cunning known, / The fool consistent and the false sincere;' (1773: 9 l. 13–15).

Pope fleshes out his theory by giving an extended example in the figure of Clodio, a portrait of a man whose actions seem wildly inconsistent but which are all explicable with reference to his 'ruling Passion' the 'Lust for Praise'. What Pope means is that although it might seem odd that Clodio is a serious political orator yet quick with low wit; is a highly religious man, and yet keen on whoring, these disparate qualities can be explained by the one thing that moves all his actions: the desire to be thought well of by everyone, no matter who they are, prelate or punk. 'Consistent in our Follies and our Sins / Here honest Nature ends as she begins (1773: 12 l. 1–2). With the ruling Passion in mind, nothing Clodio does is inconsistent: he is always trying to curry favour with whoever he is with at the time, so he acts accordingly. He is consistent in trying to please those around him, whoever they are.

Pope's overall project is to show that men (like Geometry) are rational, constant and dependable, even in their apparently wild and inconsistent actions. So long as you know his ruling Passion, you can predict what a man will do in a particular situation. He becomes a creature of reason who is logical and explicable, no matter how impetuous and capricious he may seem. This basic stereotype of masculinity is still current today and plays a crucial part in propping up Western patriarchy.

It comes as no surprise then, to find a stereotype of femininity as irrational, fickle and emotional in another of Pope's Moral Epistles *An Epistle to a Lady: On the Characters of Women* (1735). From the very first lines of the poem Pope lambastes women: 'Nothing so true than what you once let fall / Most women have no character at all / Matter too soft a lasting mark to bear / And best distinguished by black, brown or fair' (1993: 350. l. 1–4). Pope suggests that whereas men are set in stone in their dependability, women are like water-logged clay (matter too soft a lasting mark to bear), in other words, they cannot be defined by any characteristic since they cannot maintain one long enough for it to be associated with them. In fact, he opines, they are so unpredictable that they can only be distinguished by their hair colour. The poem continues with a series of thumbnail sketches of various women who behave in inconsistent ways, and whereas in the *Epistle to Cobham*, Pope draws together contradictory behaviours in a ruling Passion, which is peculiar to the man, in women, Pope finds only two ruling Passions: 'In sev'ral Men we sev'ral Passions find, / In Women, two almost divide the kind, / Those only fix'd, they first or last obey; / The Love of Pleasure or the Love of Sway' (1993: 356 l. 207–10). Although the desire for pleasure and being domineering might seem to act in the same way as in men to predict behaviour in particular circumstances, both passions are intended to define women by predicting inconsistency rather than dependability, irrationality rather than a logical mind. And Pope concludes: 'But every Woman's at heart, a Rake' (1993: 356. 216). A 'Rake' is an eighteenth-century term for someone who has loose morals, particularly in sexual matters. Thus, Pope means that women's behaviour is not only irrational, inconsistent and unaccountable, but also immoral and ultimately self-destructive.

But we can neither lay all the blame of modern gender stereotypes at Pope's feet (see, for example, Cheyne, 1733: 96), nor can we believe that Pope was wholehearted in his belief of the gender stereotypes he wrote about in these poems. The dominant trope of early eighteenth-century poetry was satire and we can be sure that Pope was not simply describing masculine or feminine characteristics as immutable. Satire's patron was Aesculapius, physician to the mythical Greek Gods, and in the same vein of curing divine ills, satirical poetry was intended to mend people's ways by showing then how silly they were being. But 'Satyr' was, as Pope's friend Jonathan Swift (1667–1745) wrote, 'a sort of Glass, wherein Beholders do generally discover everybody's Face but their own' ('Preface', *Battle of the Books* 1711: 219). Therefore, however well-intentioned a satirical piece was, it was likely to be taken at face value as an attack on someone other than the reader. So it cannot be a surprise that Pope's stereotypes, rather than his satirical stance towards the foolishness of contemporary views of masculinity and femininity, took such a hold on the imagination of eighteenth-century people, and come down to us now as the bugbears of twentieth-century feminism.

Stereotypes, as Pope mused in the *Epistle to Cobham*, are based on guesses, and draw general conclusions from individual observations. If one individual was not exactly similar to another, it did not matter – you had but to find his ruling passion to be able to understand him and predict his behaviour – but if a man did not fit the male stereotype and was instead, for example, more feminine, it was nothing short of a disaster. By the mid century, writers like John Brown (1715–66) had become so paranoid about men fitting with the masculine stereotype that they decried the whole of their society for 'sinking into effeminacy'. In his *Estimate of the Manners and Morals of the Times* (1757–8), Brown wrote of the effects of theatre going, where coarse jokes had given way to *double-entendre*:

> As Excess of Delicacy hath destroyed our *Force* of *Taste*, it hath at least one laudable Effect; for along with this it hath carried off our *Grossness* of *Obscenity*. A strong Characteristic, this, of the Manners of the Times: The untractable Spirit of Lewdness is sunk into gentle Gallantry, and *Obscenity* itself is grown Effeminate. (1757: 30)

What is important to note here is Brown's use of gender stereotypes in his language. What has been lost is the '*Force* of *Taste*', where 'force' is a masculine stereotype, and what has killed it is 'Excess of Delicacy', where 'delicacy' is a feminine stereotype. Through masculine 'force' we might expect to see the truth directly, albeit coarse and vulgar, whereas, because delicacy masks the coarseness of obscenity, the truth that coarse humour might have shown has been hidden in the double meaning that is employed for making the joke fit for women.

Brown's feeling of the growing effeminacy of his age could only be possible because of the currency in the idea of masculinity and the femininity, and as Thomas Laqueur points out in *Making Sex* (1990) the early eighteenth century was the time in which the opposition between masculine and feminine was beginning to be explored. Laqueur argues that before about 1650 a 'one-sex' theory predominated, which was based on the idea that each sperm cell in a man's semen contained a whole human being, the homunculus, which was planted into a woman's uterus and grew according to how vigorous she was during pregnancy into a male or female child. However, with the increasing number of discoveries of animals and plants throughout the world where the male was completely different from the female, a 'two-sex' theory began to emerge. Although it was not known what scientific facts accounted for the difference between the sexes, the 'two-sex' theory gave a moral basis for Pope's Epistles: an explanation of observable differences between men and women with regard to masculine and feminine gender stereotypes.

But in the effeminacy debate which raged throughout the century, women were not always irrational, inconsistent, unaccountable, immoral and ultimately self-destructive as befitted the type Pope had assigned them. At the same time that the feminine stereotype was described, women began to write against it. Mary Astell's (1666–1731) *Serious Proposal to the Ladies for the Advancement of their True and Greatest Interest* (1694), for example, rallied women to become more stereotypically masculine:

> Why are you so preposterously humble, as not to contend for one of the highest Mansions in the Court of Heaven? Believe me, Ladies, this is the only *Place* worth contending for; . . . How can you be content to be in the World like Tulips in a Garden, to make a fine *show* of yourself, and be good for nothing? (1694: 10–11)

She called for the education of women, and for women to be regarded as equal to men in all spheres of public life. After all, Queen Mary (r.1689–94) was a woman, as was her successor, Queen Anne (r.1702–14). Others, such as the poet Sarah Fyge Egerton (1670–1723), wrote bitterly against the religious and civil laws on married women's property (everything owned by a woman, including her own body, was given to her husband on their marriage to use as he wished) which produced the marriage market in which women from the middle classes upwards found themselves sold to the highest bidder into marital slavery.

> From the first dawn of life, unto the Grave
> Poor Womankind's in every State a Slave . . .
> The Husband with insulting Tyranny
> Can have ill Manners justified by Law
> For all Men join to keep the Wife in Awe . . .
> *Moses* who first our Freedom did rebuke,
> Was marry'd when he writ the Pentateuch; (1703: p. 108 l.3–4, 8–12)

Egerton's *Poems on Several Occasions* (1703) in which 'The Emulation' appeared, and from where these lines are taken, was not a hole in corner affair, as might be expected, but was widely advertised in the London daily newspapers, and appeared through highly thought of publishers and booksellers. The message of women's emancipation continued to be a subject for women poets and writers throughout the century, with the celebrated but short-lived Mary Leapor (1722–46) writing imaginatively of the way in which men had gained power over women through political thuggery:

> When our Grandsire nam'd the feather'd kind,
> Pond'ring their Names in his Careful Mind,
> 'Twas then, if on our Author we rely,
> He view'd his Consort with an Envious Eye;
> Greedy of pow'r, he hugg'd the tott'ring Throne;

> Pleas'd with Homage, and would reign alone;
> And, better to secure his doubtful Rule,
> Roll'd his wise Eyes, and pronounced her *Fool*
> ('Man the Monarch' 1751: p. 7 l.54–61).

Once again, this poem, with several more on the like theme in the collection, was published through one of the foremost publishers of the day. Moreover, the poems were so well thought of that they were published posthumously, with a preface by the celebrated poet and raconteur Christopher Smart (1722–71).

All in all it is difficult to uphold the view that in the eighteenth century, the sexes were viewed as separate and incommensurable or even were accepted as being characterized by the stereotypes that are foregrounded in the satire of Pope's Moral Epistles. Nor is it surprising the century should end with Mary Wollstonecraft's famous tract in favour of women's emancipation *A Vindication of the Rights of Woman with strictures on political and moral subjects* (1792). Her text is part of a long history of women's responses to the male domination dating at least a hundred years before its publication.

Sexuality – Heterosexuality

As we did with gender, it is probably best to begin with the conventional eighteenth-century view of this matter: that all people were heterosexual and that they either married or remained celibate. The 1662 *Book of Common Prayer* explains the demand for heterosexuality within marriage in spiritual and carnal terms. Spiritually, the marriage between a man and a woman signifies 'the mystical union that is between Christ and his Church'. Carnally, 'it was ordained for the procreation of children' and as 'a remedy against sin, and to avoid fornication, that such persons as have not the gift of continency, might marry, and keep themselves undefiled members of Christ's body'. From this starting point, it is clear to see that sexuality is bound up with morality and the family stands as its fundamental metaphor. Furthermore, though there is a moral way to express one's sexuality, it is expected that some people will fall short of it, so a moral hierarchy will develop. The most moral have 'the gift of continency' and will be celibate as was Christ. Next in the hierarchy of morality are those who lacking 'continency' will marry, as Christ was married to the Church, so they 'avoid fornication'. Fornication is a weasel word here, since it means no more than sex between any two people outside of marriage. The circularity of the moral message – that you must marry to avoid having sex outside marriage – is avoided by the mystical metaphor that Christ is married to the Church, and that one should try to be like Christ: either spiritually by being celibate, or carnally by being married to someone for the purpose of procreation so that your nuclear family resembles the family of Christ and the church.

But the religious attempt at closing off so powerful a force as sexuality was unsuccessful, as the number of prostitutes showed. Bernard Mandeville argued, in a pamphlet entitled *A Modest Defence of Public Stews* (1724), for the creation of State run brothels. 'Your Endeavours to suppress Lewdness, have only serv'd to promote it. . . . What else could we hope for, from Your persecuting of poor strolling Damsels?'(1724: p. ii). The faltering nature of sexual morality and the ubiquitous use of prostitutes may be bound up in the irresistible nature of sexuality, but may also have had something to do with the changing status of marriage in this period. Until the eighteenth century, marriage, especially in the upper echelons of society, was dominated by the dynastic model, in which the political or financial union of two families was more important than the compatibility of man and wife. The dynastic model, therefore, opened up a space for sexual liaisons outside marriage with partners who were more compatible, and a *demi-monde* of courtesans, concubines, second families and prostitutes arose. Against this tradition, Lawrence Stone, in *The Family, Sex and Marriage* (1977), argues that between 1660 and 1800, there was a rise in the companionate model of marriage in which mutual love was the dominant motive.

Nicholas Rowe's play *Jane Shore, a tragedy, written in imitation of Shakspear's* (sic) *style* (1714) dramatizes the change. Jane Shore was the mistress of Edward IV, and both were 'victims' of dynastic marriages. Shore's father, a rich merchant, married her off to Matthew Shore, an even richer mercer for economic reasons. In despite of his uncle, the Earl of Warwick, Edward married Elizabeth Woodville, causing Warwick to dethrone him for his disobedience. Rowe presents Shore's affair with Edward as a love match, legitimating the relationship in the epigraph (spoken by Mrs Oldfield, the actress who had just played the role, and died in the character of Jane) with the triplet: 'For Her Excuse too, be it understood, / That if the Woman was not quite so good / Her Lover was a King, she Flesh and Blood' (1714: 81). While the play ends with a formal declaration against marital infidelity, the import of the action is that if Edward had been free to marry Jane Shore, the love of his life, his reign would not have been fraught with the difficulties that were the result of his failure to enter the political marriage desired by his uncle, and may not have led to the disastrous reign of Richard III which followed it. We might therefore go so far as to argue that Rowe's play argued in favour of companionate over dynastic marriage: at least the topic was up for discussion. Interest in Jane Shore's story at this time – and the play ran for an unprecedented 19 London performances in 1714, and went into many editions during the century (with explanatory documents appended) suggests a growing interest in companionate marriage, and a rejection of the problems inherent in dynastic arrangements. And, in fact, a companionate marriage would seem to be the ideal to which the 1662 *Book of Common Prayer* was pointing: if the man and wife loved one another, as did Edward and Jane, they were less likely to turn to fornication to find sexual gratification, and disaster was less likely to ensue.

At the same time we find an explosion in the production of pornography and sub pornographic texts, which depict a lively debate about the pleasures and pains of sexuality within matrimony. For example, in 1706, a series of bawdy poems was published in answering pairs all using the title *The Fifteen Comforts* (2002). First there are the fifteen comforts of matrimony, which are unremittingly ironic, and told from the point of view of a disappointed husband. His wife will be a spendthrift, she will be sickly, unfaithful and shrewish; the children (who are probably not his) will disrupt his life and turn out badly. It is not only women's sexual profligacy a husband has to worry about but also the appetites of other men for his wife. *The Batchelors* (sic) *and Maids Answer to the Fifteen Comforts of Matrimony* (2002) argues the companionate case: 'When two True Hearts are both together Crown'd / All other Pleasures are but Pains to this / A Married Couple only finds the Bliss' (2002: 60).

But even in this poem, there is more than a hint of irony in the so-called comforts of matrimony: 'One minute smile, the very next a Frown, / Perhaps the next she knocks her Husband Down./ But what does this to hinder higher Charms?' (ibid.: 61). The poet even agrees that an old man takes a young wife is a fool because, sooner or later, she is bound to look elsewhere for sexual gratification. Thus, it seems safe to argue that, behind the screen of companionate marriage, the eighteenth-century heterosexual world was rife with illegitimate sexual liaisons.

In *The Fifteen Comforts of Whoring*, which is the third of the *Fifteen Comforts* series, the focus turns to men's use of prostitutes. While this poet recognizes young men's 'Native Love to Vice', (2002: 72) young men are reminded graphically of the sexually transmitted diseases that prostitutes usually carried: 'And in the Flame the Harlot lit, consumes: / Of Buboes, Nodes, and Ulcers he complains, / Of Restless Days, and Damned Nocturnal Pains' (ibid.). It is an uncomfortable fact that most newspapers of this time were financed by advertisements for cures for venereal diseases. Compounds of mercury were usual, and the 'nauseous Pills' could often do more damage to health than the disease itself. The very ubiquity of such advertisements demonstrates a like ubiquity of the diseases, but nevertheless, *The Whores and Bawd's Answer to the Fifteen Comforts of Whoring* argues that the pleasure of sexual acts will always outweigh the fear of contracting gonorrhoea or syphilis, claiming that in drinking alcohol, 'There is not half the Pleasure, that there's in, / The soft Embraces of a Woman who / Altho' she is not to one Moral true, / Does strive to please your height of amorous Lust' (ibid.: 82).

How widely distributed these poems were cannot be certain. Few of them went into second editions, but since some of them do not bear the name of a publisher, there is no real way to determine how widely they were circulated. The material itself is ephemeral, that is, bought to be read and thrown away, probably before any other family members could see them. Such poems may, however, have been bought to be read in coffee houses, the sole domain of men, so they could well have been widely known in some circles. It is difficult to be sure how representative of the contemporary view of sexuality they might have been. But we must agree with Julie Peakman, who argues:

> By the end of the eighteenth century, London was awash with all sorts of printed matter, which could be bought from a wide variety of outlets. Part of this cache of reading material was highly erotic, including licentious novels, adventurous travelogues, rude prints, ribald songs and racy poems. (2003: 12)

And this was not under the counter pornography, for as Peakman goes on, '. . . a series of advertisements for *School of Venus* [was] carried in newspapers' (ibid.: 13). Representations of sexuality were available everywhere, and in a variety of genres. Richard Payne Knight attempted a serious history of sexuality in *An Account of the remains of the Worship of Priapus* (1786) and John Wilkes used pornography in an attempt at humour in *An Essay on Woman* (1763). Probably the most famous of all pornographic texts, John Cleland's *Memoirs of a Woman of Pleasure* (1749), popularly known as *Fanny Hill*, was a novel. In fact, the sexuality of the protagonists of Cleland's book is often ambiguous, an issue we shall come to later, but for now, it is worth noting that heterosexuality portrayed in Cleland's seminal work of pornography is associated with marriage and prostitution.

Coming to London as an innocent from the country looking for work, Fanny is quickly tricked into a brothel by a bawd, who has a keen eye for the profit she will bring. Fanny does not, though, move directly to entertaining several different customers each day. She begins as the kept woman of a young man of good family, who loves her, and cannot marry her simply because she is from a lower-class background. When his support fails her, because his family find out about the relationship and send him abroad, she becomes the sole 'property' of an older, married man. During this time, Fanny begins to entertain other men in her rooms, because her keeper does not satisfy her desires, until she is discovered *in flagrante delicto*, and in the denouement of the first part of the book she is thrown out onto the streets to earn her keep with passing trade.

We can draw several important conclusions concerning attitudes towards sex and sexuality from the novel. First, it seems likely that the married man was keeping Fanny for himself so that he could enjoy sexual relations safely, and not bring venereal diseases to his wife. And this will account for his anger at finding out that Fanny was entertaining other men. Second, he feels himself allowed to enjoy sexual relations outside marriage, while he requires sexual fidelity from Fanny, and, presumably, from his wife. In both cases, his dominant sexual position appears to be based upon his economically superior position: he pays for food and lodgings for both his wife and his mistress, and he expects them, as his property, to obey him. Third, Fanny's sexuality is depicted as voracious after she has been introduced to the physical act of sex: A view which is similar to that in *The Fifteen Comforts of Matrimony*, in which it was the husband who was cheated on by his wife.

Since Fanny has seen the possibility of a perfect relationship with her first love, *Memoirs of a Woman of Pleasure* seems to suggest that the companionate marriage is best, but it is also a critique of the dynastic system. If Charles had not been constrained by the dynastic aspirations of his family and could have married Fanny, her sexuality might have been contained within the marriage. Furthermore, the catastrophe which develops in her relationship with the married man also seems to suggest the problems inherent in a dynastic marriage and the *demi-monde* which it invokes. The married man is not happy with his wife, so seeks solace with a prostitute, who is not faithful to him because he cannot be with her all the time since he must pretend to fulfil the requirements of his marriage. Moreover, the dominant position of men in marital and extra-marital relations is demonstrated as being economically based, rather than the result of any natural superiority. Just as in the *Fifteen Comforts* series, both sexual partners inside and outside the marriage seem to be equally likely to be faithful, or stray, or be sexually predatory, or sexually passive.

Sexuality – Homosexuality

Certainly the eighteenth century harshly condemned homosexuality. John Dunton (1659–1753), who might nowadays be characterized as a tabloid social commentator described the fate of a Sodomite (as male homosexuals were called at the time) thus:

> The Sodomite should be placed in a Tub, and have liquid and burning Brimstone poured down upon him till he expires in a way which Heaven has found out for the Punishment of so Unnatural a Sin. Or if it may be thought a more speedy way to suppress *Sodomy*, let every Man guilty of this Sin, have his Genitals cut off, and burnt by the common Hangman. (1703: 35)

In fact, treatment of homosexuals by society and the law was much more accepting and lenient. While sodomy, the genital penetration of one man by another, was a capital offence, only one man was hanged every ten years or so during the century, and usually for reasons other than that act itself. A man caught in the act of sodomy and brought to trial would usually bring in witnesses to his good character and get off with a fine and a short prison sentence – unless there were other reasons why he might be found guilty. For example, Thomas Poddy was indicted in 1710 for assault with sodomitical intent, upon John Sollers, but evidence was not strong enough and he was acquitted: there had to be a witness to the act of penetration so that the case did not rest upon one man's word against another's. However, when Michael Levi was accused of the like crime, though he brought eight witnesses to his good character, he was condemned and hanged – probably because he and his witnesses were all Jewish (Goldsmith, 1998).

Unlike male homosexuality which was quite frequently noticed by the law, female homosexuality is all but absent from trial records (see http://www.oldbaileyonline.org/) This reflects more the fact that sexual acts were defined by penetration, and therefore sex between two women has never been illegal. There were a few cases of fraud brought against women who dressed as men in order to marry rich women, but lesbian sex is rarely the subject of the case. This does not reflect an absence of female homosexuality in the eighteenth century, but points to two problems with using court cases as windows into contemporary ideas of sexual activity. First, sexuality and sexual activity are not fixed terms with constant referents. Just because the eighteenth-century legal mind could not imagine a sex act without penetration does not mean that women did not engage in same-sex sexual activity. But it does mean that lesbianism is all but absent from eighteenth-century trial records. And although there were 114 Old Bailey court cases for sodomy this is unlikely to reflect the extent of homosexual activity because, as we have noted, it was hard to prove penetration without a witness to the act. Furthermore, the large number of acquittals suggests that juries were less of John Dunton's homophobic bent than might be expected. In order to discover eighteenth-century views of same-sex sexual activity, therefore, we ought to search non-forensic texts which describe it. However, therein lies another problem. Since sodomy was a capital offence, no-one could publish in praise of it without being indicted. Thus, whereas there is a large body of heterosexual pornographic material, when we search texts for homosexual pornography it is unlikely we shall find any. As Julie Peakman suggests: 'Unless other material is uncovered, as far as we can tell with current available sources, fictionalized pornography directed at homosexual readers did not emerge until the nineteenth century' (2003: 3). But Peakman's suggestion is true only if we consider frank and anatomical descriptions of sexual acts between people of the same sex. Returning to Cleland's *Memoirs of a Woman of*

Pleasure, Charles is described, the first time we encounter him, in feminine terms:

> . . . his eyes closed in sleep, displayed the meeting edges of their lids beautifully bordered with long eye-lashes, over which no pencil could have describ'd two more regular arches than those that graced his forehead, which was high, perfectly white and smooth (1749: 92).

On its own, the description might pass as a stereotypically masculine man drawn from an altered sense of the aesthetics of beauty between the eighteenth and twenty-first centuries. However, with the book's narrative voice being a man ventriloquising the voice of a young woman who is interested in the penetration of small orifices by large penises, the possibility remains that Cleland is disguising homosexual pornography in a heterosexual novel. There is one scene in which Fanny witnesses sodomy between two men through a chink in a wall in a public house. It is one of the first detailed descriptions of the act in English Literature.

Other writers were less reserved in their depictions of homosexuality, albeit that they were equally circumspect. *The Adventures of Count de Vinevil and his Family* (1721) is without doubt the most moralistic of Penelope Aubin's (1679–1738) novels, however, there is something distinctly sexually ambiguous in several of the relationships described in the text. The heroine of the main plot, Ardelisa, who is dressed as a boy to protect her virginity, becomes the object of the lust of a Moslem Turk, Osmin, who is so infatuated that he does not care whether she is a boy or girl:

> 'Lovely Boy or Maid, I know not which to call you, fear not the treatment I shall give you; my Heart is made a Captive of your eyes, I will enjoy and keep you here, where nothing shall be wanting to make you happy. If you are a Man, renounce your Faith, adore the Prophet and my Great Emperor, and I will give you Honours and Wealth exceeding your Imagination; if a Woman, here are Apartments where Painting, Downy Beds, and Habits fit for to cover that soft Frame, Gardens to Walk in, and Food delicious, with faithful Slaves to wait upon you, invite your Stay; where I will feast each Sense, and make you happy as Mortality can be.' At these Words he clasped her in his Arms, and rudely opening her Breast, discovered that she was of the soft Sex. (1996: 131)

What is interesting here, and openly homosexual, is that after making the discovery that she is a woman, Osmin suddenly remembers a prior engagement he has to attend so that he does not to have sex with her. In another of Aubin's novels, *The Amorous Adventures of Lucinda* (1721), the eponymous heroine is put in a similar situation with a Turkish woman, and rather than being horrified by the thought of lesbian sex, embraces the idea, though the act itself is foiled by the untimely death of the woman's father.

There is no doubt that there are rich veins of male and female homosexual pornography carefully disguised in eighteenth-century novels. And it is just what we would expect given the huge amount of heterosexual pornographic literature produced throughout the century. If there is a general conclusion that can be drawn, it is that while heterosexual sexual activity outside marriage was thought morally wrong, but unavoidable, same-sex sexual activity, which was by definition outside marriage, was not only thought morally wrong, but also something to be kept hidden. Furthermore, even if fornication was morally wrong, it was not going to go away – in whatever form it took.

Ethnicity

(See p. 107, Chapter 5, Case Studies in Reading 2: Key Theoretical and Critical Texts: Empire and Affect; see p. 187, Chapter 10, Mapping the Current Critical Landscape)

We have already glimpsed some of the eighteenth-century givens of ethnicity in the examples from Penelope Aubin's novels: her Turks were outlandishly dressed and sexually reckless and ambiguous. But we might go further to suggest that the eighteenth-century mind understood people of non-white racial backgrounds to be radically different from white Europeans, maybe even as not human. Felicity Nussbaum draws our attention to the elision of black people and animals in the writing of the philosopher David Hume, who:

> . . . drawing a comparison between a Negro and a parrot in a notorious footnote to the 1753–4 edition of his essay, 'Of National Characters' singles out a Jamaican man of learning as an exceptional being akin to a speaking parrot: he claims that the educated Negro . . . a freakish example of his species, resembles a parrot in his ability to imitate a few words (2003: 136).

However, advertisements from the *Daily Courant* of 1706 demonstrate that where a sea-captain is searching for an escaped 'servant' (which occurred every month or so), the description of the escapee is always given in terms of their clothes rather than skin colour. This would seem to suggest that black people were not uncommon in eighteenth-century London. They were carried from Africa to America and from America to Britain. Thus, while there were never large numbers of black slaves in Britain, they cannot have been so uncommon as to have caused a stir because of their skin colour.

At the same time it must not be forgotten that much of Britain's national wealth in the eighteenth century, and most of the stately homes dating from this century, were built with money gained from the slave trade. Disgust at the trade in fellow human beings built gradually until slavery was finally abolished in 1833. Hence we ought to take David Hume's comment about the educated Jamaican being like a talking parrot in the same vein as John Dunton's polemic against homosexuals: as a personal opinion, not an indication of the general eighteenth-century view. Certainly, by 1772, Lord Mansfield's decision in the *habeas corpus* case of James Sommersett made slavery *de facto* and *de jure* illegal in Britain. Sommersett was a slave who escaped from his master, Charles Stewart, while they were in Britain. While free, Sommersett was baptized and became friends with a number of abolitionists in particular Granville Sharp. He was recaptured by Stewart, and imprisoned on a ship bound for Virginia, but Sharp intervened, bringing a case of *habeas corpus* against Stewart which was heard at the Court of King's Bench. Lord Mansfield's decision in the case argues the irrationality and odiousness of slavery, at the same time pointing out that since there was no statute law instituting slavery, then ownership of slaves had no legal basis. Furthermore, he argued that there could be no claim that slavery was natural, and therefore instituted by practice through time immemorial through the Common Law. The end of Mansfield's decision is oft quoted, but is worth repeating here:

> The state of slavery is of such a nature, that it is incapable of being introduced on any reasons, moral or political, but only positive law; . . . It's so odious that nothing can be suffered to support it, but positive law. Whatever inconveniences, therefore, that may follow from a decision, I cannot say this case is allowed or approved by the law of England; and therefore the black must be discharged. (1772) 20 State Trials: 22.

Thus, as in the cases of gender and sexuality, although we might find a stereotypical negative view of non-white races that appears to be commonly held in the eighteenth century, we also find a number of positive views. In fact we might argue that only the century that produced such great wealth from the evils of the slave trade could have produced the counter energy that would bring forth abolition.

In the same manner as in the cases of gender and sexuality, it is the drive to taxonomic rigour in which we find the basis of the negative stereotype. In separating out the different types of Homo sapiens in his *Systema Natura* (1735) the great Swedish natural philosopher Carolus Linnaeus – or Carl von Linne – (1707–78) listed six sets of characteristics by which to distinguish racial types.

(1) Homo
(2) Four-footed, mute, hairy. *Wild Man.*
(3) Copper-coloured, choleric, erect. *American.*
Hair black; straight, thick; *nostrils* wide; *face* harsh; *beard* scanty; *obstinate*, content, free. *Paints* himself with fine red lines. *Regulated* by customs.
(4) Fair, sanguine, brawny *European.*
Hair yellow; brown, flowing; *eyes* blue; *gentle*, acute, inventive.
Covered with close vestments. *Governed* by laws.
(5) Sooty, melancholy, rigid. *Asiatic.*
Hair black; *eyes* dark; *severe*, haughty, covetous. *Covered* with loose garments. *Governed* by opinions.
(6) Black, phlegmatic, relaxed. *African.*
Hair black, frizzled; *skin* silky; *Nose* flat; *lips* tumid; *crafty*, indolent, negligent, *Anoints* himself with grease. *Governed* by caprice (1802: 9).

In the descriptions, none of the terms is without ambiguity. The skin colours 'Copper coloured', 'Fair', 'Sooty' and 'Black' are as generalized and inaccurate to specific individuals as the designations of social organization of each racial group by 'customs', 'laws', 'opinions' and 'caprice'. So it is no surprise that when we explore representations of different racial groups in literature, we find many challenges to the negative stereotype represented by David Hume and Carolus Linnaeus: black people are not always shown to be crafty, indolent, negligent and governed by caprice.

Turning once again to Penelope Aubin's popular novels of the 1720s, we find in *Charlotta du Pont* (1723) Isabinda's story, which tells of a white woman marrying a black man. Isabinda is the daughter of Virginia planter, and Domingo one of her father's slaves. Domingo kidnaps Isabinda and carried her away to a small island where, as she says 'he proceeded to kiss me, [so that] my Distraction was such, that I swooned; [and] he took the Advantage of those unhappy Minutes, when I was unable to resist, and, in fine, has kept me here two whole Years'. (1723: 29) We know the marriage has been consummated during her swoon because Isabinda has a 'Molotto' child. But this cannot be seen as the child of a rape since Isabinda is determined to marry Domingo: 'I would now willingly consent to be his Wife, having Treasure sufficient to purchase us a good settlement in any Place' (1723: 71). In fact, Charlotta sees Domingo as a potential victim since his treatment of Isabinda is likely to get him hanged, even though they are now in love and want to live happily ever after. She decides to help them, and says:

> 'No, my dear *Isabinda*', said she, 'you will part no more; *Domingo* shall be carried hence to a Place we are bound to, where he may safely and lawfully

> possess you; since you now love, as I perceive, and have forgiven him his Crime in getting you, we will assist him to be happy. The selling of human Creatures is a Crime my Soul abhors; and wealth so got never thrives. Though he is black, yet the Almighty made him as well as us, and Christianity ne'er taught us Cruelty'(1723: 71).

The early date of this abolitionist sentiment maybe due to the fact that Aubin's husband's family were involved in trade between America and Britain, so she may have had first-hand experience of the treatment of slaves, and of meeting black people. What is important here is Aubin regards black men as human, and more than that, as sexually attractive and potential life partners for white women, in the same way as Aphra Behn (1640–89) in the previous century, in her novel *Oroonoko* (c.1688). In fact, the question of why people might be regarded as more or less human or not is not addressed in terms of race, but in terms of sensibility.

Brycchan Carey (2005) explores the question of sensibility with regard to abolitionist discourse, noting that it was sensibility, rather than education that defined worthy humanity. Carey gives a useful definition of sensibility: 'Eighteenth-century sensibility was a discourse which celebrated the passions over the intellect, which valued untutored response over considered reply, and which favoured "natural genius" to learned philosophical and critical procedures' (2005: 4). The vogue for sensibility after 1760 gave rise to the Romantic movement at the end of the century, with a developing interest in working-class poets such as Stephen Duck (1705–56) and Mary Collier (?1690–1762). But uneducated black people fitted easily into the mould of 'natural genius'. For example, Ignatius Sancho (1729–80) was an orphan slave who was not allowed an education in order to ensure his docility, by the three maiden ladies who kept him in Greenwich. He was, in fact, educated under the auspices of the Earl of Montagu, but the aura of 'natural genius' remained with him as he rose through service to become the owner of a grocery shop. While he ran the shop, he wrote two plays and a book of music theory, as well as being a well-known journalist and doyen of the arts. Above all he took advantage of the late century fascination for the cult of sensibility, and his race played into that social trend.

In both these examples, we see a positive version of a non-white person, one textual and one actual. The Aubin text seems to draw upon a history of representations of black men as 'Splendid savages' and the case of Sancho can be seen to be a timely phenomenon arising from the cult of sensibility. But however they are explained, both the textual Domingo and the real life of Sancho demonstrate that the negative stereotype of the non-white races being less than human was criticized during the eighteenth century, and that positive views of people of different races were not unknown.

Conclusions

What has been demonstrated is that where a stereotype of gender, sexuality or ethnicity exists in eighteenth-century culture, there are also counter examples that suggest that the stereotypes were not the only way people thought of these issues. What remains to be considered is whether the counter examples represent exceptions that prove the rule, or are part of a newly discovered parallel history of cultural values.

The answer might seem to be to count the number of occurrences of positive and negative stereotypes and perform a calculation to discover which was the dominant viewpoint. But as we have seen, especially in the case of homosexuality, which was illegal, studying court records gives a skewed view of the numbers of incidences as it only picks up on those which were discovered, and positive literary representations may be encoded or even fenced off with formal denunciations. It remains to be seen whether there will be further cases of positive viewpoints of women, homosexuals and non-whites will emerge, however, the existence of the ones that have been discovered already suggests that the negative stereotypes of gender, sexuality and ethnicity were always mitigated by positive representations.

10 Mapping the Current Critical Landscape

Donna Landry

Chapter Overview

Training a global optic on the long eighteenth century (1688–1832) presents exciting prospects. Britain's new-found importance in the world economy, commerce with increasingly exotic trading partners, scientific and commercial voyaging, far-flung colonial settlements, and burgeoning print culture had important ramifications for country as well as city, and for women of vision as well as men of feeling. We can best predict the future by examining the newest, most resonant developments whose potential has yet to be fully explored. Three kinds of criticism point the way forward for eighteenth-century studies in a globalized world: postcolonial and Black Atlantic criticism, green or ecological criticism, and criticism attentive to the relations between capitalism and subjectivity, or affects and economics. Jane Austen's novel *Mansfield Park* (first published 1814; second edition, with Austen's corrections, 1816) offers itself as a particularly fruitful case study for glimpsing the potential of these new forms of critical practice.

Postcolonial Approaches: The Instance of the Black Atlantic

Postcolonial criticism investigates the history of empire from the perspective of anti-colonial resistance and decolonization. Edward Said's *Orientalism*

(1978 second edition 1995) is a foundational text for this kind of criticism, and one of the most fertile fields of long eighteenth-century studies will undoubtedly continue to be East-West relations, particularly relations between Britain and, Said's primary focus, the Islamic world. The idea of a Black Atlantic, to adopt Paul Gilroy's formulation, although related to the Saidian critique of empire, shifts the question of African peoples in diaspora from too narrow a focus on their enslavement and transport as chattel, and makes it possible to attend to Black writing and cultural production beyond the nationalist boundaries that often segregate 'British' from 'American' literature (1992 and 1993) (see pp. 96f. Chapter 5, Case Studies in Reading 2: Key Theoretical and Critical Texts).

The growth of print culture opened up opportunities for women, labourers and artisans, and slaves or former slaves to recount their experiences to a wider audience. Much has been achieved in recent years in bringing some of these authors to light. Phillis Wheatley's (?1735–84) brilliant mastery of English poetic forms, for example, or Olaudah Equiano's (1745–97) textual virtuosity, were important aesthetic achievements in themselves as well as testimony to the intellectual capabilities of African subjects and reasons to abolish the slave trade. But there is still plenty of work to do if authors who were important during the eighteenth century but who have since been forgotten, or whose importance has been downplayed by previous scholarship are to receive the recognition they deserve. Although Gilroy's model of how African diasporic writers constituted a new public sphere may be a bit too idealistic, given the continuing dominance of white abolitionists within the movement, and the continuous suffering of millions within the institution of slavery, even after the abolition of the transatlantic slave trade, the concept of a Black Atlantic does at least offer an alternative historical vision to a complacently Anglo- and imperial one (see pp. 168f. Chapter 9, Gender, Sexuality and Ethnicity).

Mansfield Park is particularly open to postcolonial and Black Atlantic-inspired readings because it subtly portrays relationships between Britain and the West Indies, the effects of colonial income upon society and family life in the English countryside, and the moral, ethical and environmental consequences of wealth linked to the slave trade. Marcus Wood (2002) has recently argued that *Mansfield Park* may be a more profoundly radical novel than it has previously been thought to be. From Wood's perspective, in *Mansfield Park* Austen reveals herself as both knowledgeable about – and highly critical of – the effects the slave trade and wealth derived from plantation slave-labour were having on British society in the first decades of the nineteenth century. Wood claims that Austen's oblique approach to the question of slavery should be understood not as political disengagement or detachment or a lack of interest in questioning 'the realities of the colonial context' (2002: 296) but rather as an ingenious critique.

Wood radicalizes Austen's politics in an exciting way by paying close attention to the structure and meaningful repetitions of her prose, remarking that 'Austen's critique emerges in nuanced and ironic punning on key terms which can equally be used to describe wealth, domestic and foreign property, breeding, aesthetics, and personal ethics' (2002: 298–9). He shows Austen employing a language of 'improvement' in relation to Fanny Price's adoption by Sir Thomas Bertram that exposes Fanny's metaphorical, but also material, status as property. As property, Fanny is a commodity to be invested in and 'improved' in the hopes of a good return when she marries. In so far as she is a poor white relation at Mansfield Park, and amongst those governed by the proprietorship of Sir Thomas, Fanny also bears some resemblance to the slaves owned in Antigua. For Wood, Austen's exposure of how the income from slavery insidiously corrupts life at Mansfield Park harks back to the exposure of slavery as a form of monopoly capitalism by Adam Smith (1723–90) in *The Wealth of Nations* (1776 and 1976). Smith, who lectured in rhetoric and *belles-lettres* before turning his attention to economic matters, decried how mercantile monopolists were the enemies of improvement, especially once one grasped the greater productivity to be gained by investment in technological innovation and increased specialization through the division of labour. Plantation slave labour was the antithesis of Smith's vision of the new and improved labour force who worked ever harder from self-interest and the desire of self-improvement; slavery encouraged moral degeneracy as well as representing bad commercial policy. Wood's reading of Fanny within the language of improvement, a language deployed obliquely and ironically but tellingly by Austen, is set in train by the following 'grammatically intricate sentence' (2002: 304):

> The time was now come when Sir Thomas expected his sister-in-law to claim her share in their niece, the change in Mrs. Norris's situation, and the improvement in Fanny's age, seeming not only to do away any former objection to their living together, but even to give it the most decided eligibility; and as his own circumstances were rendered less fair than heretofore, by some recent losses on his West India estate, in addition to his eldest son's extravagance, it became not undesirable to himself to be relieved from the expense of her support, and the obligation of her future provision. (1998: 19)

Wood notes how a 'fiscal vocabulary' dominates the description of family relations from first to last, with Fanny's fate being explicitly entailed upon the fortunes of Sir Thomas's sugar plantation. As we learn from the outset, '[i]f the sugar money stops coming in, Fanny will be one of the first excess expenditures Sir Thomas will have to dispense with' (Wood: 2002: 306). The intricate grammar of the sentence, and its circumlocutory syntax, are dictated by Sir Thomas's 'linguistic code', which like his rules of conduct, presupposes a generosity and benevolence predicated on income derived from landed property, whether foreign or domestic; according to this code, 'it is not appropriate to express loss positively, nor is it proper ever to state that Sir Thomas cannot afford to do something' (ibid.: 305). The climax of Wood's reading of Fanny in terms of 'improvement', bound up with the exigencies of plantation slavery, occurs when Sir Thomas returns from Antigua after attempting to sort out his less than fair prospects. Fresh from the world of slave markets and the slave-owner's constant appraisal of human flesh, Sir Thomas takes an entirely new approach to Fanny, now entering into womanhood:

> Sir Thomas was at that moment looking round him, and saying, 'But where is Fanny? – Why do I not see my little Fanny?' And on perceiving her, came forward with a kindness which astonished and penetrated her, calling her his dear Fanny, kissing her affectionately, and observing with decided pleasure how much she was grown! Fanny knew not how to feel, nor where to look. She was quite oppressed. He had never been so kind, so *very* kind to her in his life. His manner seemed changed; his voice was quick from the agitation of joy; and all that had been awful in his dignity seemed lost in tenderness. He led her nearer the light and looked at her again – inquired particularly after he health, and then correcting himself, observed that he need *not* inquire, for her appearance spoke sufficiently on that point. A fine blush having succeeded the previousness paleness of her face, he was justified in his belief of her equal improvement in health and beauty. (1998: 123)

Wood illuminates this passage by noting that '[n]othing has prepared us for the amorous ferocity of Sir Thomas', and that '[t]his is the most overtly sexual writing in the novel', an epiphany of 'emotional arousal' (2002: 311). Wood finds Sir Thomas behaving only just within the limits of gentlemanly acceptability, with a connoisseur's eye directed to Fanny's parts in a manner that Fanny finds confusing and oppressive. Even Fanny's blush under the glare of this appraisal is reminiscent of the blushes of 'beautiful mulatto or quadroon slave girls on the auction block' (ibid.: 313).

What is particularly convincing about Wood's reading of this scene is that, however disconcerted Fanny may at first feel, this encounter undoubtedly draws Fanny and Sir Thomas closer together than ever before and establishes her as newly important to him as a companion and interlocutor.

Ironically, their new-found closeness manifests itself in nothing so much as their mutual pleasure in talking about Antigua and the question of slavery, a subject which, within the Bertram family circle, appears only of compelling interest to Fanny. Austen's irony plays wickedly here, in that Fanny's status as a poor relation, forever indebted to Sir Thomas's beneficence, combines with Fanny's own humility and class deference to make her obligation to Sir Thomas not the object of resentment but a bond to be invested with all her most delicate feelings, even eroticized. Their relationship is not formally that of slave-holder to slave, of course, and hence not subject to the exploitations and abuses of that relation. Sir Thomas and Fanny will come to behave in such a way that any erotic charge between them will be kept within appropriate bounds of avuncular concern and affection. Embarrassed by her own increasing desirability, Fanny takes refuge in a relationship with Sir Thomas safeguarded by the very reserved and dignified propriety that had formerly made him seem so cold and intimidating.

Fanny's advancement in Sir Thomas's estimation produces the moment in the novel that has most readily captured the attention of critics interested in questions of empire and led to the most speculation about Austen's views on slavery. Fanny and Edmund discuss how quiet the evenings at Mansfield Park now are, after Sir Thomas's return; the amateur theatricals have been interrupted and abandoned, the coming and going of guests has ceased; Sir Thomas is enjoying presiding at his own fireside. Fanny defends this new regime, somewhat disingenuously, given that she knows how Edmund must be missing the company of Mary Crawford:

> 'The evenings do not appear long to me. I love to hear my uncle talk of the West Indies. I could listen to him for an hour together. It entertains *me* more than many other things have done – but then I am unlike other people I dare say.'
>
> 'Your uncle is disposed to be pleased with you in every respect; and I only wish you would talk to him more. – You are one of those who are too silent in the evening circle.'
>
> 'But I do talk to him more than I used. I am sure I do. Did not you hear me ask him about the slave-trade last night?'
>
> 'I did – and was in hopes the question would be followed up by others. It would have pleased your uncle to have been inquired of farther.'
>
> 'And I longed to do it – but there was such a dead silence! And while my cousins were sitting by without speaking a word, or seeming at all interested in the subject, I did not like – I thought it would appear as if I wanted to set myself off at their expense, by shewing a curiosity and pleasure in his information which he must wish his own daughters to feel.' (1998: 135–36)

Once again fiscal language echoes within the language of feeling: Fanny ventures to express how she is afraid to compete for Sir Thomas's approval since that would mean pleasing him at her cousins' 'expense'. When the slave trade is at last actually mentioned at Mansfield Park, and the infamous 'dead silence' falls upon the company, only Fanny and Sir Thomas are prepared to engage with the issue. It is as if they were the only two properly serious people present; the others are all thinking of flirtations past, present and future, or, in the case of the eldest son Tom, of hunting, racing and gambling. This scene establishes the very note of complicity between Sir Thomas and Fanny with which the novel will eventually end. After these two moments in the novel – his return from Antigua, and her fascination with his experiences there – Fanny and Sir Thomas will be bound together in a meeting of minds, preferences and principles, consolidated most happily, once Fanny marries Edmund, by their becoming father-in-law and daughter-in-law. Although the negotiating of this fondness is not without its pitfalls, such as her refusal to marry Henry Crawford and thus capitalize on Sir Thomas's investment in her upbringing, Fanny and Sir Thomas will, after these two encounters, be essentially on the same side.

Whatever Sir Thomas's 'information' might consist of, we are not to be made privy to it, nor to how Fanny, who appears to be, like Austen, 'a friend of the abolition' (Southam in Johnson, 1998: 498) must feel about Sir Thomas's continuing to have slaves. Wood suggests such omissions imply not so much a dearth of knowledge or understanding on the part of Austen's characters (and, implicitly, her readers), but rather an all too recent deluge of information on the subject. By the time of the novel's publication in 1814, an outpouring of visual and verbal representations of the horrors of slavery had been inspiring a public outcry for decades. Arguments for and against the slave trade had been in circulation since the 1770s, the movement for abolition had recently achieved a victory in 1807, and the question of the institution of slave labour itself was becoming a thorny issue with which Austen's audience would have been all too familiar. It might be boredom with the known, Wood suggests, rather than a lack of curiosity about the unknown that produces that deathly hush in the Mansfield Park drawing room when Fanny asks Sir Thomas about the slave trade. If this were so, and Wood makes a very convincing case, we might conclude that a kind of Black Atlantic traffic in people, ideas and images, some of them produced by freed slaves who became authors, had seeped into the consciousness of Austen and her readers in a profound way.

Wood's close reading shows the way towards ever more subtle understandings of the diffusion of slavery, abolition, and the developing discourse of racial difference and race prejudice throughout long eighteenth-century literature. Even *Mansfield Park*, so meticulously analysed by Wood, will continue to yield new insights if read within a Black Atlantic paradigm. Consider, for example, Maria Bertram's comments on the locked gate in the park at Sotherton, on the day that the Bertrams and Crawfords visit Maria's future husband Mr Rushworth at home. '[U]nluckily that iron gate, that ha-ha, gives me a feeling of restraint and hardship' (1998: 71), Maria remarks to Henry Crawford. Then she echoes the passage about a caged starling in Laurence Sterne's *A Sentimental Journey* (1768): 'I cannot get out, as the starling said' (ibid.: 71). If we trace the origin of this quotation back to Sterne's novel, we will discover that this passage was Sterne's attempt to please his friend Ignatius Sancho, a man of letters and former slave, who had requested that Sterne strike a blow against slavery.

Eighteenth-century writing will continue to yield richly complex new insights within global and Black Atlantic perspectives.

A Green Revolution: Ecological Approaches

Attendant upon the growing awareness of the imperial and the global, environmental or ecological approaches to the long eighteenth century will also continue to grow in urgency and importance.

If, like an estate, Fanny is 'improved' by Sir Thomas's investment in her education and upbringing, her being instilled with good taste and refined manners and a properly genteel sense of how life should be lived tranquilly and harmoniously, that improvement manifests itself at least partly in relation to Fanny's relation to landscape and the natural world. Fanny in the green world occupies a particular social and economic position, but her observations open the text to a reading sensitive to broader questions of how humans relate to the natural world at large. This is the domain of ecocriticism or ecological readings.

Ecological approaches to eighteenth-century studies are new in one sense, but not in another. For instance the work of Raymond Williams, John Barrell and James Grantham Turner established, in the 1970s and early 1980s, sophisticated ways of understanding how nature was artificially produced or constructed in actual landscapes, as well as in literary and artistic representations of them. As characterized by Raymond Williams in *The Country and the City* (1973), Austen's attitude towards society and landscape should be understood in the context of her location as one of the three contemporaries who lived 'around Farnham': the naturalist Gilbert White (1720–93) and the radical journalist William Cobbett (1763–1835). Focusing on her attitude to landscape, Williams showed that Austen was more attuned to social injustice and the workings of capital than previous commentators had allowed. John Barrell (1972) has memorably characterized how the writing of landscape displays both the material contours of the lie of the land and a syntax for grasping it.

Author of the famous poem 'The Seasons' (1726–30), James Thomson (1700–48) gives a commanding view of a whole countryside which is quite different from the circular parish-bound sense of the land that we get from the poet and agricultural labourer John Clare (1793–1864) who conveys an intimate knowledge of footpaths, mole hills and individual birds and wild flowers. Barrell (1980) has also revealed the politics of culture at work in English landscape painting, especially the presence or absence of labour and labourers therein. James Grantham Turner (1980) has brilliantly shown how inseparable are the very tropes most typical of poetic representation of land from the politics of its ownership, its working, and its erotic symbolization.

It would be hard, in this regard, to ignore the landscape of Mansfield Park, even though the politics underlying it are not immediately apparent. Rural labour is nearly as shadowy in its representation as plantation slave labour, gestured towards in conversation, as when Mary Crawford complains that she has not been able to transport her harp because all the local carts were engaged in haymaking. Indeed, rural labourers are figured most often in terms of their desirable absence; talk of the improvement of estates consists first and foremost in separating gentlemen's houses from their farmyards, as even Edmund agrees when discussing Thornton Lacey.

In *Mansfield Park*, more attention is paid to the green world as signifying something beyond the human than is paid to actual labourers labouring within view. Raymond Williams memorably elevated a phrase from John Clare, the 'green language', into a whole new movement of thought and sensibility and way of looking at the world – for Williams, a new 'structure of feeling' – in the late eighteenth century. Austen incorporated the Romantic interest in nature into all her novels in various ways, but Fanny's observations about land and landscape are particularly revealing. Talking to Mary Crawford in the Parsonage shrubbery, Fanny praises the growth of the laurels and other evergreens which shelter them:

> How beautiful, how welcome, how wonderful the evergreen! – When one thinks of it, how astonishing a variety of nature! – In some countries we know the tree that sheds its leaf is the variety, but that does not make it less amazing, that the same soil and the same sun should nurture plants differing in the first rule and law of their existence. (1998: 144)

She then apologizes to Mary for rhapsodizing, observing that when she is sitting out of doors, she is 'very apt to get into this sort of wondering strain', whereby '[o]ne cannot fix one's eyes on the commonest natural production without finding food for a rambling fancy' (ibid.). Fanny's ramblings ironically comment on the very different species of human beings currently coexisting in and around Mansfield Park. Not surprisingly, Fanny prefers the constancy of the evergreen, the odd species out in a world of marked seasonal change and deciduous foliage – a seasonal shedding akin to Mary's restless preoccupation with fashion.

Fanny's comment emphasizes the figure in the landscape, the question of the human in relation to non-human nature, from the point of view of an observer who derives pleasure from contemplation of natural phenomena as landscape–whether planted pleasure grounds, such as the shrubbery, or more expansive prospects. The natural world as a picture, composed and framed for the spectator, who is then composed and refreshed by the image presented, had become a dominant mode of engaging with nature by the late eighteenth century. Michael McKeon calls this mode of apprehending the natural world both pastoral and Romantic, arguing that today, in the post-industrialized West, this attitude remains the dominant one, founded on a contradiction between 'the dream of a direct apprehension of nature' and 'the inevitability of nature's imaginative construction' (1998: 289). We construct nature imaginatively, and even manufacture it, but hope to look upon this construction unobtrusively, maintaining the conceit that this picture is entirely 'natural' and requires no intervention by humans.

The picturesque encouraged a pictorial rather than a sensory approach to the natural world. Picturesque theory anticipated today's ecocriticism by advocating a visual, hands-off kind of interaction with nature: take only pictures, leave only footprints. Inspired by, among others, William Gilpin (1724–1804), schoolmaster, vicar and author of a series of illustrated tours, seekers after the picturesque kept diaries and sketchbooks of scenes, like photograph albums. Rather than bagging game, hunting or gathering, these tourists took away with them only an aesthetic experience of nature, as memory or *aide memoire*.

Such an aestheticized approach became popular in direct proportion to the intensification of agriculture in the late eighteenth and early nineteenth century. Between 1750 and the early 1800s, the taste of the nation shifted towards wilder prospects once – to borrow terms from the historian Robert C. Allen (1992) – the second, or landlords' agricultural revolution occurred. This process involved the final wave of parliamentary enclosures of common lands, and intensified engrossments and emparkments of land by wealthy owners of large estates. Cultivated landscapes were no longer really fashionable as objects of aesthetic appreciation precisely because they bespoke utility rather than a nature that exceeded human capacity to master it.

Fanny appears to have a 'natural' taste for landscape, in that we do not observe her receiving instruction in nature worship, the theories of William Gilpin regarding picturesque beauty, or other fashionable approaches to the subject. She quotes William Cowper (1731–1800), a poet who suffered terribly from depression, as readily as she responds to a prospect with aesthetic appreciation and feeling. She is above being swayed by the new fashion for estate 'improvement' that was being promoted by the professional landscape gardener Humphry Repton (1752–1818) and paid for lavishly by those devoted to redesigning their estates in order to impress. When Mr Rushworth observes that he believes Humphry Repton would be bound to advise cutting down the avenue at Sotherton, Fanny exclaims quietly to Edmund, 'Cut down an avenue! What a pity! Does it not make you think of Cowper? "Ye fallen avenues, once more I mourn your fate unmerited" ' (1998: 41). Fanny revels in sitting in the carefully planted 'wilderness' at Sotherton, observing that 'to sit in the shade on a fine day, and look upon verdure, is the most perfect refreshment' (ibid.: 68). Back at Mansfield Park, she will attempt to distract Edmund from Mary Crawford's charms by getting him to notice the beauty of the woods and the night sky.

> Here's what may tranquillize every care, and lift the heart to rapture! When I look out on such a night as this, I feel as if there could be neither wickedness nor sorrow in the world; and there certainly would be less of both if the sublimity of Nature were more attended to, and people were carried more out of themselves by contemplating such a scene. (ibid.: 80)

The appeal to Edmund works, in so far as he replies that he pities those who 'have not been taught to feel in some degree as you do – who have not at least been given a taste for nature in early life. They lose a great deal' (ibid.: 81).

This scene is almost cruelly revealing of how Fanny herself attributes her strong affective attachment to the natural world entirely to Edmund's teaching. She replies, simply: '*You* taught me to think and feel on the subject, cousin' (1998: 81). We recognize with a shock that even her love of non-human nature, the world of trees, plants and celestial bodies, is for Fanny completely bound up with a mimetic relation to her first human love. Liking Edmund and striving to be like him has meant Fanny regards the natural world in a particularly intense way. Nature becomes their common ground, on which to enact their mutual liking.

Once again we notice how Fanny has been shaped by her dependence on the Bertram family's benevolence, and how she has been largely produced as a sensitive, feeling being attuned to the natural world by the material environment of Mansfield Park. This is never more obvious than during Fanny's exile among her immediate family in Portsmouth, which is both a demotion in social class and a deprivation of those material advantages of beauty, tranquillity and good manners Fanny has learned to value. The beauties of the English countryside, as experienced from the grounds of a baronet's estate, can never be surpassed within Austen's representation of the world, though they are forever at risk of corruption from the entanglements of economics and empire. The implications of this vision suggest that Austen can indeed be productively read as a contemporary of her fellow dwellers around Farnham, William Cobbett and Gilbert White. The project of accounting for Austen and other writers in terms of social ecology and the roots of ecological thinking has barely begun.

Affects and Economics: Approaches Grounded in Histories of Feeling and the Marketplace

We have already noted that in *Mansfield Park* the very language of sentiment and affect is also an economic language. Austen subtly foregrounds, within the texture of her prose, the contradictions arising between imperial ambitions, mentalities and manners derived from the capitalist marketplace, and traditional community and family structures. New work in the field of the history of the emotions, mapping the circulation of 'affects' and their theorization in the eighteenth century, represents an exciting rethinking of the old debate about reason versus the passions during the Enlightenment. This source of new understandings of the eighteenth century has only just begun to be tapped and promises long-term replenishment for interpreting canonical texts as well as discovering newly interesting ones (see p. 111, Chapter 5, Case Studies in Reading 2: Key Theoretical and Critical Texts: Passion and Emotion).

The bond between Sir Thomas and Fanny is a bond of deference and dependency on her side, and of patronage on his. It is a strongly affective bond, shot through with power, and as the novel progresses, Fanny's fear and Sir Thomas's distance develop into mutual liking, in spite of, and across, but also *through* the relations of social and economic power that link them. We might say that the bond between them has everything to do with sympathy – the term that Adam Smith theorized as crucial for both the social fabric and the market.

In his *Theory of Moral Sentiments* (1759), Smith argued that people could only project themselves into experiencing some semblance of recognition of the suffering of others by imagining what they themselves might feel in the same circumstances. He defines sympathy as follows:

> As we have no immediate experience of what other men feel, we can form no idea of the manner in which they are affected, but by conceiving what we ourselves should feel in the like situation. Though our brother is upon the rack, as long as we ourselves are at our ease, our senses will never inform us of what he suffers. . . . [I]t is by the imagination only that we can form any conception of what are his sensations. (1976: 9)

In *The Wealth of Nations* (1776), Smith claimed that this imaginative sympathy should not be pushed too far, but that individuals were alike in acting according to their own self-interest. Binding together these otherwise separate and competitive subjects of self-interested striving, was the market:

> It is not from the benevolence of the butcher, the brewer, or the baker, that we expect our dinner, but from their regard to their own self interest. We address ourselves, not to their humanity but to their self-love, and never talk to them of our own necessities but of their advantages. (ibid.: 26–7)

The division of labour in the workplace is another example of how each individual, concentrating on his or her own task, nevertheless co-operates in the production of the finished product. It is also a means of increasing productivity. Smith notes that pin making can be divided into eighteen distinct operations. If each of these is assigned to different individuals, they will produce more pins than just one person working on his or her own. The division of labour, then, is a good illustration of the interdependency of individuals which in turn is one condition for a successful economy. Anyone who understood the limited operations of sympathy would rejoice in this benevolent conception of the regulative fairness of the division of labour in which each had only to labour diligently for all to thrive.

In *Novel Relations* (2004), Ruth Perry has brilliantly shown how, during the later decades of the eighteenth century, 'the emotional capital' of kinship was being rewritten, and the consanguineal or extended family displaced by the conjugal couple and its offspring. As with Smith's notion of the workforce as relatively atomized individuals, so also with the nuclear family as the sole focus of family feeling: a lopping off of formerly more capacious branches of social connectedness and mutual obligation ensues. This is precisely what does not happen at Mansfield Park, and Fanny is the chief beneficiary of this resistance to the new political economic imperatives.

One of the peculiarities of this text is that although Sir Thomas is a slave-owner, and, as we have seen, Austen's text is far from uncritical of slavery, we as readers are not allowed to dislike or dismiss him. One consequence of Austen's skilful narration is that we will likely see things largely from Fanny's point of view and, as a further consequence, often feel as she does. From Fanny's vantage point, Sir Thomas, who has been from the first her benefactor, and who struggles to maintain a just balance between personal feeling, imaginative sympathy, and the entitlements of obligation when dealing with her, emerges as more sympathetic than he would from some of the other characters' perspectives, especially the insurgent Maria's.

Sir Thomas is introduced as a man of principle – in fact, in Perry's terms, a good old-fashioned sort who considers his wife's extended family as well within the purview of his principled benevolence. His motivation for seeking to help the Price family goes beyond mere family pride, the narrator assures us; it derives also from 'principle' – 'from a general wish of doing right, and a desire of seeing all that were connected with him in situations of respectability' (5). Indeed what Fanny and Sir Thomas share is a strong commitment to controlling their feelings according to principle, rather than uncritically pursuing their own emotional self-interest.

'Principle', 'interest': the language of finance is inescapably bound up with the language of feeling; in this work at least, there is no language of feeling other than the language of the marketplace. It is as if Austen were playfully satirizing Smith's twin preoccupations, in his two famous treatises, the first on 'moral sentiments', the second on political economy and the 'wealth of nations'. In a concluding passage, Austen's narrator enters Sir Thomas's consciousness to observe: 'Fanny was indeed the daughter that he wanted. His charitable kindness had been rearing a prime comfort for himself. His liberality had a rich repayment, and the general goodness of his intentions by her, deserved it' (1998: 320). If the 'rich repayment' he had initially envisaged, as a return on his investment in her upbringing, was Fanny's marriage to the rich Henry Crawford, the outcome of her 'cousins in love' (ibid.: 7) marriage to Edmund is now perceived by him as superior to any monetary enrichment. The text stresses the affective bonds that have superseded economic ones:

> He might have made her childhood happier; but it had been an error of judgment only which had given him the appearance of harshness, and deprived him of her early love; and now, on really knowing each other, their mutual attachment became very strong. (ibid.: 320)

We are left with the impression that Fanny's destiny is to spend at least as much time in the company of Sir Thomas as in her husband Edmund's, so 'strong' is this 'mutual attachment' that contravenes the new nuclear familial ideology: 'After settling her at Thornton Lacey with every kind attention to her comfort, the object of almost every day was to see her there, or to get her away from it' (ibid.). However witty the tone, and however brief the description of Fanny and Sir Thomas as strongly attached, we are left with the distinct impression that this affection is a good thing, despite the contradiction between the circumstances that produced it and the principles of those involved.

Thus does Austen engage in some powerful manipulation of readerly affinities and sentiments, but to what end? We are, perforce, made not only to tolerate a slave owner but to like and admire him. Fanny is first a dependent then mistress of an estate that itself depends on the unfree labour of unseen others thousands of miles away as well as the unseen labour of countless servants. And yet we are not allowed to close the book by merely condemning this dependency, though we may be troubled by it. By revealing the inseparable entanglements of the flows of capital and feeling, of benevolence and the attachments that form within economic and social bonds, Austen both exposes the contradictions that produce her world and insists upon their vexing complexity. As Alexander Pope proclaimed in his 'Epistle to Burlington' (1731) 'Tis use alone that sanctifies expence', (1950–69: 149) and this distinctly eighteenth-century sentiment continues to resonate throughout Austen's fiction. Once again, the teasing out of these complex networks of affect and economics remains a project only just begun.

Conclusion

The eighteenth century has emerged as the lodestone of our most urgent modern preoccupations. Global perspectives, including a focus on East-West relations and Britain and the Muslim world, will continue to compel audiences for some time to come. Black Atlantic writing offers exciting archival challenges while rewriting imperial history as we have known it. Given current concerns with planetary crisis management, a Green revolution in literary studies is more likely to be perpetual than short-lived, just as the critique of empire has a long time to run, given the halting progress of decolonization. So long as the micro-electronically networked financialization of the globe continues to intensify, the market for reinventions of the history of capitalism and emotion will be huge.

Glossary

Teresa Barnard and Gary Day

Augustan Age: The Augustan period is named for the Roman emperor Augustus Caesar, who ruled from 27 BCE (before common era) to 14 CE (common era). During his reign, Rome saw what many consider its greatest literary and cultural achievements: Augustan poets include Virgil (famous for his poem *The Aeneid*), Ovid (famous for his mythological poem *The Metamorphoses* and his erotic poetry) and Horace (famous for his odes). Sometimes the term *Augustan* is applied to the late seventeenth and early eighteenth centuries in England, the period also called Neoclassical, and sometimes, more controversially, even to the entire eighteenth century. The work of writers belonging to this period is characterized by a striving for balance, harmony and refinement.

Blue Stocking: A group which met at the London homes of Elizabeth Montagu, Elizabeth Vesey and Frances Boscawen. The name derives from the blue worsted stockings of the botanist Benjamin Stillingfleet who attended the meetings but was too poor to afford the white silk stockings required for formal wear. The main female members of the circle were the scholar and classical translator Elizabeth Carter, the novelist Fanny Burney and the writer and dramatist Hannah More. Male members included Samuel Johnson and Sir Joshua Reynolds. The sole purpose of the blue stocking evening was conversation, though there should be no reference to politics or scandal. And swearing was not allowed. Hannah More proclaimed conversation to be 'That noblest commerce of mankind / Whose precious merchandise is MIND!'

Ballad: Ballad is a narrative verse restored from medieval times or written contemporarily and intended to be recited or sung. Its origins are in the oral tradition and poets frequently used the form to reflect the language of common people. Ballads of love, adventure and comedy were intended to entertain and amuse. Executions of criminals were a favourite subject and the execution broadside or 'last words' of the condemned was a recognized genre, often including a prose description of the crime and the last hours of the criminal alongside verses expressive of his or her repentance on the gallows. Many purporting to deliver shocking news were fakes, and a tale of disastrous flood, earthquake or Act of God might be reprinted several times with the location and the names of individuals changed to make the story seem new. Ballads commented, usually satirically, on events and famous people rather than presenting new information. One, for example, related the story of a lady who fell in love with her serving man. Ballads began to be studied seriously in the eighteenth century and were collected and valued as expressions of authentic national identity.

Coffee House: Coffee houses did not just serve coffee, they also offered their customers chocolate, wine, brandy and punch. They were centres of conversation and business. The modern stock-market, for example, originated at Jonathan's coffee house in Exchange Alley. Besides being meeting places, coffee houses provided a wide range of newspapers, pamphlets and periodicals for customers to read. In this respect they were like many institutions which sprang up all over Europe devoted to the discussion and exploration of ideas such as academies, learned societies and so on. Coffee houses were at the heart of what Jurgen Habermas calls the public sphere, a space ideally accessible to all and characterized by rational discourse and the free exchange of opinion.

Didactic: Literary works that intend to instruct. Eighteenth-century readers generally expected and valued moral didacticism in novels. Samuel Richardson's *Pamela, or, Virtue Rewarded* (1740) prompted a cult following from many readers, although it also attracted a cynical response from anti-Pamela novels such as Henry Fielding's *Shamela* (1741).

Elegy: A formal meditative poem of lamentation that explores mortality through grief expressed at the death of a public figure or of a close friend and seeks consolation. More generally, the elegy focuses on the transience of the world. The most famous example in the eighteenth century is Thomas Gray's 'Elegy Written in a Country Churchyard (1751). It contains some of the best-known lines in English literature such as 'Full many a Flower is born to blush unseen / And waste its Sweetness on the desart Air.' The title of Thomas Hardy's *Far from the Madding Crowd* also comes from the poem.

Essay: Although essay writing was not unknown before the eighteenth century, it was the period during which the form became widespread. The English Renaissance writer Francis Bacon saw essays as extended precepts or pointed reflections. The word essay comes from the Latin *exagere* which means to weigh, to sift, to winnow. It becomes *essayer* in French which means to try or attempt. It was another Renaissance writer, Michel de Montaigne, who gave the essay its name and its characteristic personal tone. Addison and Steele, in the early part of the eighteenth century, extended the form by adding the persona, that is a narrative voice not their own. The essay was highly adaptable to a range of subjects and an ideal means for conveying to a large audience the latest discoveries or thinking on topics as diverse as opera and deportment. Johnson also used a persona in his essays, that of the idler or the rambler, but he uses the essay more as a means of enforcing opinion on the reader rather than conversing with him or her. The following gives an example of his style. 'Criticism is a study by which men grow important and formidable at very small expense. The power of invention has been conferred by nature upon few, and the labour of learning those sciences which may, by mere labour, be obtained, is too great to be willingly endured; but every man can exert such judgement as he has upon the works of others; and he whom nature has made weak, and idleness keeps ignorant, may yet support his vanity by the name of a critic' (The *Idler* 60 [1759]).

Grand Tour: This began in the sixteenth century and became a fashion in the eighteenth. It was a leisurely journey through the cultural centres of Europe, undertaken by the sons of the aristocracy, with the aim of acquainting them with the classical past. The tour, which began to include the wealthy middle class, inspired the new genre of guide book writing.

Grub Street: In his *Dictionary*, Johnson declared this was originally the name of a street near Moorfields in London 'much inhabited by writers of small histories, dictionaries and temporary poems whence any mean production is called grub-street'. Johnson's comment is not just a reflection on the quality of literature produced by inhabitants of that area but also on the emergence of a literary marketplace. Prior to the eighteenth century a writer mostly relied on a patron to promote his or her work. The expansion of publishing and the increase in the audience for printed works was one of the key factors in the decline of patronage. Some regarded its passing with regret, believing that the support of a king or nobleman enabled the writer to produce work of the highest standard while others saw patronage as a form of literary prostitution. One commented that gentlemen 'kept a bard, just as they keep a whore'. But the demands of the market could also cause a writer to prostitute his or her talent because their first responsibility was to the book-seller, not to their art. If he or she is to make any kind of living, Johnson notes elsewhere, the writer 'is compelled to accept any task that is thrown before him'.

Kit-Kat Club: The Kit-Kat Club was founded in William III's reign, largely by Lord Somers, the Lord Chancellor, and the publisher Jacob Tonson, who became its secretary. Its aim was to support the 1688 Revolution, which brought William III to the throne, and to uphold the Protestant succession. Its members included Joseph Addison, Richard Steele and William Congreve. They met at the house of one Christopher Cat (or Kat) a cook, whose mutton pies were known as 'kit-kats'.

Literary Club: The most influential club of the second half of the eighteenth century. Set up by Johnson in 1764, its members included the painter Joshua Reynolds, the botanist Joseph Banks, the actor David Garrick and the writer Oliver Goldsmith. They produced work in a variety of fields, placed contemporaries in relation to their predecessors and shaped a series of traditions across different disciplines and created a valuable cultural heritage.

Muse: Originally from Greek mythology, the Muses were invoked for inspiration within different genres, for example, *Thalia* for comedy and *Melpomene* for tragedy.

Nature: This term has many different meanings in the eighteenth century. In one view nature is a self-contained system of laws created by, but not controlled by God. The workings of nature are thus seen as independent of divine providence. This is the scientific view of nature which leads ultimately to its exploitation for man's benefit. The artistic view of nature saw it more as a guide to human action. In his 'Essay on Criticism', Pope advises the would-be poet to 'First follow Nature, and your judgement frame / By her just standard which is still the same' (l. 68–9). It is this view of nature which feeds into Wordsworth's belief that nature is a moral force which should shape our actions. Both scientists – the eighteenth-century term would be natural philosopher – and poets and painters regarded nature as a symbol of order. The job of the scientist was to describe nature, that of the poet to imitate it. At the same time both believed that nature needed to be improved by human action. Dryden thought that art completes what nature leaves imperfect. Nature, he wrote, offers 'a brazen world – the poets only deliver a golden'. A good example of art improving nature is landscape gardening, which went through a number of phases in this period from formal settings to styles more in harmony with 'the genius of place'. Finally, there was a view of nature as sublime, as something too vast and powerful for humans to comprehend, never mind control. It is a view which becomes prominent in some aspects of Romanticism.

Ode: The word comes from the Greek meaning 'song': A lyric poem in a high style on a serious subject. Odes are usually classed as Pindaric (after the Greek poet Pindar (522–433 BC)) or Horatian (after the Roman poet Horace (65–8 BC)). The Pindaric ode was reserved for public occasions, such as celebrations of a victory, whereas the Horatian ode was more private and meditative. This was reflected in the language. The Pindaric ode was assured, elaborate and sonorous while the Horatian one was more subdued and thoughtful. Generally, the Pindaric ode was favoured in the early part of the long eighteenth century though it was not without its critics. From the 1740s the Horatian becomes more popular. There is a move from praise of persons to communing with the natural world or personifications of human qualities like 'Mercy'.

Pastoral: Poetry or drama or prose fiction that deals with country pleasures. The weather is always sunny and the trees and flowers are always in bloom. The earliest example of the pastoral is the *Idylls* of Theocritus in which shepherds live an idealized existence of love and song. Virgil, in his *Eclogues*, introduced a more realistic note and also made the pastoral a vehicle for social commentary. The pastoral fell out of favour in the middle ages but reappeared during the Renaissance. Samuel Johnson thought the pastoral sufficiently important to devote two *Rambler* essays to it. He defines it as 'the representation of passion or action by its effects upon country life' and accounts for its appeal by saying that it is a reminder of the joys of childhood and is a comfort in age. He also thought the pastoral did not lend itself to development because the countryside largely remains the same and he felt that the genre was suffering at the hands of those who wrote about the countryside without having first-hand experience of it. The history of the pastoral seems to consist of correcting the idyllic portrayal of the countryside by injecting a note of realism. James Thomson, author of *The Seasons*, extolled country pleasures and represented rural trades as enjoyable, but George Crabbe (1754–1832) found the poem to be more ideal than real. His response was 'The Village' (1783) which sought to give a detailed picture of rural poverty.

Picaresque: The word comes from the Spanish *picaro*, a wily trickster, and refers to novels with an unscrupulous but captivating protagonist who has a series of adventures, escaping downfall through trickery and deceit, but who eventually repents the error of his or her ways. Daniel Defoe's *Moll Flanders* (1722) is an example of the genre. Today the term signifies episodic novels, especially those of Fielding and Smollett which describe the adventures of a lively and resourceful hero on a journey.

Picturesque: A term which came into fashion in the late eighteenth century and was used to describe scenery that is rough and irregular. The picturesque was part of a change in the representation of landscape, where the aim was to evoke a frisson, a feeling of awe in the viewer. But mountains, lakes and forests were not just inspiring, they were also the setting for ruined castles and abbeys and therefore had a historical significance either as evidence of a barbaric past or as fragments of a native culture whose recovery was a matter of pride.

Politeness: One of the problems for eighteenth-century moralists and social commentators was how to avoid the divisive effects of politics and religion that, in the previous century, had led to civil war. Their answer was politeness. In the eighteenth century this term meant much more than saying 'please' and 'thank you'. It embodied the idea of what a true gentleman and lady should be: gracious, refined, courteous. A study of the arts would help people to become polite, as would conversation. Politeness, explained one contemporary manual, 'is a system of behaviour, polished by good breeding and disposes us on all occasions to render ourselves agreeable. It does not constitute merit, it shows it to advantage, as it equally regulates that manner of speaking and acting which conveys grace and commands respect'. Addison recommended keeping a diary as a means of cultivating politeness. But however it was to be achieved, its purpose remained the same, 'to replace', in the words of John Brewer, 'political zeal and religious bigotry with mutual tolerance and understanding' (1997: 102).

Religion: The Enlightenment is often regarded as marking the rise of the sciences and the decline of religion. But the picture is more complicated than that. Most books published in the period were religious in character. And while increasing knowledge of nature's laws undermined the belief in miracles, those very laws could also be seen as proof of an intelligent creator. The existence of God was thus more a matter of reason than revelation. However, events like the Lisbon earthquake in 1775 which killed 10,000 people, shattered this cosy assumption. Either God had created a faulty world or else he was not benevolent. The attempt to create a 'reasonable' Christianity was also reaction to the sectarian strife of the seventeenth century. A religion based on demonstrable evidence coupled with, in England, the Toleration Act of 1689, went some way to soften sectarian divisions. But this does not mean that faith ceased to play a dramatic role in social life. The Gordon riots of 1780 were a protest against the repeal of some of the laws that discriminated against Catholics and the tensions between the Anglican church and the various dissenting bodies like Baptists, Quakers and Unitarians, never quite disappeared. The greatest nonconformist movement of the eighteenth century, Methodism, began within the Church of England. Founded by John Wesley, its basic doctrine was that man could be saved if he believed in the gospels and performed good works. Methodism appealed mainly to the lower orders deflecting their energies away from political protest to the salvation of their souls.

Scriblerus Club: A literary grouping which included the royal physician John Arbuthnot, John Gay, Alexander Pope and Jonathan Swift. Members met mainly from January 1714 to July of the same year. According to Pope, the aim of the club was to ridicule 'all the false tastes in learning, under the character of a man of capacity enough that had dipped in every art and science, but injudiciously in each'.

Wit: Derived from the Anglo-Saxon *gewit*, the term originally signified mind, reason and intelligence, meanings which still cling to the late seventeenth- and early eighteenth-century use of the word. According to John Locke, wit is also the power of combining ideas; judgement is the power of discriminating between them. For Dryden, wit was synonymous with imagination while for Pope it was the best form of expression. But wit also had a class dimension. From 1660–1700 it was associated with the aristocracy. The main vehicle for their wit was Restoration comedy, a flamboyant celebration of aristocratic values after sober, puritan rule. In these plays, wit was used as a tool of seduction and mockery raising the question of whether or not it could be compatible with goodness. Wit was a highly prized quality at the start of the period but later came to be seen as a form of insincerity and self-aggrandizement. The more important qualities for the new era were integrity, morality, prudence and commercial humanism, that is the cultivation of manners and pleasures.

Appendix: Teaching and Learning Strategies

Ian McCormick

Chapter Overview

Ian McCormick is a Professor and member of the School of the Arts at The University of Northampton. His recent work has been in the field of deconstruction and drama, and in pedagogical aspects of eighteenth-century studies. Professor McCormick's critical editions of Robert Graves's novels *Antigua, Penny, Puce* and *They Hanged my saintly Billy* (Carcanet) were published in 2003.

Notes on Contributors

Teresa Barnard is a lecturer in English at the University of Derby, teaching Eighteenth-Century Literature and Local Writers. Her research areas are in eighteenth-century women's writing, especially Anna Seward; regional identity, and life writing. She has published several articles and chapters and her book, *Anna Seward: A Constructed Life*, will be published with Ashgate in 2009.

Gavin Budge is a Senior Lecturer in English Literature at the University of Hertfordshire. Recent publications include a monograph, *Charlotte M. Yonge: Religion, Feminism and Realism in the Victorian Novel* (Lang 2007) and an edited collection of essays, *Romantic Empiricism: Poetics and the Philosophy of Common Sense* (Bucknell University Press 2007). He is the Executive Secretary of the British Society for Eighteenth-Century Studies.

Michael Caines is the Bibliography Editor of the *Times Literary Supplement*. He has edited an anthology of plays by eighteenth-century women (2004) and a book about the actor David Garrick (2008), and co-edited anthologies on Shakespeare (2003) and the Romantics (2004).

Anne Chandler is an Associate Professor of English at Southern Illinois University Carbondale. Her research interests include Gothic and Didactic fiction, Revolution-era feminism, and British responses to Rousseau. She has published on Thomas Day, Mary Wollstonecraft and many other figures. Her current projects include the lingering influence of the Burke-Paine controversy.

Daniel Cook obtained his PhD from Queens' College, Cambridge. He has worked as an AHRC Research Fellow on the 'Cambridge Edition of the Works of Jonathan Swift' project and has edited a critical anthology on Swift for Bloom's Classic Critical Views (2009). He has also written on a range of eighteenth-century writers including Isaac D'Israeli and Thomas Tyrwhitt.

Gary Day is a Principal Lecturer in English at De Montfort University. He is the general editor of the Wiley Encyclopaedia of Eighteenth-Century Literature and his most recent book is *Literary Criticism: A New History* (2008). He is at present working on a study of Modernism.

Amber Haschenburger studied Art and History at Hastings College before obtaining her Bachelors degree in English Literature. She then received a Masters Degree in the same field from Creighton University. Now she works at a library and is actively compiling a literary canon of her own devising.

Bridget Keegan is Professor of English at Creighton University. She is the author of *British Labouring-Class Nature Poetry: 1730–1837* (2008) and is the editor of *Eighteenth Century Labouring-Class Poets*, Volume 2 (2003). She has published extensively on John Clare, labouring-class, writing and environmental literary criticism. She is currently collaborating on a bibliographical project devoted to non-canonical eighteenth century poetry and is beginning work on a new monograph on eighteenth-century British Catholic Culture.

Kelly Kramer completed her PhD at the University of Leeds. She is currently teaching at the University of Leeds and Leeds Metropolitan University. Her research focuses on questions of the law and property and the effects of these on representations of community and notions of belonging in eighteenth-century literature and culture.

Donna Landry is a Professor of English and Director of the Centre for Studies in the Long Eighteenth Century at the University of Kent. Her many publications include *The Muses of Resistance* (1990), *The Invention of the Countryside* (2001) and *Noble Brutes: How Eastern Horses Transformed English Culture* (2008). Her current project is *The Evliya Çelebi Way* http://www.kent.ac.uk/english/evliya/index.html.

Ruth M. Larsen is a lecturer in History at the University of Derby. Her primary areas of research are the domestic and social roles of aristocratic women in the long eighteenth century, and she has published various articles on these topics. She also edited with Edward Royle an edition of the 1865 Visitation Returns of the Archbishop of York.

Bonnie Latimer is a lecturer in Eighteenth-Century Literature at the University of Leeds. She has just completed a book on Samuel Richardson (2009), and has also published essays on Richardson, Alexander Pope, Sarah Scott and Mary Wollstonecraft. Her next project is a study of satire and alchemy in the early eighteenth century.

Ian McCormick is a Professor and member of the School of the Arts at The University of Northampton. His recent work has been in the field of deconstruction and drama, and in pedagogical aspects of eighteenth-century studies. Professor McCormick's critical editions of Robert Graves's novels *Antigua, Penny, Puce* and *They Hanged my saintly Billy* (Carcanet) were published in 2003.

Chris Mounsey is the author of *Christopher Smart: Clown of God* and editor of several collections of essays on the History of Sexuality. Chris runs the Queer People series of conferences with Caroline Gonda, and is currently researching into French erotic theatre of the eighteenth century. Chris also edits the *Journal for Eighteenth-Century Studies*.

Steve Newman is an Associate Professor of English at Temple University. His first book was *Ballad Collection, Lyric, and the Canon: The Call of the Popular from the Restoration to The New Criticism* (2007). His current project is a book about competing ideas of time and value in the humanities from the Scottish Enlightenment to the present.

Philip Smallwood is a Professor of English at Birmingham City University where he teaches the poetry and prose of Dryden, Pope and Johnson, literary thought, and the history of literary criticism. He is the co-editor of *Johnson after 300 Years* (2009) and is finishing a book on eighteenth-century criticism.

Richard Terry is currently Professor of Eighteenth-Century English Literature at Northumbria University, having worked for many years at the University of Sunderland. He has published extensively on literary historiography and on eighteenth-century mock-heroic. He has recently completed a study of the plagiarism allegation in English literature between Dryden and Sterne.

Bibliography

General Reference

There are some helpful volumes in the *Cambridge Companion* series, especially the following:

Richetti, J. (ed.) (1996), *The Cambridge Companion to the Eighteenth-Century Novel*. Cambridge: Cambridge University Press.

Sitter, J. (ed.) (2001), *The Cambridge Companion to Eighteenth-Century Poetry*. Cambridge: Cambridge University Press.

Zwicker, S. N. (ed.) (1998), *The Cambridge Companion to English Literature, 1650–1740*. Cambridge: Cambridge University Press.

Biographies, Autobiographies and Life Writing

Harding's chapter on biography and autobiography gives an overview of mid- to late-eighteenth-century life writing culture with a focus on Johnson and Wollstonecraft together with a relevant bibliography. Birkbeck Hill's edition of Boswell's *Life* is the leading version, with DeMaria Jr., Johnston and Wain providing contemporary accounts of Johnson and his circle. Montagu and Williams express themselves through epistolary autobiography and Rousseau also explores his social identities through his autobiographical writing. A good resource for biographies is the *Oxford Dictionary of National Biography*, which can be accessed online through your university website subscription or in hard copy at a larger library.

Bate, W. J. (1977), *Samuel Johnson*. New York and London: Harcourt Brace.

Boswell, J. (1934–65), *The Life of Samuel Johnson*, 6 vols. G. Birkbeck Hill (ed.). Oxford: Clarendon.

DeMaria Jr., R. (1993), *The Life of Samuel Johnson: A Critical Biography*. Oxford: Blackwell.

Doody, M. A. (1988), *Frances Burney: The Life in the Works*. New Brunswick, NJ: Rutgers University Press.

Harding, H. (2005), 'Biography and Autobiography'. *Romanticism: An Oxford Guide*. N. Roe (ed.). Oxford: Oxford University Press, 445–62.

Johnson, S. (1905), *The Lives of the Poets (1779–81)*, 3 vols. G. Birkbeck Hill (ed.). Oxford: Clarendon.

—— (2006), *The Lives of the Most Eminent English Poets*, 4 vols. R. Lonsdale (ed.). Oxford: Clarendon.

Johnston, F. (2005), *Samuel Johnson and the Art of Sinking, 1709–1791*. Oxford: Oxford University Press.

McConnell, A. (2004), 'Beckford, William Thomas (1760–1844)', *Oxford Dictionary of National Biography*. Oxford: Oxford University Press, online edition: http://www.oxforddnb.com/view/article/1905.

Mack, M. (1985), *Alexander Pope: A Life*. New Haven, CT and London: Yale University Press.

Martin, P. (1999), *A Life of James Boswell*. London: Weidenfeld & Nicolson.

Montagu, Lady M. W. (1994), *The Turkish Embassy Letters*. London: Virago Press.

Rousseau, J.-J. (1996), *Confessions*. (First published in 1781.) London: Wordsworth Editions.

Todd, J. (2000), *Mary Wollstonecraft: a Revolutionary Life*. London: Weidenfeld & Nicolson.

Wain, J. (1974), *Samuel Johnson*. London: Macmillan.

Williams, H. M. (2002), *Letters Written in France in the Summer of 1790 to a Friend in England; containing various anecdotes relative to the French Revolution*. N. Fraistat and S. S. Lanser (eds). Peterborough, ON: Broadview.

Childhood

O'Malley looks at pedagogical reform, class and children's literature and Müller's collection of essays takes a comparative and broad interdisciplinary approach to the representation of childhood.

Müller, A. (ed.) (2006), *Fashioning Childhood in the Eighteenth Century: Age and Identity*. London: Ashgate.

O'Malley, A. (2003), *The Making of the Modern Child: Children's Literature in the Late Eighteenth Century*. New York and London: Routledge.

Contemporary Writing

The following selection of influential contemporary writing includes the subjects of philosophy (Burke, Hume), feminism (Astell, Wollstonecraft), politics (Defoe, Smith), together with several essays on culture, all of which informed and shaped eighteenth-century literature.

Astell, M. (1694), *A Serious Proposal to the Ladies*. London: R. Wilkes.

Brown, J. (1757), *An Estimate of the Manners and Principles of the Times*. Dublin: Exshaw.

Burke, E. (1998), *A Philosophical Enquiry into the Origin of Our Ideas on the Sublime and the Beautiful*. A. Phillips (ed.). (First Published in 1757.) Oxford: Oxford University Press.

Cowley, A. (1989 and 1992), *The Collected Works of Abraham Cowley*, 2 vols. to date. T. O. Calhoun, L. Hayworth, and A. Pritchard (eds). Newark: University of Delaware Press.

Defoe, D. (1709), *A Review of the State of the British Nation*, in W. A. Speck (1977), *Stability and Strife: England 1714–1760*. London: Edward Arnold.

Dryden, J. (2000), *Preface to Fables Ancient and Modern*, in *The Works of John Dryden*, vol. 7. V. A. Dearing (ed.). (First published in 1700.) Berkeley, CA: University of California Press.

—— (1958), *The Poems and Fables of John Dryden*. J. Kinsley (ed.). London: Oxford University Press.

Fielding, H. (1751), *An enquiry into the causes of the late increase of robbers, &c. with some proposals for remedying this growing evil*. Dublin: printed for G. Faulkner, P. Wilson, R. James, and M. Williamson.

Hume, D. (1985), *A Treatise on Human Nature: Being an Attempt to Introduce the Experimental Method of Reasoning into Moral Subjects*. E. C. Mossner (ed.). (First published in 1739–40.) London: Penguin Books.

Johnson, S. (1958–), *The Yale Edition of the Works of Samuel Johnson*. J. Middendorf (gen. ed.). New Haven, CT and London: Yale University Press.

Richardson, J. (1719), *Two Discourses. I. An essay on the whole art of criticism as it relates to painting; II. An argument in behalf of the science of a connoisseur*. London: printed for W. Churchill.

Smith, A. (1976), *An Inquiry into the Nature and Causes of the Wealth of Nations*. R. H. Campbell and A. S. Skinner (gen. eds), W. B. Todd (textual ed.) 2 vols. (First published in 1776.) Oxford: Clarendon.

—— (1976), *The Theory of Moral Sentiments*. D. D. Raphael and A. L. Macfie (eds). (First published in 1759.) Oxford: Clarendon.

Trenchard, J. and Gordon, T. (1995), *Cato's Letters: Essays on Liberty, Civil and Religious and Other Important Subjects*. R. Hamowy (ed.). (First published in 1720–23.) Indianapolis, IN: Liberty Fund Inc.

Warton, Joseph (1756), *An Essay on the Genius and Writings of Pope*. London: M. Cooper.

Wollstonecraft, M. (2004), *A Vindication of the Rights of Woman*. M. Brody (ed.). (First published in 1792.) London: Penguin Books.

Young, E. (1978), *'Conjectures on Original Composition' in England and Germany*. (First published in 1759.) Norwood, PA: Norwood Editions.

Culture

Brewer's readable work and Sambrook's comprehensive study cover the general aspects of culture. More specific books include Ellis's history of coffee houses, which refers to the advent of eighteenth-century debating coteries, and Vickery's meticulous examination of women's letters, diaries and account books which produces a definitive work on how genteel society lived. Klein, Sekora, Berg and Eger look at luxury and the emerging consumer society.

Andrew, D. T. (1996), 'Popular culture and public debate: London 1780'. *Historical Journal*, 39, 405–23.

Berg, M. (2005), *Luxury and Pleasure in Eighteenth-Century Britain*. Oxford: Oxford University Press.

Berg, M. and Eger, E. (eds). (2007), *Luxury in the Eighteenth Century: Debates, Desires and Delectable Goods*. Basingstoke: Palgrave Macmillan.

Brewer, J. (1997), *The Pleasures of the Imagination: English Culture in the Eighteenth Century*. Chicago, IL: University of Chicago Press.

—— (1995), '"The most polite age and the most vicious": attitudes towards culture as a commodity, 1660–1800', A. Bermingham and J. Brewer (eds). *The Consumption of Culture 1600–1800: Image, Object, Text*. London: Routledge, 341–61.

Carter, P. (1997), 'Men about town: representations of foppery and masculinity in early eighteenth-century urban society', in H. Barker and E. Chalus (eds). *Gender in Eighteenth-Century England: Roles, Representations and Responsibilities*. London: Longman, 31–57.

Collini, S. (1999), *English Pasts: Essays in History and Culture*. Oxford: Oxford University Press.

Earle, P. (1994), 'The middling sort in London', in J. Barry and C. W. Brooks (eds). *The Middling Sort of People: Culture, Society and Politics in England, 1550–1800*. Basingstoke: Macmillan, 145–58.

Ellis, M. (2004), *The Coffee-House: A Cultural History*. London: Weidenfeld & Nicolson.

Ellis, M. (2001), 'The coffee-women, *The Spectator* and the public sphere in the early eighteenth century', in E. Eger, C. Grant, C. Ó Gallchóir, and P. Warburton (eds). *Women, Writing and the Public Sphere, 1700–1830*. Cambridge: Cambridge University Press, 27–52.

Klein, L. E. (1995), 'Politeness for plebes: consumption and social identity in early eighteenth-century England', in A. Bermingham and J. Brewer (eds). *The Consumption of Culture 1600–1800: Image, Object, Text*. London: Routledge, 362–82.

Langford, P. (1989), *A Polite and Commercial People: England 1727–1783*. Oxford: Oxford University Press.

Manning, S. (2001), 'Whatever Happened to Pleasure', *The Cambridge Quarterly*, 30, 3, 215–32.

McKeon, M. (2005), *The Secret History of Domesticity: Public, Private, and the Division of Knowledge*. Baltimore, MD: Johns Hopkins University Press.

Perry, R. (2004), *Novel Relations: The Transformation of Kinship in English Literature and Culture, 1748–1818*. Cambridge and New York: Cambridge University Press.

Sambrook, J. (1993), *The Eighteenth Century: The Intellectual and Cultural Context of English Literature 1700–1789* (Second edition). London: Longman.

Sekora, J. (1997), *Luxury: The Concept in Western Thought from Eden to Smollett*. Baltimore, MD: Johns Hopkins University Press.

Vickery, A. (1998), *The Gentleman's Daughter. Women's Lives in Georgian England*. New Haven, CT: Yale University Press.

Wroth, W. (1979), *The London Pleasure Gardens of the Eighteenth Century*. Assisted by Arthur Edgar Wroth. (First published in 1896.) London: Macmillan.

Drama and the Theatre

The major transformations in English theatre from the Restoration to the eighteenth century are described by both Bevis and Webster. Hughes's six volume anthology is an excellent resource for the work of post-Aphra Behn women dramatists and Webster's book offers an historical background to the plays of this era. The idea of ethnicity in drama is explored effectively by Worrall.

Bevis, R. W. (1988), *English Drama: Restoration and Eighteenth-Century, 1660–1789*. London: Longman.

Congreve, W. (2006), *The Way of the World and Other Plays*. E. Rump (ed.). (First published in 1700.) London: Penguin Books.
Hughes, D. (gen. ed.) (2001), *Eighteenth-Century Women Playwrights*, 6 vols. London: Pickering and Chatto.
Webster, J. W. (2005), *Performing Libertinism in Charles II's Court: Politics, Drama, Sexuality*. Basingstoke: Palgrave Macmillan.
Worrall, D. (2007), *Harlequin Empire: Race, Ethnicity, and the Drama of the Popular Enlightenment*. London: Pickering & Chatto.

French Revolution

The main British observers of the impact of the French Revolution are considered by Butler and Hodson. Jones gives an historical overview of the setting, the war and the consequent search for stability.

Butler, M. (1984), *Burke, Paine, Godwin, and the Revolution Controversy*. Cambridge: Cambridge University Press.
Hodson, J. (2007), *Language and Revolution in Burke, Wollstonecraft, Paine, and Godwin*. London: Ashgate.
Jones, P. M. (2003), *The French Revolution 1787–1804*. Harlow and London: Pearson Education.

Gender and Sexuality

The general idea of separate (public and private) spheres is examined in Kerber, Rendall and Vickery, while Clery looks specifically at women and the leisure culture within the same context. Women's identity and societal roles are discussed in Barker and Chalus, Fletcher and also in Nussbaum, with Cook focusing on self-expression through women's writings. Clark and Rumbold are concerned with representations of women's personal relationships with male writers.

Barker, H. and Chalus, E. (1997), 'Introduction'. H. Barker and E. Chalus (eds). *Gender in Eighteenth-Century England: Roles, Representations and Responsibilities*. London: Longman, 1–28.
Bohstedt, J. (1988), 'Gender, household and community politics: women in English riots, 1790–1810'. *Past & Present*, 120, 88–122.
Clarke, N. (2000), *Dr Johnson's Women*. London: London and Hambleton.
Clery, E. (2004), *The Feminization Debate in Eighteenth-Century England: Literature, Commerce and Luxury*. Basingstoke and New York: Palgrave Macmillan.
Collier, J. (1994), *An Essay on the Art of Ingeniously Tormenting: With Proper Rules for the Exercise of that Pleasant Art*. (Facsimile of 1753 edition.) M. M. Roberts (ed.). Bristol: Routledge Thoemmes Press.
Cook, E. H. (1996), *Epistolary Bodies: Gender and Genre in the Eighteenth-Century Republic of Letters*. Palo Alto, CA: Stanford University Press.
Dunton, J. (1703), *The Shortest-way with Whores and Rogues, Or, A New Project for Reformation*. London: unknown publisher.
Fletcher, A. J. (1995), *Gender, Sex and Subordination in England 1500–1800*. New Haven, CT.: Yale University Press, 222–46; 376–400.

Goldsmith, N. M. (1998), *The Worst of Crimes: Homosexuality and the Law in Eighteenth-Century London*. Aldershot: Ashgate.

Jones, V. (ed.) (1990), *Women in the Eighteenth Century: Constructions of Femininity*. London: Routledge.

Kerber, L. (1988), 'Separate spheres, female worlds, woman's place: the rhetoric of women's history'. *Journal of American History*, 75, 9–39.

Nussbaum, F. A. (2003), *The Limits of the Human: Fictions of Anomaly, Race and Gender in the Long Eighteenth Century*. Cambridge and New York: Cambridge University Press.

Pettit, A. and Spedding, P. (eds) (2002), *Eighteenth-Century British Erotica*. London: Pickering and Chatto.

Rendall, J. (1999), 'Women and the public sphere'. *Gender and History*, 11, 475–488.

—— (1990), *Women in an Industrializing Society: England 1750–1850*. Oxford: Blackwell.

—— (1985), *The Origins of Modern Feminism: Women in Britain, France and the United States, 1780–1860*. Basingstoke: Macmillan.

Rumbold, V. (1989), *Women's Place in Pope's World*. Cambridge: Cambridge University Press.

Tague, I. H. (2002), *Women of Quality: Accepting and Contesting Ideals of Femininity in England, 1690–1760*. Woodbridge: Boydell.

Vickery, A. (1993), 'The Golden Age to separate spheres? A review of the categories and chronology of English women's history'. *The Historical Journal*, 36, 383–404.

Gothic

Botting traces the cultural significance of gothic literature with an emphasis on origins and forms. Castle's main focus is on the celebration and transgression of the carnivalesque. Some of the contemporary influential gothic genre writers are included here: Beckford, Radcliffe, Walpole and 'Monk' Lewis.

Beckford, W. (1998), *Vathek*. R. Lonsdale (ed.). (First published in 1786.) Oxford: Oxford University Press.

Botting, F. (1996), *Gothic*. Oxford and New York: Routledge.

Castle, T. (1986), *Masquerade and Civilisation: Carnivalesque in Eighteenth-Century Culture and Fiction*. Palo Alto, CA: Stanford University Press.

Lewis, M. (2008), *The Monk*. E. McEvoy (ed.). (First published in 1796.) Oxford: Oxford University Press.

Radcliffe, A. (1998), *The Mysteries of Udolpho*, B. Dobree (ed.). (First published in 1794.) Oxford: Oxford University Press.

Walpole, H. (1998), *The Castle of Otranto*. W. S. Lewis (ed.). (First published in 1765.) Oxford: Oxford University Press.

Heritage and Landscape: Urban and Rural

For visual representations of the rural landscape, Barrell's work takes a fresh look at the paintings of Constable, Gainsborough and Morland. Allen considers the effects of economic development and the enclosure laws while Andrews and

Copley and Garside are concerned with aesthetics. Christie, Duckworth, Kennedy and Saumarez Smith provide overviews of the historic and literary advance of the country house. Williams takes a theoretical approach to the perceived boundaries between the urban and the rural.

Allen, R.C. (1992), *Enclosure and the Yeoman: Agricultural development of the South Midlands, 1450–1850*. Oxford: Clarendon.

Andrews, M. (1989), *The Search for the Picturesque: Landscape Aesthetics and Tourism in Britain, 1760–1800*. Aldershot: Scolar Press.

Barrell, J. (1980), *The Dark Side of the Landscape: The Representation of the Rural Poor in English Painting*. Cambridge: Cambridge University Press.

Borsay, P. (1990), 'Introduction'. *The Eighteenth-Century Town: A Reader in English Urban History 1688–1820*. P. Borsay (ed.). London: Longman, 1–38.

Christie, C. (2000), *The British Country House in the Eighteenth Century*. Manchester: Manchester University Press.

Copley. S. and Garside, P. (eds) (1994), *The Politics of the Picturesque: Literature, Landscape, and Aesthetics since 1770*. Cambridge: Cambridge University Press.

Duckworth, A.M. (1994), *The Improvement of the Estate: A Study of Jane Austen's Novels*. Baltimore, MD and London: Johns Hopkins University Press.

Kennedy, C. (1982), *Harewood: The Life and Times of an English Country House*. London: Hutchinson.

Landry, D. (2008), *Noble Brutes: How Eastern Horses Transformed English Culture*. Baltimore, MD and London: Johns Hopkins University Press.

—— (2001), *The Invention of the Countryside: Hunting, Walking, and Ecology in English Literature, 1671–1831*. Basingstoke and New York: Palgrave.

Saumarez Smith, C. (1990), *The Building of Castle Howard*. London: Pimlico.

Williams, R. (1973), *The Country and the City*. New York: Oxford University Press.

History

Speck gives a sound outline of eighteenth-century history in his first chapter while Sharpe's book centres on cultural and spiritual aspects. Nussbaum's collection of essays presents clear accounts of the complex issues related to social histories of race and ethnicity.

Borsay, P. (1977), *Stability and Strife: England 1714–1760*. London: Edward Arnold.

Kenyon, J. P. (1989), 'Introduction', *By Force or by Default? The Revolution of 1688–1689*, E. Cruickshanks (ed.). Edinburgh: John Donald, 1989, 1–7.

Langford, P. (2002), 'Introduction: time and space'. *The Eighteenth Century, 1688–1815*. P. Langford (ed.). Oxford: Oxford University Press, 1–34.

Nussbaum, F. A. (ed.) (2003), *The Global Eighteenth Century*. Baltimore, MD and London: Johns Hopkins University Press.

Sharpe, J. A. (1997), *Early Modern England: A Social History, 1550–1760* (Second edition). London: Edward Arnold.

Speck, W. A. (1993), *A Concise History of Britain 1707–1975*. Cambridge: Cambridge University Press.

Literature and Literary Theory

The history of the literature of this period is examined in detail by Barrell, Brown, DeMaria, Gross, Perry and Rogers. Attridge considers the relation of literature to ethics and Moi takes a feminist approach to theoretical concepts of women's writing. Both Hagstrum and Deutsch write of the Age of Johnson and Womersley's anthology covers the poetry of Dryden and Pope, as well as Johnson's.

Attridge, D. (2004), *The Singularity of Literature*. London: Routledge.
Barrell, J. (1983), *English Literature in History, 1730–1780: An Equal Wide Survey.* London: Hutchinson.
Bennington, G. (2007), 'Derrida's "Eighteenth Century"'. *Eighteenth-Century Studies*, 40, 3, 381–93.
Brown, L. (2001), *Fables of Modernity: Literature and Culture in the English Eighteenth Century.* Ithaca, NY and London: Cornell University Press.
Clingham, G. (ed.) (1997), *The Cambridge Companion to Samuel Johnson*. Cambridge: Cambridge University Press.
Crane, R.S. (1968), *The Idea of the Humanities*, 2 vols. Chicago, IL: University of Chicago Press.
DeMaria Jr., R. (2001), *British Literature 1640–1789* (Second edition). Oxford: Blackwell.
Deutsch, H. (2005), *Loving Dr Johnson*. Chicago: Chicago University Press.
Eagleton, T. (2003), *After Theory*. New York: Basic Books.
Ellis, F. H. (1951), 'Gray's *Elegy*: The Biographical Problem in Literary Criticism'. *PMLA*. 66, 971–1008.
Ellis, J. M. (1997), *Literature Lost: Social Agendas and the Corruption of the Humanities.* New Haven, CT: Yale University Press.
Greene, J. (2007), 'Hors d'Oeuvre'. *Eighteenth-Century Studies*, 40, 3, 367–79.
Gross, J. J. (1969), *The Rise and Fall of the Man of Letters: Aspects of English Literary Life since 1800.* London: Weidenfeld & Nicolson.
Hagstrum, J. (1967), *Samuel Johnson's Literary Criticism* (Second edition). Chicago, IL: University of Chicago Press.
Hammond, B. (1997), *Professional Imaginative Writing in England, 1670–1740: Hackney for Bread.* Oxford: Clarendon.
Hawes, C. (2005), *The British Eighteenth Century and Global Critique*. New York and Basingstoke: Palgrave Macmillan.
Hopkins, D. and Gillespie, S. (eds) (2005), *Oxford History of Literary Translation in English (1660–1790).* Oxford: Oxford University Press.
Leavis, F.R. (1952), *The Common Pursuit.* London: Chatto and Windus.
—— (1995), 'Historicizing Patriarchy: The Emergence of Gender Difference in England, 1660–1760'. *Eighteenth-Century Studies*, 28, 3, 295–322.
—— (1989), 'A Defense of Dialectical Method in Literary History'. *Diacritics*, 19, 1, 82–96.
Moi, T. (1985), *Sexual/Textual Politics: Feminist Literary Theory (New Accents).* London: Methuen.
Nussbaum, F. A. (2003), *The Limits of the Human.* Cambridge: Cambridge University Press.

Nussbaum, F. A. and Brown, L. (1988), *New Eighteenth Century: Theory, Politics, English Literature*. New York and London: Routledge.

Perry, R. (1999), 'De-familiarizing the Family; or, Writing Family History from Literary Sources', in M. Brown (ed.). *Eighteenth-Century Literary History: An MLQ Reader*. Durham, NC: Duke University Press, 159–71.

Rogers P., (ed.) (1978), *The Eighteenth Century (Context of English Literature)*. London: Methuen.

Sitter, J. (1982), *Literary Loneliness in Mid-Eighteenth-Century England*. Ithaca, NY and London: Cornell University Press.

Southam, B. (1995), 'The Silence of the Bertrams', *Times Literary Supplement*, 17 February, 1995.

Stallybrass, P. and White, A. (1986), *The Politics and Poetics of Transgression*. Ithaca, NY: Cornell University Press.

Warner, W.B. (1990), 'Taking Dialectic with a Grain of Salt: A Reply to McKeon'. *Diacritics*, 20, 1, 103–7.

—— (1989), 'Realist Literary History: McKeon's New Origins of the Novel'. *Diacritics* 19, 1, 62–81.

Wellek, R. (1955–92), *History of Modern Criticism: 1750–1950*, 8 vols. London: Jonathan Cape.

Womersley, D. (1997), *Augustan Critical Writing*. London: Penguin Books.

Zunshine, L. (2006), *Why We Read Fiction: Theory of Mind and the Novel*. Columbus: Ohio State University Press.

National Identity and Englishness

Ideas about the self and identity are thoroughly explored in Wahrman, Yadav and in Wilson's book which deals specifically with identity in terms of gender. Markley takes ethnicity as his starting point in his study of literature while Matar's research looks at the influence of Islam on national identity. Colley's book provides an excellent comprehensive and readable guide to identity and issues of nationality, covering Englishness, gender, war, religion and culture.

Colley, L. (2003), *Britons: Forging the Nation 1707–1837*. London: Pimlico.

Hudson, N. (2003), *Samuel Johnson and the Making of Modern England*. Cambridge: Cambridge University Press.

Markley, R. (2006), *The Far East and the English Imagination, 1600–1730*. Cambridge and New York: Cambridge University Press.

Matar, N. (1998), *Islam in Britain, 1558–1685*. Cambridge and New York: Cambridge University Press.

Wahrman, D. (2004), *The Making of the Modern Self: Identity and Culture in Eighteenth-Century England*. New Haven, CT: Yale University Press.

Wilson, K. (2003), *The Island Race: Englishness, Empire and Gender in the Eighteenth Century*. London: Routledge.

Yadav, A. (2004), *Before the Empire of English: Literature, Provinciality, and Nationalism in Eighteenth-Century Britain*. New York and Basingstoke: Palgrave Macmillan.

Novels and Novelists

As well as a selection of the most popular and significant novels from the major authors of the long eighteenth century, such as Austen, Burney, Defoe, Richardson and Swift, this section of the bibliography covers works on plot (Barney), context (Hammond and Regan) and the rise of the novel (Watt). Armstrong places novels written by women especially for women readers in terms of the development of female authority and Bender takes an interesting view on the rise of the novel in conjunction with the rise of the penitentiary.

Austen, J. (2005), *The Cambridge Edition of the Works of Jane Austen*, 3 vols. J. Todd (gen. ed.). Cambridge: Cambridge University Press.

Austen, J. (1998), *Mansfield Park*. C. Johnson (ed.). (First published in 1816.) New York: W. W. Norton.

Armstrong, N. (1989), *Desire and Domestic Fiction: A Political History of the Novel*. New York and Oxford: Oxford University Press.

Barney, R. A. (1999), *Plots of the Enlightenment: Education and the Novel in Eighteenth-Century England*. Palo Alto, CA: Stanford University Press.

Behn, A. (1997), *Oroonoko or, The Royal Slave: A True History*. J. Lipking (ed.). (First published in 1688.) New York and London: W. W. Norton.

Bender, J. (1989), *Imagining the Penitentiary: Fiction and the Architecture of the Mind in Eighteenth-Century England*. Chicago, IL: University of Chicago Press.

Bunyan, J. (2007), *The Life and Death of Mr Badman*. (First published in 1680.) London: Hesperus Press.

Burney, F. (1998), *Evelina, Or the History of a Young Lady's Entrance into the World*. S. J. Cooke (ed.). (First published in 1778.) New York: W. W. Norton.

—— (1999), *Cecilia, Or Memoirs of an Heiress*. M. A. Doody and P. Sabor (eds.). (First published in 1782.) Oxford: Oxford University Press.

Cleland, J. (c. 1760), *Fanny Hill, Memoirs of a Woman of Pleasure*. London: R. Griffiths.

Coetzee, J.M. (1986), *Foe*. London: Secker and Warburg.

Defoe, D. (2005), *The Life, Adventures and Piracies of the Famous Captain Singleton*. (First published in 1720.) Boston, MA: Adamant Media Corporation.

Fielding, S. (1998), *The Adventures of David Simple*. P. Sabor (ed.). (First published in 1744.) Lexington, KY: University Press of Kentucky.

Gay, J. (1986), *The Beggar's Opera*. B. Loughray (ed.). (First published in 1728.) London: Penguin Books.

Goethe, J. W. von (2006), *The Sorrows of Young Werther*. Trans. by M. Hulse. (First published in 1774.) London: Penguin Books.

Hammond, B. and Regan, S. (2006), *Making the Novel: Fiction and Society in Britain, 1660–1789*. Basingstoke and New York: Palgrave Macmillan.

Hays, M. (2000), *Memoirs of Emma Courtney*. E. Ty (ed.). (First published in 1796.) Oxford: Oxford University Press.

Hunter, J. P. (1992), *Before Novels: Cultural Contexts of Eighteenth-Century English Fiction*. New York: W. W. Norton.

Inchbald, E. (1988), *A Simple Story*. J. M. S. Tompkins (ed.). (First published in 1791.) Oxford: Oxford University Press.

McGirr, E. M. (2007), *Eighteenth-Century Characters: A Guide to the Literature of the Age*. Basingstoke: Palgrave Macmillan.

McKeon, M. (2002), *The Origins of the English Novel, 1600–1740*. Baltimore, MD and London: Johns Hopkins University Press.

Richardson, S. (2001), *Pamela; or, Virtue Rewarded*. T. Keymer and A. Wakely (eds). (First published in 1740.) Oxford: Oxford University Press.

Swift, J. (1999), *A Tale of a Tub and Other Works*. (First published in 1711.) Oxford: Oxford University Press.

Thompson, J. (1996), *Models of Value: Eighteenth-Century Political Economy and the Novel*. Durham, NC: Duke University Press.

—— (1998), *Between Self and World: The Novels of Jane Austen*. University Park, PA: Pennsylvania State University Press.

Warner, W. (1998), *Licensing Entertainment: The Elevation of Novel Reading in Britain, 1684–1750*. Berkeley and Los Angeles: University of California Press.

Watt, I. (2000), *The Rise of the Novel: Studies in Defoe, Richardson and Fielding*. London: Pimlico.

Philosophy

Of the philosophical works relating to the era, Potkay, Salovey and Sluyter consider emotional aspects, and Vermeule's study of writers and artists looks at moral philosophy, particularly in the works of Johnson, Hume and Pope. Israel's work of philosophy moves from the Enlightenment and the French Revolution to the making of Modernity by considering religion and morality in a European context.

Anderson, H. and Shea, J.S. (eds) (1967), *Studies in Criticism and Aesthetics, 1660–1800: Essays in Honor of Samuel Holt Monk*. Minneapolis, MN: University of Minnesota Press.

Freire, P. (2005), *Education for Critical Consciousness*. London: Continuum.

Gardner, H. (2000), *Intelligence Reframed: Multiple Intelligences for the 21st Century*. London: Basic Books.

Hamby, B.W. (2007), *The Philosophy of Anything: Critical Thinking in Context*. Dubuque, IA: Kendall Hunt Publishing Company.

Hanrahan, H. and Madsen, D.L. (eds) (2006), *Teaching, Technology, Textuality: Approaches to New Media*. Basingstoke: Palgrave Macmillan.

Hindery, R. (2001), *Indoctrination and Self-deception or Free and Critical Thought*. New York: Mellen Press.

Israel, J. I. (2006), *Enlightenment Contested: Philosophy, Modernity and the Emancipation of Man 1670–1752*. Oxford: Oxford University Press.

Potkay, A. (2007), *The Story of Joy: From the Bible to Late Romanticism*. Cambridge: Cambridge University Press.

—— (2000), *The Passion for Happiness: Samuel Johnson and David Hume*. Ithaca, NY: Cornell University Press.

Salovey, P. and Sluyter, D. (1997), *Emotional Development and Emotional Intelligence: Educational Implications*. London: Basic Books.

Schor, I. (1992), *Empowering Education: Critical Teaching for Social Change*. Chicago, IL: University of Chicago Press.

Vermeule, B. (2000), *The Party of Humanity: Writing Moral Psychology in Eighteenth-Century Britain*. Baltimore, MD: Johns Hopkins University Press.

Poetry and Poets

There are many anthologies of eighteenth-century poetry and Davison's, Fairer and Gerrard's and Kaul's are particularly useful. A focus on female poets is found in Backscheider, Lonsdale, Spacks and Wu, while Landry concentrates on the achievements of working-class women poets such as Mary Leapor and Elizabeth Hands. Fulford presents a fascinating study of the idealisation of Native Americans in Romantic poetry. A range of works from the significant poets of the period includes Chatterton, Dryden, Duck and Cowley.

Ackroyd, P. (1987), *Chatterton*. London: Hamish Hamilton.

Backscheider, P. R. (2005), *Eighteenth-Century Women Poets and their Poetry*. Baltimore, MD: Johns Hopkins University Press.

Barrell, J. (1972), *The Idea of Landscape and the Sense of Place, 1730–1840: An Approach to the Poetry of John Clare*. Cambridge: Cambridge University Press.

Bloomfield, R. (1800), *The Farmer's Boy: A Rural Poem*. London: printed for Vernor and Hood.

Chatterton, T. (1971), *The Complete Works of Thomas Chatterton: A Bicentenary Edition*. 2 vols. D. S. Taylor (ed.). Oxford: Clarendon.

Davison, D. (ed.) (1973), *The Penguin Book of Eighteenth-Century English Verse*. Harmondsworth: Penguin.

Dryden, J. (1995–2005), *The Poems of John Dryden*, 5 vols. P. Hammond and D. Hopkins (eds). Harlow: Pearson Longman.

Duck, S. (1730), *Poems on Several Subjects* (Second edition). London: printed for J. Roberts.

Egerton, S. F. (1703), *Poems on Several Occasions*. London: J. Nutt.

Eskine-Hill, H. (1996), *Poetry of Opposition and Revolution: Dryden to Wordsworth*. Oxford: Clarendon.

Fulford, T. (2006), *Romantic Indians: Native Americans, British Literature, and Transatlantic Culture 1756–1830*. Oxford: Oxford University Press.

Gerrard, C. and Fairer, D. (eds) (2004), *Eighteenth-Century Poetry: An Annotated Anthology*. Malden, MA and Oxford: Blackwell.

Gleckner, R.F. (1997), *Gray Agonistes: Thomas Gray and Masculine Friendship*. Baltimore, MD: Johns Hopkins University Press.

Hammond, P. (1999), *Dryden and the Traces of Classical Rome*. Oxford: Oxford University Press.

Kaul, S. (2000), *Poems of Nation, Anthems of Empire: English Verse in the Long Eighteenth Century*. Charlottesville: University Press of Virginia.

Landry, D. (1990), *The Muses of Resistance: Laboring Class Women's Poetry in Britain, 1739–1796*. Cambridge: Cambridge University Press.

Leapor, M. (1751), *Poems on Several Occasions*. London: J. Roberts.

Lonsdale, R. (ed.) (1990), *Eighteenth-Century Women Poets*. Oxford: Oxford University Press.

Lord, G. de F. (gen. ed.) (1963–75), *Poems on Affairs of State: Augustan Satirical Verse, 1660–1714*, 7 vols. New Haven, CT and London: Yale University Press.

Mason, H.A. (1972), *To Homer through Pope: An Introduction to Homer's 'Iliad' and Pope's Translation*. London: Chatto and Windus.

Mason, T. and Hopkins, D. (eds) (1994), *Selected Poems of Abraham Cowley*. Manchester: Fyfield.

McLaverty, J. (2001), *Pope, Print and Meaning*. Oxford: Clarendon.
Percy, T. (1767), *Reliques of Ancient English Poetry* (Second edition). London: J. Dodsley.
Pope, A. (1963), *The Poems of Alexander Pope*. J. Butt (ed.). London: Methuen.
—— (1950–1969), 'Epistle to Burlington', in F. W. Bateson (ed.), *Epistles to Several Persons (Moral Essays)* in *The Twickenham Edition of the Poems of Alexander Pope*, 11 vols. J. Butt (gen. ed.). London: Methuen.
Spacks, P. M. (1967), *The Poetry of Vision: Five Eighteenth-Century Poets*. Cambridge, MA: Harvard University Press.
Starr, H.W. (ed.) (1968), *Twentieth Century Interpretations of Gray's Elegy: A Collection of Critical Essays*. Englewood Cliffs, NJ: Prentice-Hall.
Turner, J.G. (1978), *The Politics of Landscape: Rural Scenery and Society in English Poetry, 1630–1660*. Oxford: Blackwell.
Williams, A. (2005), *Poetry and the Creation of a Whig Literary Culture 1681–1714*. Oxford: Oxford University Press.
Winn, J. A. (1987), *John Dryden and his World*. New Haven, CT and London: Yale University Press.
Wu, D. (ed.) (1998), *Romantic Women Poets: An Anthology*. Oxford and Malden, MA: Blackwell.
Yearsley, A. (1785), *Poems, on Several Occasions*. London: printed for T. Cadell.

Pornography

For a wide-ranging survey of erotic literature and pornography, particularly in relation to sexual stereotypes, the books of Peakman and McCormick are invaluable. Mowry provides an interesting backdrop to historical cultural constructions of sexuality.

McCormick, I. (1997), *Secret Sexualities: A Sourcebook of 17th and 18th Century Writing*. London and New York: Routledge.
Mowry, M. M. (2004), *The Bawdy Politic in Stuart England, 1660–1714: Political Pornography and Prostitution*. Burlington, VT and Aldershot: Ashgate.
Peakman, J. (2003), *Mighty Lewd Books: The Development of Pornography in Eighteenth-Century England*. Basingstoke: Palgrave Macmillan.

Publishing and Print Culture

For practical information on eighteenth-century print culture, Green's book is useful in its survey of intellectual property rights and Rivers' collection of essays covers various aspects of readership, including biographies, journals and theological books.

Greene, J. (2005), *The Trouble with Ownership: Literary Property and Authorial Liability in England 1660–1730*. Philadelphia: University of Pennsylvania Press.
Rivers, I. (ed.) (2003), *Books and their Readers in the Eighteenth Century: New Essays*. London: Continuum.

Romanticism

The *Oxford Guide* presents a comprehensive dictionary and series of essays covering the literary history, culture and society during the Romantic period, together with a wide-ranging bibliography. Butler's specific focal point is the literature and individuality of a group of writers including Shelley, Scott and Coleridge.

Butler, M. (1981), *Romantics, Rebels, and Reactionaries: English Literature and its Background 1760–1830*. Oxford: Oxford University Press.

Roe, N. (ed.) (2005), *Romanticism: An Oxford Guide*. Oxford: Oxford University Press.

Science

Fara's book explains concisely the work of women who participated in scientific experiments, mostly in their own homes. Golinski also looks at the social setting of chemistry in his historical study. Uglow's work on the Birmingham Lunar Group friends who drove the Industrial Revolution forward is informative and exceptionally detailed. Contemporary works include Cheyne's fascinating thoughts on diet and Linnaeus' definitive botanic taxonomy.

Cheyne, G. (1733), *English Malady, or A Treatise of Nervous Diseases of all Kinds*. London: George Strahan.

Fara, P. (2005), *Pandora's Breeches: Women, Science and Power in the Enlightenment*. London: Pimlico.

Golinski, J. (1999), *Science as Public Culture: Chemistry and Enlightenment in Britain, 1760–1820*. Cambridge: Cambridge University Press.

Henrey, B. (1975), *British Botanical and Horticultural Literature before 1800*. Oxford: Clarendon.

Linnaeus, C. (1802), *Systema Naturae*. Translated by William Turton. (Originally published in 1735.) London: Lackington, Allen and Co.

Newton, I. (1726), *The Mathematical Principles of Natural Philosophy*. Translated by Andrew Motte. London: Benjamin Motte.

Uglow, J. (2002), *The Lunar Men: The Friends who made the Future, 1730–1810*. London: Faber and Faber.

Sensibility and Sentiment

Todd's book is a basic but very concise guide to the complexities of sensibility, as is McGann's, which focuses on the poetry of the era. For general information on sensibility and sentiment, Barker-Benfield, Mullan, Pinch and Rawson provide a range of study materials. Ellison's book looks at the trans-Atlantic status of emotional expression and Phillips' book is particularly relevant for the study of historiography, biography and the history of lives and manners.

Barker-Benfield, J. G. (1992), *The Culture of Sensibility: Sex and Society in Eighteenth-Century Britain*. Chicago, IL: University of Chicago Press.

Ellis, M. (1996), *The Politics of Sensibility: Race, Gender and Commerce in the Sentimental Novel*. Cambridge and New York: Cambridge University Press.

Ellison, J. K. (1999), *Cato's Tears and the Making of Anglo-American Emotion*. Chicago, IL: University of Chicago Press.
Harkin, M. (1994) 'Mackenzie's *Man of Feeling*: Embalming Sensibility'. *English Literary History*, 61, 2, 317–40.
Marshall, D. (1985), *The Surprising Effects of Sympathy: Marivaux, Diderot, Rousseau, and Mary Shelley*. Chicago, IL: University of Chicago Press.
McGann, J. J. (1996), *The Poetics of Sensibility: A Revolution in Literary Style*. Oxford: Clarendon.
Mullan, J. (1988), *Sentiment and Sociability: The Language of Feeling in the Eighteenth Century*. Oxford: Clarendon.
Phillips, M. S. (2000), *Society and Sentiment: Genres of Historical Writing in Britain, 1740–1820*. Princeton, NJ: Princeton University Press.
Pinch, A. (1996), *Strange Fits of Passion: Epistemologies of Emotion from Hume to Austen*. Palo Alto, CA: Stanford University Press.
Rawson, C. (2000), *Satire and Sentiment 1660–1830. Stress Points in the English Augustan Tradition*. New Haven, CT and London: Yale University Press.
Sterne, L. (2003), *A Sentimental Journey and Other Writings*, I. Jack and T. Parnell (eds). (First published in 1793.) Oxford and New York: Oxford University Press.
Todd, J. (1986), *Sensibility: An Introduction*. London: Methuen.

Slavery, Abolitionism and Empire

Said and Fanon provide accessible theoretical frameworks for the subject and make an excellent starting point to the study of abolitionist literature. Ferguson, Fraiman, Park and Rajan examine the works of Austen in terms of colonialism and Joseph, Brown and Ferguson consider the representation of women in literature with themes of slavery. Ballaster looks at the narrative and form of Oriental tales while Carey's book studies the sentimental rhetoric attached to eighteenth-century fiction and non-fiction writing. Maclean and Pratt explore travel writing and Walvin looks closely at the consequences of Britain's part in the international slave trade.

Andrade, S. Z. (1994), 'White Skin, Black Masks: Colonialism and the Sexual Politics of *Oroonoko*'. *Cultural Critique*, 27, 189–214.
Aravamudan, S. (1999), *Tropicopolitans: Colonialism and Agency, 1688–1804*. Durham, NC: Duke University Press.
Ballaster, R. (2005), *Fabulous Orients: Fictions of the East in England, 1662–1785*. Oxford and New York: Oxford University Press.
Brown, L. (1993), *Ends of Empire: Women and Ideology in Early Eighteenth-Century Literature*. Ithaca, NY: Cornell University Press.
Carey, B. (2005), *British Abolitionism and the Rhetoric of Sensibility: Writing, Sentiment, and Slavery, 1760–1807*. Basingstoke and New York: Palgrave Macmillan.
Carretta, V. (ed.) (1995), *Olaudah Equiano: The Interesting Narrative and Other Writings*. London and New York: Penguin Books.
—— (2005), *Equiano the African: Biography of a Self-made Man*. Athens, GA: University of Georgia Press.
Coleman, D. (2005), *Romantic Colonization and British Anti-Slavery*. Cambridge: Cambridge University Press.

Edwards, P. and Walvin, J. (1983), *Black Personalities in the Era of the Slave Trade.* Basingstoke: Macmillan.

Fanon, F. (2008), *Black Skin, White Masks.* K. W. Appiah (ed.). (First published in 1952.) New York: Grove Press.

Ferguson, M. (1993), *Colonialism and Gender Relations from Mary Wollstonecraft to Jamaica Kincaid: East Caribbean Connections.* New York: Columbia University Press.

—— (1992), *Subject to Others: British Women Writers and Colonial Slavery, 1670–1834.* New York and London: Routledge.

—— (1991), '*Mansfield Park*: Slavery, colonialism, and gender', *Oxford Literary Review,* 13, 118–39.

Fraiman, S, (1995), 'Jane Austen and Edward Said: Gender, Culture, and Imperialism'. *Critical Inquiry,* 21, 4, 805–21.

Gilroy, P. (1993), *The Black Atlantic: Modernity and Double Consciousness.* Cambridge, MA.: Harvard University Press.

Grossberg, L., Nelson, C. and Treichler, P. A. (eds) (1992), *Cultural Studies.* New York and London: Routledge.

Joseph, B. (2004), *Reading the East India Company, 1720–1840: Colonial Currencies of Gender.* Chicago, IL and London: University of Chicago Press.

MacLean, G. (2004), *The Rise of Oriental Travel: English Visitors to the Ottoman Empire, 1580–1720.* Basingstoke and New York: Palgrave Macmillan.

—— (2007), *Looking East: English Writing and the Ottoman Empire before 1800.* Basingstoke and New York: Palgrave Macmillan.

Park, Y. and Rajan, R. S. (eds) (2000), *The Postcolonial Jane Austen.* London and New York: Routledge.

Pratt, M. L. (2007), *Imperial Eyes: Travel Writing and Transculturation.* London: Routledge.

Richardson, A. and Lee, D. (eds) (2004), *Early Black British Writing: Olaudah Equiano, Mary Prince, and Others.* Boston and New York: Houghton Mifflin.

Said, E.W. (1995), *Orientalism: Western Conceptions of the Orient.* London: Penguin.

—— (1993), *Culture and Imperialism.* New York: Alfred A. Knopf.

Schama, S. (2005), *Rough Crossings. Britain, the Slaves, and the American Revolution.* London: BBC Books.

Sussman, C. (2000), *Consuming Anxieties: Consumer Protest, Gender, and British Slavery, 1713–1833.* Palo Alto, CA: Stanford University Press.

Walvin, J. (2000), *Britain's Slave Empire.* Stroud: Tempus.

—— (1986), *England, Slaves and Freedom: 1776–1838.* Basingstoke: Macmillan.

Wood, M. (2002), *Slavery, Empathy, and Pornography.* Oxford and New York: Oxford University Press.

—— (2000), *Blind Memory: Visual Representations of Slavery in England and America, 1780–1865.* Manchester: Manchester University Press.

Society, Politics and Class

For an overview of eighteenth-century society, O'Gorman, Davidoff and Hall provide insightful accounts and Porter's books are packed with relevant and interesting facts. Other constructive information can be found on women's roles in society (Chalus, A. Clark, Foreman, Hunt, Reynolds, Richardson), war and rebellion (J.C.D. Clark, Conway, Cookson, Cruickshank and Black, Duffy, McKeon, Miller, Stevenson, Williams), the consumer society and commerce (Hunt, Langford, McKendrick, Brewer, Plumb, Ormrod) and Hay and Rogers' study, which considers the implications of demography, labour and law on the working classes. One of the most comprehensive guides to society is found in Stone's book, which looks at the inception of the nuclear family unit and the widespread shift in the approach to religion and politics.

Appleby, J. O. (1976), 'Ideology and theory: the tension between political and economic liberalism in seventeenth-century England'. *American Historical Review*, 81, 499–515.

Baugh, D. A. (1976), 'Introduction: the social basis of stability'. D. A. Baugh (ed.). *Aristocratic Government and Society in Eighteenth-Century England: the Foundations of Stability*. New York: New Viewpoints, 1–18.

Besterman, T. (ed.) (1976), *Selected Letters of Voltaire*. London: Thomas Nelson, Ltd.

Chalus, E. (2005), *Elite Women in English Political Life c. 1754–1790*. Oxford: Clarendon.

—— (2000), 'Elite women, social politics, and the political world of late eighteenth-century England'. *Historical Journal*, 43, 3, 669–98.

Clark, A. (1995), *The Struggle for the Breeches: Gender and the Making of the British Working Class*. London: Rivers Oram Press.

Clark, J. C. D. (1986), *Revolution and Rebellion: State and Society in England in the Seventeenth and Eighteenth Centuries*. Cambridge: Cambridge University Press.

—— (1985), *English Society, 1688–1832*. Cambridge: Cambridge University Press.

Conway, S. (2006), *War, State, and Society in Mid-Eighteenth-Century Britain and Ireland*. Oxford: Oxford University Press.

Cookson, J. E. (1999), 'War'. *An Oxford Companion to the Romantic Age: British Culture, 1776–1832*. I. McCalman, J. Mee, G. Russell, and C. Tuite (eds). Oxford: Oxford University Press, 26–33.

Corfield, P.J. (2000), *Power and the Professions in Britain, 1700–1850*. London: Routledge.

Cruickshanks, E. and Black, J. (1988) (eds), 'Introduction'. *The Jacobite Challenge*. Edinburgh: John Donald, 1–6.

Davidoff, L. and Hall, C. (2002), *Family Fortunes: Men and Women of the English Middle Class 1780–1850* (Revised edition). London: Routledge.

Duffy, M. (2002), 'Contested empires 1756–1815', *The Eighteenth Century, 1688–1815*. P. Langford (ed.). Oxford: Oxford University Press, 213–44.

Foreman, A. (1997), 'A politician's politician: Georgiana, Duchess of Devonshire and the Whig party'. *Gender in Eighteenth-Century England: Roles, Representations and Responsibilities*. H. Barker and E. Chalus (eds). London: Longman, 179–204.

Habermas, J. (1989), *The Structural Transformation of the Public Sphere: An Inquiry into a Category of Bourgeois Society*. Translated by T. Burger. London: Polity Press.

Hay, D. and Rogers, N. (1997), *Eighteenth-Century English Society: Shuttles and Swords*. Oxford: Oxford University Press.

Hunt, M. R. (1996), *The Middling Sort: Commerce, Gender, and the Family in England, 1680–1780*. Berkeley, CA: University of California Press.

Jones, G. W. (1974), 'Introduction: the Office of Prime Minister'. *The Prime Ministers. Volume 1: Sir Robert Walpole to Sir Robert Peel*. H. Van Thal (ed.). London: George Allen and Unwin Ltd, 11–26.

Lamb, J. (2001), *Preserving the Self in the South Seas, 1680–1840*. Chicago, IL and London: University of Chicago Press.

Langford, P. (1989), *A Polite and Commercial People: England 1727–83*. Oxford: Oxford University Press.

McKendrick, N., Brewer, J., and Plumb, J. H. (1982), *The Birth of a Consumer Society: The Commercialization of Eighteenth-Century England*. London: Hutchinson.

McKeon, M. (1998), 'The Pastoral Revolution'. *Refiguring Revolutions: Aesthetics and Politics from the English Revolution to the Romantic Revolution*. K. Sharpe and S. N. Zwicker (eds). Berkeley, Los Angeles and London: University of California Press, 267–90.

Miller, J. (1988), 'Proto-Jacobitism? The Tories and the Revolution of 1688–9'. *The Jacobite Challenge*. E. Cruickshanks and J. Black (eds). Edinburgh: John Donald, 7–23.

O'Gorman, F. (1997), *The Long Eighteenth Century: British Political and Social History 1688–1832*. London: Edward Arnold.

—— (1989), *Voters, Patrons and Parties: The Unreformed Electoral System of Hanoverian England, 1734–1832*. Oxford: Clarendon.

Ormrod, D. (2003), *The Rise of Commercial Empires: England and the Netherlands in the Age of Mercantilism, 1650–1770*. Cambridge: Cambridge University Press.

Porter, R. (2005), *Flesh in the Age of Reason: How the Enlightenment Transformed the Way We See Our Bodies and Souls* (Second edition). London: Penguin Books.

—— (1990), *English Society in the Eighteenth Century* (Revised edition). Harmondsworth: Penguin Books.

Reynolds, K. D. (1998), *Aristocratic Women and Political Society in Victorian Britain*. Oxford: Clarendon.

Richardson, S. (1996), 'The role of women in electoral politics in Yorkshire during the eighteen-thirties'. *Northern History*, 32, 133–51.

Rogers, N. (1994), 'The middling sort in eighteenth-century politics'. *The Middling Sort of People: Culture, Society and Politics in England, 1550–1800*. J. Barry and C. W. Brooks (eds). Basingstoke: Macmillan, 159–80.

Russell, G. (2001), '"Keeping place": servants, theatre [sic] and sociability in mid-eighteenth-century Britain'. *The Eighteenth Century: Theory and Interpretation*, 42, 1, 21–42.

Stevenson, J. (1992), *Popular Disturbances in England, 1700–1832* (Second edition). London: Longman.

Stone, L. (1977), *The Family, Sex and Marriage in England 1500–1800*. New York: Harper and Row.

Stone, L. and Fawtier Stone, J. C. (1994), *An Open Elite? England 1540–1880*. Oxford: Clarendon.

Wahrman, D. (1995), *Imagining the Middle Class: The Political Representation of Class in Britain c. 1780–1840*. Cambridge: Cambridge University Press.

Williams, D. (ed.) (1999), *The Enlightenment.* Cambridge: Cambridge University Press.

Williams, R. (1961), *The Long Revolution.* New York: Columbia University Press.

Travel Writing

Bohls and Duncan provide an anthology of travel writings that were originally inspired by travel literature. Their authors include Defoe, Mary Wortley Montagu, Scott, Boswell and Wordsworth.

Bohls, E. A. and Duncan, I. (eds) (2005), *Travel Writing 1700–1830: An Anthology.* Oxford: Oxford University Press.

Women's Writing

Clark and Connolly examine epistolary writing and Turner's study is of professional authorship and the development of the woman novelist. Gallagher analyses the work of writers such as Burney and Lennox in terms of their relation to authorship and Lanser expands on this subject by looking specifically at the female narrative voice. Todd's book examines women's writing from the Restoration to the end of the eighteenth century, referring to Haywood, Lennox, Fielding and Brooke amongst other well-known writers.

Brown, M. G. (1986), 'Fanny Burney's "Feminism": Gender or Genre?'. *Fetter'd or Free? British Women Novelists, 1670–1815.* M. A. Schofield and C. Macheski (eds). Athens, OH: Ohio University Press, 29–39.

Clarke, N. (2004), *The Rise and Fall of the Woman of Letters.* London: Pimlico.

Connolly, C. (ed.) (1993), *Letters for Literary Ladies* [Maria Edgeworth (1795)]. London: Everyman.

Fraiman, S. (1993), 'Getting Waylaid in *Evelina*'. *Unbecoming Women: British Women Writers and the Novel of Development.* New York: Columbia University Press, 32–58.

Gallagher, C. (1994), *Nobody's Story: The Vanishing Acts of Women Writers in the Marketplace, 1670–1820.* Berkeley, CA: University of California Press.

Lanser, S. S. (1992), *Fictions of Authority: Women Writers and Narrative Voice.* Ithaca, NY: Cornell University Press.

Poovey, M. (1985), *The Proper Lady and the Woman Writer: Ideology as Style in the Works of Mary Wollstonecraft, Mary Shelley, and Jane Austen.* Chicago, IL: University of Chicago Press.

Rooney, E. (ed.) (2006), *The Cambridge Companion to Feminist Literary Criticism.* Cambridge: Cambridge University Press.

Spencer, J. (1986), *The Rise of the Woman Novelist from Aphra Behn to Jane Austen.* Oxford: Blackwell.

Todd, J. (1989), *The Sign of Angellica: Women, Writing and Fiction, 1660–1800.* New York: Columbia University Press.

Turner, C. (1992), *Living by the Pen: Women Writers in the Eighteenth Century.* London: Routledge.

Journals

The journals listed here are the most valuable for the study of eighteenth-century literature and theory and are available by subscription in most university libraries.

Journal for Eighteenth-Century Studies.
Cambridge Quarterly.
Eighteenth Century: Theory and Interpretation.
Eighteenth-Century Life.
English: the Journal of the English Association.
Essays in Criticism.
Review of English Studies.
Studies in Eighteenth-Century Culture.
Studies in English Literature: 1500–1900.

Internet Resources

Of the many web sites, Google Book Search and Rutgers provide a wide range of digitalised books and literary resources. The MLA International Bibliography site gives a classified listing of books and articles on literature, linguistics and folklore and Intute links to a database of Arts and Humanities resources. It is always worth checking your university's library catalogue for electronic resources in the first instance.

http://andromeda.rutgers.edu/~jlynch/18th/index.html
http://books.google.com
http://bubl.ac.uk
http://www.intute.ac.uk/artsandhumanities
http://www.mla.org/bibliography
http://vos.ucsb.edu/browse.asp?id=3
http://www.vts.intute.ac.uk

References

Chapter 1: Introduction

Brewer, J. (1997), *The Pleasures of the Imagination: English Culture in the Eighteenth Century*. London: HarperCollins.

Kramnick, I. (ed.) (1995), *The Portable Enlightenment Reader*. Harmondsworth: Penguin Books.

Ross, T. (2000), *The Making of the English Literary Canon from the Middle Ages to the Late Eighteenth Century*. Montreal and Kingston: McGill-Queen's University Press.

Sim, S. (2008), *The Eighteenth Century Novel and Contemporary Social Issues*. Edinburgh: Edinburgh University Press.

Chapter 2: Contexts, Identities and Consumption: Britain 1688–1815

Primary Works

Bloomfield, R. (1800), *The Farmer's Boy. A Rural Poem*. London: printed for Vernor and Hood.

Defoe, D. (1709), *A Review of the State of the British Nation*, quoted in W. A. Speck (1977), *Stability and Strife: England 1714–1760*. Cambridge, MA: Harvard University Press.

Duck, S. (1730), *Poems on Several Subjects* (Second edition). London: printed for J. Roberts.

Fielding, H. (1751), *An enquiry into the causes of the late increase of robbers, &c. with some proposals for remedying this growing evil*. Dublin: printed for G. Faulkner, P. Wilson, R. James, and M. Williamson.

Richardson, J. (1719), *Two Discourses. I. An essay on the whole art of criticism as it relates to painting; II. An argument in behalf of the science of a connoisseur*. London: printed for W. Churchill.

Yearsley, A. (1785), *Poems, on Several Occasions*. London: printed for T. Cadell.

Secondary Works

Freud, S. (1979), *Civilisation and its Discontents* (Revised edition.) Translated by J. Riviere. J. Strachey (ed.). London: Hogarth Press.

Consumerism

Andrew, D. T. (1996), 'Popular culture and public debate: London 1780'. *Historical Journal*, 39, 405–23.

Bermingham, A. and Brewer, J. (eds.) (1995), *The Consumption of Culture 1600–1800: Image, Object, Text*. London: Routledge.

Berg, M. (2005), *Luxury and Pleasure in Eighteenth-Century Britain*. Oxford: Oxford University Press.

Brewer, J. (1995), '"The most polite age and the most vicious": attitudes towards culture as a commodity, 1660–1800'. A. Bermingham and J. Brewer (eds) *The Consumption of Culture 1600–1800: Image, Object, Text*. London: Routledge, 341–61.

Brewer, J. (1997), *The Pleasures of the Imagination: The Emergence of English Culture in the Eighteenth Century*. London: HarperCollins.

Eger, E., Grant, C., Ó Gallchóir, C., and Warburton, P. (eds) (2001), *Women, Writing and the Public Sphere, 1700–1830*. Cambridge: Cambridge University Press.

Ellis, M. (2004), *The Coffee-House: A Cultural History*. London: Weidenfeld & Nicolson.

McKendrick, N., Brewer, J., and Plumb, J. H. (1982), *The Birth of a Consumer Society: The Commercialization of Eighteenth-Century England*. London: Hutchinson.

Wroth, W. (1979), *The London Pleasure Gardens of the Eighteenth Century* (Assisted by Arthur Edgar Wroth. First published in 1896.) Hamden, CT: Archon Books.

Social Structure

Barry, J. and Brooks, C. W. (eds) (1994), *The Middling Sort of People: Culture, Society and Politics in England, 1550–1800*. Basingstoke: Macmillan.

Bender, J. (1996), 'Introduction' in J. Bender and S. Stern (eds), *Tom Jones by Henry Fielding*. Oxford: Oxford University Press, ix–xxxiv.

Bohstedt, J. (1988), 'Gender, household and community politics: women in English riots, 1790–1810', *Past & Present*, 120, 88–122.

Corfield, P. J. (2000), *Power and the Professions in Britain, 1700–1850*. London: Routledge.

Earle, P. (1994), 'The middling sort in London', in J. Barry and C. W. Brooks (eds), *The Middling Sort of People: Culture, Society and Politics in England, 1550–1800*. Basingstoke: Macmillan, 156–71.

Habermas, J. (1989), *The Structural Transformation of the Public Sphere: An Inquiry into a Category of Bourgeois Society*, translated by T. Burger. Cambridge: Polity Press. (Originally published in German in 1962.)

Hay, D. and Rogers, N. (1997), *Eighteenth-Century English Society: Shuttles and Swords*. Oxford: Oxford University Press.

Hunt, M. R. (1996), *The Middling Sort: Commerce, Gender, and the Family in England, 1680–1780*. Berkeley: University of California Press.

Rogers, N. (1994), 'The middling sort in eighteenth-century politics', in J. Barry and C. W. Brooks (eds). *The Middling Sort of People: Culture, Society and Politics in England, 1550–1800*. Basingstoke: Macmillan, 159–80.

Speck, W. A. (1977), *Stability and Strife: England 1714–1760*. London: Edward Arnold.

Feminism

Barker-Benfield, G. J. (1992), *The Culture of Sensibility: Sex and Society in Eighteenth-Century Britain*. Chicago, IL: University of Chicago Press.

Barker, H. and Chalus, E. (eds) (1997), *Gender in Eighteenth-Century England: Roles, Representations and Responsibilities*. London: Longman.

Carter, P. (1997), 'Men about town: representations of foppery and masculinity in early eighteenth-century urban society', in H. Barker and E. Chalus (eds). *Gender in Eighteenth-Century England: Roles, Representations and Responsibilites*. London: Longman, 31–57.

Chalus, E. (2000), 'Elite women, social politics, and the political world of late eighteenth-century England'. *Historical Journal*, 43, 3, 669–71.

Clark, A. (1995), *The Struggle for the Breeches. Gender and the Making of the British Working Class*. London: Rivers Oram Press.

Davidoff, L. and Hall, C. (2002), *Family Fortunes: Men and Women of the English Middle Class 1780–1850* (revised edition). London: Routledge.

Jones, V. (ed.) (1990), *Women in the Eighteenth Century: Constructions of Femininity*. London: Routledge.

Kerber, L. (1988), 'Separate spheres, female worlds, woman's place: the rhetoric of women's history'. *Journal of American History*, 75, 9–39.

Lewis, J. S. (2003), *Sacred to Female Patriotism: Gender, Class, and Politics in Late Georgian Britain*. London: Routledge.

Rendall, J. (1985), *The Origins of Modern Feminism: Women in Britain, France and the United States, 1780–1860*. Basingstoke: Macmillan.

—— (1990), *Women in an Industrializing Society: England 1750–1850*. Oxford: Blackwell.

—— (1999), 'Women and the public sphere'. *Gender and History*, 11, 475–88.

Stone, L. (1977), *The Family, Sex and Marriage in England 1500–1800*. New York: Harper and Row.

Tague, I. H. (2002), *Women of Quality: Accepting and Contesting Ideals of Femininity in England, 1690–1760*. Rochester, NY and Woodbridge: Boydell.

Todd, J. (2000), *Mary Wollstonecraft: a Revolutionary Life*. London: Weidenfeld & Nicolson.

Vickery, A. (1993), 'The Golden Age to separate spheres? A review of the categories and chronology of English women's history', *The Historical Journal* 36, 383–404.

—— (1998), *The Gentleman's Daughter. Women's Lives in Georgian England*. New Haven, CT: Yale University Press.

Wahrman, D. (2004), *The Making of the Modern Self: Identity and Culture in Eighteenth-Century England*. New Haven, CT: Yale University Press.

Slavery

Edwards, P. and Walvin, J. (1983), *Black Personalities in the Era of the Slave Trade*. Basingstoke: Macmillan.

Schama, S. (2005), *Rough Crossings. Britain, the Slaves, and the American Revolution*. London: BBC Books.

Walvin, J. (1986), *England, Slaves and Freedom: 1776–1838*. Basingstoke: Macmillan.

—— (2000), *Britain's Slave Empire*. Stroud: Tempus.

General Histories

Baugh, D.A. (ed.) (1976), *Aristocratic Government and Society in Eighteenth-Century England: the Foundations of Stability*. New York: New Viewpoints.

Chalus, E. (2005), *Elite Women in English Political Life c. 1754–1790*. Oxford: Clarendon.

Christie, C. (2000), *The British Country House in the Eighteenth Century*. Manchester: Manchester University Press.

Clark, J. C. D. (1986), *Revolution and Rebellion: State and Society in England in the Seventeenth and Eighteenth Centuries*. Cambridge: Cambridge University Press.

Colley, L. (1992), *Britons: Forging the Nation, 1707–1837*. New Haven, CT: Yale University Press.

Conway, S. (2006), *War, State, and Society in Mid-Eighteenth-Century Britain and Ireland*. Oxford: Oxford University Press.

Langford, P. (1989), *A Polite and Commercial People: England 1727–1783*. Oxford: Oxford University Press.

—— (ed.) (2002), *The Eighteenth Century, 1688–1815*. Oxford: Oxford University Press.

O'Gorman, F. (1989), *Voters, Patrons and Parties: The Unreformed Electoral System of Hanoverian England, 1734–1832*. Oxford: Clarendon.

—— (1997), *The Long Eighteenth Century: British Political and Social History 1688–1832*. London: Edward Arnold.

Porter, R. (1990), *English Society in the Eighteenth Century* (revised edition). Harmondsworth: Penguin Books.

Sambrook, J. (1993), *The Eighteenth Century. The Intellectual and Cultural Context of English Literature 1700–1789* (Second edition). London: Longman.

Sharpe, J. A. (1997), *Early Modern England: A Social History, 1550–1760* (Second edition). London: Edward Arnold.

Smyth, J. (2001), *The Making of the United Kingdom 1660–1800: State, Religion and Identity in Britain and Ireland*. London: Longman.

Stevenson, J. (1992), *Popular Disturbances in England, 1700–1832* (Second edition). London: Longman.

Thompson, E. P. (1993), *Customs in Common*, Harmondsworth: Penguin Books.

Wahrman, D. (2004), *The Making of the Modern Self: Identity and Culture in Eighteenth-Century England*. New Haven, CT: Yale University Press.

Glorious Revolution

Cruickshanks, E. and Black, J. (eds) (1988), *The Jacobite Challenge*. Edinburgh: John Donald.

Cruickshanks, E. (ed.) (1989), *By Force or by Default? The Revolution of 1688–1689*. Edinburgh: John Donald.

Kenyon, J. P. (1989), 'Introduction', in E. Cruickshanks (ed.), *By Force or by Default? The Revolution of 1688–1689*. Edinburgh: John Donald, 1–7.

Miller, J. (1988), 'Proto-Jacobitism? The Tories and the Revolution of 1688–9', in E. Cruickshanks and J. Black (eds), *The Jacobite Challenge*. Edinburgh: John Donald, 7–23.

Van Thal, H. (ed.) (1974), *The Prime Ministers. Volume 1: Sir Robert Walpole to Sir Robert Peel*. London: George Allen and Unwin Ltd.

Chapter 3: Literary and Cultural Figures, Genres and Contexts

Burney

Chisholm, K. (1998), *Fanny Burney: Her Life, 1752–1840*. London: Chatto & Windus.
Cutting-Gray, J. (1992), *Woman as 'Nobody' and the Novels of Fanny Burney*. Gainesville: University Press of Florida.
Doody, M. A. (1988), *Frances Burney: The Life in the Works*. Cambridge: Cambridge University Press.
Harman, H. (2000), *Fanny Burney: A Biography*. London: HarperCollins.
Johnson, C. L. (1995), *Equivocal Beings: Politics, Gender, and Sentimentality in the 1790s: Wollstonecraft, Radcliffe, Burney, Austen*. Chicago, IL: University of Chicago Press.
Nicolson, N. (2002), *Fanny Burney: The Mother of English Fiction*. London: Short Books.
Rogers, K. M. (1990), *Frances Burney: The World of 'Female Difficulties'*. New York: Harvester Wheatsheaf.
Thaddeus, J. R. (2000), *Frances Burney: A Literary Life*. Basingstoke: Macmillan.

Defoe

Alkon, P. K. (1979), *Defoe and Fictional Time*. Athens, GA: University of Georgia Press.
Backscheider, P. R. (1989), *Daniel Defoe: His Life*. Baltimore, MD and London: Johns Hopkins University Press.
Bastian, F. (1981), *Defoe's Early Life*. London: Macmillan.
Furbank, P N. (2006), *A Political Biography of Daniel Defoe*. London: Pickering & Chatto.
Meier, T. K. (1987), *Defoe and the Defense of Commerce*. Victoria, BC: University of Victoria.
Novak, M. E. (2003), *Daniel Defoe: Master of Fictions; His life and ideas*. Oxford: Oxford University Press.
Richetti, J, (ed.) (2008), *The Cambridge Companion to Daniel Defoe*. Cambridge: Cambridge University Press.
—— (2005), *The Life of Daniel Defoe*. Malden, MA: Blackwell.
Watt, I. (1957), *The Rise of the Novel: Studies in Defoe, Richardson and Fielding*. London: Chatto & Windus.

Fielding

Battestin, M. C. (2000), *A Henry Fielding Companion*. Westport, CT and London: Greenwood Press.
Bell, I. A. (1994), *Henry Fielding: Authorship and Authority*. London: Longman.
Bertelsen, L. (2000), *Henry Fielding at Work: Magistrate, Businessman, Writer*. Basingstoke: Palgrave.
Pagliaro, H. (1998), *Henry Fielding: A Literary Life*. Basingstoke: Macmillan.
Paulson, R. (2000), *The Life of Henry Fielding: A Critical Biography*. Oxford: Blackwell.
Rawson, C. (ed.) (2007), *The Cambridge Companion to Henry Fielding*. Cambridge: Cambridge University Press.

Johnson

Clingham, G., (ed.) (1997), *The Cambridge Companion to Samuel Johnson*. Cambridge: Cambridge University Press.
Crystal, D. (2005), *Dr Johnson's Dictionary*. London: Penguin Books.
DeMaria Jr, R. (1997), *Samuel Johnson and the Life of Reading*. Baltimore, MD and London: Johns Hopkins University Press.
Lipking, L. (1988), *Samuel Johnson: The Life of an Author*. Cambridge, MA: Harvard University Press.
Parker, F. (2003), *Scepticism and Literature: An Essay on Pope, Hume, Sterne and Johnson*. Oxford: Oxford University Press.
Smallwood, P. (2004), *Johnson's Critical Presence: Image, History, Judgement*. Aldershot, UK and Burlington, VT: Ashgate.
Weinbrot, H. D. (2005), *Aspects of Samuel Johnson: Essays on His Arts, Mind, Afterlife, and Politics*. Newark, DE: University of Delaware Press.

Pope

Baines, P. (2000), *The Complete Critical Guide to Alexander Pope*. London and New York: Routledge.
Erskine-Hill, H. (2008), *The Life of Alexander Pope*. Oxford: Blackwell.
Fairer, D. (1989), *The Poetry of Alexander Pope*. Harmondsworth: Penguin Books.
Goldsmith, N. M. (2002), *Alexander Pope: The Evolution of a Poet*. Aldershot: Ashgate.
Mack, M. (1985), *Alexander Pope: A Life*. New York: W. W. Norton.
Pope, A. (2006), *The Major Works*. P. Rogers (ed.). Oxford: Oxford University Press.
Rogers, P. (2004), *The Alexander Pope Encyclopedia*. Westport, CT: Greenwood.
—— (ed.) (2007), *The Cambridge Companion to Alexander Pope*. Cambridge: Cambridge University Press.
Thomas, C. N. (1994), *Alexander Pope and His Eighteenth-Century Women Readers*. Carbondale, IL: Southern Illinois University Press.
Weinbrot, H. D. (1982), *Alexander Pope and the Traditions of Formal Verse Satire*. Princeton, NJ: Princeton University Press.

Richardson

Castle, T. (1982), *Clarissa's Ciphers: Meaning and Disruption in Richardson's Clarissa*. Ithaca, NY: Cornell University Press.
Doody, M. A. and Sabor, P. (eds.) (1989), *Samuel Richardson: Tercentenary Essays*. Cambridge: Cambridge University Press.
Eagleton, T. (1982), *The Rape of Clarissa: Writing, Sexuality and Class Struggle in Samuel Richardson*. Oxford: Blackwell.
Flynn, C. H. and Copeland, E. (eds) (1999), *Clarissa and Her Readers*. New York: AMS Press.
Harris, J. (1987), *Samuel Richardson*. Cambridge: Cambridge University Press.
Keymer, T. (1992), *Richardson's Clarissa and the Eighteenth-Century Reader*. Cambridge: Cambridge University Press.

Keymer, T. and Sabor, P. (2005), *'Pamela' in the Marketplace: Literary Controversy and Print Culture in Eighteenth-Century Britain and Ireland*. Cambridge: Cambridge University Press.
Rivero, A J. (ed.) (1996), *New Essays on Samuel Richardson*. Basingstoke: Macmillan.
Tassie, T. (1993), *Samuel Richardson's Fictions of Gender*. Palo Alto, CA: Stanford University Press.

Swift

Crook, K. (1998), *A Preface to Swift*. London and New York: Longman.
Ehrenpreis, I. (1962–83), *Swift: The Man, his Works, and the Age*, 3 vols. London: Methuen.
Fox, C. (ed.) (2003), *The Cambridge Companion to Jonathan Swift*. Cambridge: Cambridge University Press.
Glendinning, V. (1999), *Jonathan Swift*. London: Pimlico.
Higgins, I. (2004), *Jonathan Swift*, 'Writers and their Work'. Horndon: Northcote.
Kelly, A. C. (2002), *Jonathan Swift and Popular Culture: Myth, Media, and the Man*. New York and Basingstoke: Palgrave.
McMinn, J. (1991), *Jonathan Swift: A Literary Life*. Basingstoke: Macmillan.
Nokes, D. (1985), *Jonathan Swift, a Hypocrite Reversed: A Critical Biography*. Oxford: Oxford University Press.
Swift, J. (1999–), *The Correspondence of Jonathan Swift, D.D.*, D. Woolley (ed.). Frankfurt am Main and Oxford: P. Lang.
—— (2003), *Major Works*, A. Ross and D. Woolley (eds). Oxford: Oxford University Press.

GENRES

Eighteenth-century Poetry

Doody, M. A. (1985), *The Daring Muse: Augustan Poetry Reconsidered*. Cambridge: Cambridge University Press.
Fairer, D. and Gerrard, C. (eds) (2004), *Eighteenth-Century Poetry: An Annotated Anthology* (Second edition). Oxford: Blackwell.
Fairer, D. (2003), *English Poetry of the Eighteenth Century, 1700–1789*. London: Longman.
Gerrard, C. (2006), *A Companion to Eighteenth-Century Poetry*. Oxford: Blackwell.
Keymer, T. and Mee, J. (eds) (2004), *The Cambridge Companion to English Literature 1740–1830*. Cambridge: Cambridge University Press.
Lonsdale, R. (ed.) (1984), *The New Oxford Book of Eighteenth-Century Verse*. Oxford: Oxford University Press.
Nisbet, H. B. and Rawson, C. (eds) (1997), *The Cambridge History of Literary Criticism, Volume 4: The Eighteenth Century*. Cambridge: Cambridge University Press.
Richetti, J. (ed.) (2005), *The Cambridge History of English Literature, 1660–1780*. Cambridge: Cambridge University Press.
Sitter, J. (ed.) (2001), *The Cambridge Companion to Eighteenth-Century Poetry*. Cambridge: Cambridge University Press.

Weinbrot, H. D. (1993), *Britannia's Issue: The Rise of British Literature from Dryden to Ossian*. Cambridge: Cambridge University Press.

Novel

Backscheider, P. R. and Ingrassia, C. (eds) (2005), *Companion to the Eighteenth-Century English Novel and Culture*. Oxford: Blackwell.
Barchas, J. (2003), *Graphic Design, Print Culture, and the Eighteenth-Century Novel*. Cambridge: Cambridge University Press.
Barney, R. A. (1999), *Plots of Enlightenment: Education and the Novel in Eighteenth-Century England*. Palo Alto, CA: Stanford University Press.
Bellamy, L. (1998), *Commerce, Morality and the Eighteenth-Century Novel*. Cambridge: Cambridge University Press.
London, A. (1999), *Women and Property in the Eighteenth-Century English Novel*. Cambridge: Cambridge University Press.
Richetti, J. J. (ed.) (1996), *The Cambridge Companion to the Eighteenth-Century Novel*. Cambridge: Cambridge University Press.
Skinner, J. (2001), *An Introduction to Eighteenth-Century Fiction: Raising the Novel*. Basingstoke: Palgrave Macmillan.
Van Sant, A. J. (1993), *Eighteenth-Century Sensibility and the Novel: The Senses in Social Context*. Cambridge: Cambridge University Press.
Zimmerman, E. (1996), *The Boundaries of Fiction: History and the Eighteenth-Century British Novel*. Ithaca, NY: Cornell University Press.

Theatre

Brewer, J. (1997), *The Pleasures of the Imagination: English Culture in the Eighteenth Century*. London: HarperCollins.
Dobson, M. (1992), *The Making of the National Poet: Shakespeare, Adaptation and Authorship, 1660–1769*. Oxford: Clarendon.
Hume, R. D. (ed.) (1980), *The London Theatre World, 1660–1800*. Carbondale: Southern Illinois University Press.
Kelly, L. (1980), *The Kemble Era: John Philip Kemble, Sarah Siddons and the London Stage*. London: Bodley Head.
Nicoll, A. (1980), *The Garrick Stage*. Manchester: Manchester University Press.
Price, C. (1973), *Theatre in the Age of Garrick*. Oxford: Clarendon.
Shepherd, S. and Womack, P. (1996), *English Drama: A Cultural History*. Oxford: Blackwell.
Thomas, D. and Hare, A. (1989), *Theatre in Europe: A Documentary History: Restoration and Georgian England, 1660–1788*. Cambridge: Cambridge University Press.

CONTEXTS

Print Culture

Barker, H. (1998), *Newspapers, Politics and Public Opinion in Late Eighteenth-century England*. Oxford: Clarendon.

Hammond, B. (1997), *Professional Imaginative Writing in England, 1670–1740: Hackney for Bread*. Oxford: Clarendon.

McDowell, P. (1998), *The Women of Grub Street: Press, Politics, and Gender in the London Literary Marketplace, 1678–1730*. Oxford: Clarendon.

Raven, J. (2007), *The Business of Books: Booksellers and the English Book Trade 1450–1850*. New Haven, CT: Yale University Press.

Rivers, I. (ed.) (1982), *Books and Their Readers in Eighteenth-Century England*. Basingstoke: Palgrave Macmillan.

Rogers, P. (1972), *Grub Street: Studies in a Subculture*. London: Methuen.

Rose, M. (1993), *Authors and Owners: The Invention of Copyright*. Cambridge, MA: Harvard University Press.

Eighteenth-Century Science

Christie, J. and Shuttleworth, S. (eds) (1989), *Nature Transfigured: Science and Literature 1700–1900*. Manchester and New York: Manchester University Press.

Fox, C., Porter, R. and Wokler, R. (eds) (1995), *Inventing Human Science: Eighteenth-Century Domains*. Berkeley, CA: University of California Press.

Golinski, J. (1991), *Science as Public Culture: Chemistry and Enlightenment in Britain, 1760–1900*. Cambridge: Cambridge University Press.

Jaco, M. C. and Stewart, L. (2004), *Practical Matter: Newton's Science in the Service of Industry and Empire, 1687–1851*. Cambridge, MA: Harvard University Press.

Porter, Roy, (ed.) (2003), *Science in the Eighteenth Century*. Cambridge: Cambridge University Press.

Rousseau, G. S. (1991), *Enlightenment Borders: Pre- and Post-Modern Discourses; Medical, Scientific*. Manchester: Manchester University Press.

Rousseau, G. S. and Porter, R. (eds) (1980), *The Ferment of Knowledge: Studies in the Historiography of Eighteenth-Century Science*. Cambridge: Cambridge University Press.

Soupel, S. and Hambridge, R. A. (eds) (1982), *Literature and Science and Medicine*. Los Angeles: University of California Press.

Vickers, I. (1996), *Defoe and the New Sciences*. Cambridge: Cambridge University Press.

Walmsley, P. (2003), *Locke's Essay and the Rhetoric of Science*. Lewisburg, PA: Bucknell University Press.

Chapter 4: Case Studies in Reading 1: Key Primary Literary Texts

Secondary works

Brown, M. G. 'Fanny Burney's "Feminism" Gender or Genre?' in M. A. Schofield and C. Macheski (eds). *Fetter'd or Free? British Women Novelists 1670–1815*. Athens, OH: Ohio University Press, 29–39.

Clingham, G. (ed.) (1997), *The Cambridge Companion to Samuel Johnson*. Cambridge: Cambridge University Press.

Doody, M. A. (1988), *Frances Burney: The Life in the Works*. New Brunswick, NJ: Rutgers University Press.

Ellis, F. (1981), 'Gray's Elegy: The Biographical Problem in Literary Criticism', *PMLA* 66, 971–1008.

Fraiman S. (1993), 'Getting Waylaid in *Evelina*', in *Unbecoming Women: British Women Writers and the Novel of Development*. New York: Columbia University Press, 32–58.

Gleckner, R. F. (1997), *Gray Agonistes: Thomas Gray and Masculine Friendship*. Baltimore, MD: Johns Hopkins University Press.

Hagstrum, J. (1967), *Samuel Johnson's Literary Criticism* (Second edition). Chicago, IL: University of Chicago Press.

Korshin, P. J. (1997) 'Johnson, the essay and the Rambler' in G. Clingham (ed.), *The Cambridge Companion to Samuel Johnson*. Cambridge: Cambridge University Press, 51–66.

Mack, M. (1985), *Alexander Pope: A Life*. New York: W. W. Norton.

Meyer Spacks, P. (1967), *The Poetry of Vision: Five Eighteenth-Century Poets*. Cambridge, MA: Harvard University Press.

Starr, H. W. (ed.) (1968), *Twentieth Century Interpretations of Gray's* Elegy. Englewood Cliffs, NJ: Prentice-Hall.

Schofield, M. A. and Macheski, C. (eds) (1986), *Fetter'd or Free? British Women Novelists, 1670–1815*. Athens, OH: Ohio University Press.

Spencer J. (1986), *The Rise of the Woman Novelist: From Aphra Behn to Jane Austen*. Oxford: Blackwell.

Todd, J. (1986), *Sensibility: An Introduction*. London: Methuen.

Womersley, D. (ed. intro.) (1997), *Augustan Critical Writing*. Harmondsworth: Penguin Books.

Chapter 5: Case Studies in Reading 2: Key Theoretical and Critical Texts

Aravamudan, S. (1999), *Tropicopolitans: Colonialism and Agency 1688–1804*, Durham, NC: Duke University Press.

Armstrong, N. (1987), *Desire and Domestic Fiction: A Political History of the Novel*. New York: Oxford University Press.

Backscheider, P. (2005), *Eighteenth-Century Women Poets and their Poetry: Inventing Agency, Inventing Genre*. Baltimore, MD: Johns Hopkins University Press.

Barker-Benfield, G. J. (1992), *The Culture of Sensibility: Sex and Society in Eighteenth-Century Britain*. Chicago, IL: University of Chicago Press.

Bender, J. (1987), *Imagining the Penitentiary: Fiction and the Architecture of Mind in Eighteenth-Century England*. Chicago, IL: University of Chicago Press.

Brown, L. (1993), *Ends of Empire: Women and Ideology in Early Eighteenth-Century Literature*. Ithaca, NY: Cornell University Press.

Brown, L. and Nussbaum, F. A. (1987), *The New Eighteenth Century: Theory, Politics, English Literature*. London and New York: Methuen.

Castle, T. (1986), *Masquerade and Civilization: The Carnivalesque in Eighteenth-century English Culture and Fiction*. Palo Alto, CA: Stanford University Press.

Clark, J. C. D. (1985), *English Society, 1688–1832*. Cambridge: Cambridge University Press.

Deutsch, H. (2005), *Loving Dr. Johnson*. Chicago, IL: University of Chicago Press.

Ellison, J. K. (1999), *Cato's Tears and the Making of Anglo-American Emotion*. Chicago, IL: University of Chicago Press.

Fanon, Frantz [1952] (2008), *White Skin, Black Masks*. New York: Grove Press.

Ferguson, M. (1992), *Subject to Others: British Women Writers and Colonial Slavery, 1670–1834*. New York: Routledge.

Fulford, T. (2006), *Native Americans, British Literature, and Transatlantic Culture 1756–1830*. Oxford: Oxford University Press.

Gallagher, C. (1994), *Nobody's Story: The Vanishing Acts of Women Writers in the Marketplace, 1670–1820*. Berkeley, CA: University of California Press.

Green, J. (2005), *The Trouble with Ownership: Literary Property and Authorial Liability in England, 1660–1730*. Philadelphia, PA: University of Pennsylvania Press.

Hawes, C. (2005), *The British Eighteenth Century and Global Critique*. New York: Palgrave Macmillan.

Hunter, J. P. (1992), *Before Novels: Cultural Contexts of Eighteenth-Century English Fiction*. New York and London: W. W. Norton.

Joseph, B. (2004), *Reading the East India Company, 1720–1840*. Chicago, IL and London: University of Chicago Press.

Langford, P. (1989), *A Polite and Commercial People: England 1727–83*. Oxford: Oxford University Press.

Marshall, D. (1985), *The Surprising Effects of Sympathy: Marivaux, Diderot, Rousseau, and Mary Shelley*. Chicago, IL: University of Chicago Press.

McGann J. (1996), *The Poetics of Sensibility: A Revolution in Literary Style*. Oxford: Clarendon.

McKeon, M. (1987, 2nd ed. 2002), *The Origins of the English Novel, 1660–1740*. Baltimore, MD and London: Johns Hopkins University Press.

—— (2005), *The Secret History of Domesticity: Public, Private, and the Division of Knowledge*. Baltimore, MD: Johns Hopkins University Press.

Mowry, M. (2004), *The Bawdy Politic in Stuart England: Political Pornography and Prostitution 1660–1714*. London: Ashgate.

Pinch, A. (1996), *Strange Fits of Passion: Epistemologies of Emotion, from Hume to Austen*. Palo Alto, CA: Stanford University Press.

Potkay, A. (2000), *The Passion for Happiness: Samuel Johnson and David Hume*. Ithaca, NY: Cornell University Press.

—— (2007), *The Story of Joy*. Cambridge: Cambridge University Press.

Pratt, M. L. (1992), *Imperial Eyes: Travel Writing and Transculturation*. London: Routledge.

Said, E. (1978, 2nd ed. 2003), *Orientalism: Western Conceptions of the Orient*. Harmondsworth: Penguin Books.

Todd, J. (1989), *The Sign of Angelica: Women, Writing and Fiction 1660–1800*. London: Virago.

Vermeule, B. (2000), *The Party of Humanity: Writing Moral Psychology in Eighteenth-Century Britain*. Baltimore, MD: Johns Hopkins University Press.

Watt, I. (1957, 2nd ed. 2000), *The Rise of the Novel: Studies in Defoe, Richardson and Fielding*, Berkeley, CA: University of California Press.

Wahrman, D. (1995), *Imagining the Middle Class: The Political Representation of Class in Britain c. 1780–1840*. Cambridge: Cambridge University Press.

Warner, W. (1998), *Licensing Entertainment: The Elevation of Novel Reading in England*. Berkeley, CA and London: University of California Press.

Williams, R. (1961, 2nd ed. 1963), *The Long Revolution*. New York: Columbia University Press and London: Pelican.

Zunshine, L. (2006), *Why We Read Fiction: Theory of Mind and the Novel*. Columbus, OH: Ohio State University Press.

Chapter 7: 'Dead Keen on Reason?'

1650–1850: Ideas, Aesthetics and Inquiries in the Early Modern Era.
Ackroyd, P. (1987), *Chatterton*. London: Hamish Hamilton.
Anderson, H. and Shea, J. S. (eds) (1967), *Studies in Criticism and Aesthetics, 1660–1800: Essays in Honor of Samuel Holt Monk*. Minneapolis, MN: University of Minnesota Press.
Austen, J. (2005), 3 vols. *The Cambridge Edition of the Works of Jane Austen*, J. Todd (gen. ed.). Cambridge: Cambridge University Press.
Bate, W. J. (1977), *Samuel Johnson*. New York and London: Harcourt Brace.
—— (1946), *From Classic to Romantic*. Cambridge, MA: Harvard University Press.
Bennington, G. (2007), 'Derrida's "Eighteenth Century"'. *Eighteenth-Century Studies*, 40, 3, 381–93.
British Journal for Eighteenth-Century Studies.
Cambridge Quarterly.
Chatterton, T. (1971), 2 vols. *The Complete Works of Thomas Chatterton: A Bicentenary Edition*, D. S. Taylor (ed.). Oxford: Clarendon.
Clarke, N. (2000), *Dr Johnson's Women*. London: London and Hambleton.
—— (2004), *The Rise and Fall of the Woman of Letters*. London: Pimlico.
Cleland, J. (c. 1760), *Fanny Hill, Memoirs of a Woman of Pleasure*. London: printed for R. Griffiths.
Coetzee, J.M. (1986), *Foe*. London: Secker and Warburg.
Collini, S. (1999), *English Pasts*. Oxford: Oxford University Press.
Connolly, C. (ed.) (1993), *Letters for Literary Ladies* [Maria Edgeworth (1795)]. London: Everyman.
Cowley, A. (1989 and 1992), 2 vols. *The Collected Works of Abraham Cowley*, T. O. Calhoun, L. Hayworth, and A. Pritchard (eds). Newark, DE: University of Delaware Press.
Crane, R. S. (1968), 2 vols. *The Idea of the Humanities*. Chicago, IL: University of Chicago Press.
Davison, D. (ed.) (1973), *The Penguin Book of Eighteenth-Century English Verse*. Harmondsworth: Penguin Books.
DeMaria Jr., R. (1993), *The Life of Samuel Johnson: A Critical Biography*. Oxford: Blackwell.
—— (2001), *British Literature 1640–1789* (Second edition). Oxford: Blackwell.
Dryden, J. (1700), Preface to *Fables Ancient and Modern*. In *The Works of John Dryden*, vol. 7 (2000). V. A. Dearing (ed.). Berkeley, CA: University of California Press.
—— (1958), *The Poems and Fables of John Dryden*, J. Kinsley (ed.). London: Oxford University Press.
—— (1995–2005), 5 vols. *The Poems of John Dryden*, P. Hammond and D. Hopkins (eds). Harlow: Pearson Longman.
Eighteenth Century: Theory and Interpretation.

Eighteenth-Century Life.
Ellis, J. M. (1997), *Literature Lost: Social Agendas and the Corruption of the Humanities.* New Haven, CT: Yale University Press.
English: the Journal of the English Association.
Eskine-Hill, H. (1996), *Poetry of Opposition and Revolution: Dryden to Wordsworth.* Oxford: Clarendon.
Essays in Criticism.
Fairer, D. and Gerrard, C. (eds) (1999), *Eighteenth-Century Poetry: An Annotated Anthology.* Oxford: Blackwell.
Greene, J. (2007), 'Hors d'Oeuvre', *Eighteenth-Century Studies*, 40, 3, 367–79.
Gross, J. J. (1969), *The Rise and Fall of the Man of Letters: Aspects of English Literary Life since 1800.* London: Weidenfeld & Nicolson.
Hammond, B. (1997), *Professional Imaginative Writing in England, 1670–1740: Hackney for Bread.* Oxford: Clarendon.
Hammond, P. (1999), *Dryden and the Traces of Classical Rome.* Oxford: Oxford University Press.
Hopkins, D. and Gillespie, S. (eds) (2005), *Oxford History of Literary Translation in English (1660–1790).* Oxford: Oxford University Press.
Hudson, N. (2003), *Samuel Johnson and the Making of Modern England.* Cambridge: Cambridge University Press.
Johnson, S. (1905), 3 vols. *The Lives of the Poets (1779–81)*, G. Birkbeck Hill (ed.). Oxford: Clarendon.
—— (1958–), *The Yale Edition of the Works of Samuel Johnson*, J. Middendorf (gen. ed.). New Haven, CT and London: Yale University Press.
—— (2006), 4 vols. *The Lives of the Most Eminent English Poets*, Roger Lonsdale (ed.). Oxford: Clarendon.
Johnston, F. (2005), *Samuel Johnson and the Art of Sinking, 1709–1791.* Oxford: Oxford University Press.
Korshin, P. J., and Lynch, J. (eds) (2006), *Age of Johnson, The: An Annual.* New York: AMS Press.
Leavis, F. R. (1952), *The Common Pursuit.* London: Chatto & Windus.
Mack, M. (1985), *Alexander Pope: A Life.* New Haven, CT and London: Yale University Press.
Manning, S. (2001), 'Whatever Happened to Pleasure', *The Cambridge Quarterly*, 30, 3, 215–32.
Mason, H. A. (1972), *To Homer through Pope: An Introduction to Homer's 'Iliad' and Pope's Translation.* London: Chatto & Windus.
Mason, T. and Hopkins, D. (eds) (1994), *Selected Poems of Abraham Cowley.* Manchester: Fyfield.
McLaverty, J. (2001), *Pope, Print and Meaning.* Oxford: Clarendon.
Nussbaum, F. (ed.) (2003), *The Global Eighteenth Century.* Baltimore, MD and London: Johns Hopkins University Press.
Perry, R. (1999), 'De-familiarizing the Family; or, Writing Family History from Literary Sources' in *Eighteenth-Century Literary History: An MLQ Reader*, M. Brown (ed.). Durham, NC: Duke University Press, 159–71.
Plath, S. (2005), *The Bell Jar.* (1963). London: Faber and Faber.
Poems on Affairs of State: Augustan Satirical Verse, 1660–1714 (1963–75), 7 vols.

G. de Forest Lord (gen. ed.). New Haven, CT and London: Yale University Press.
Pope, A. (1963), *The Poems of Alexander Pope*. J. Butt (ed.). London: Methuen.
Review of English Studies.
Richetti, J. (ed.) (2005), *The Cambridge History of English Literature, 1660–1780*. Cambridge: Cambridge University Press.
Rivers, I. (ed.) (2001), *Books and their Readers in the Eighteenth Century: New Essays*. London and New York: Leicester University Press.
Rumbold, V. (1989), *Women's Place in Pope's World*. Cambridge: Cambridge University Press.
Studies in Eighteenth-Century Culture.
Studies in English Literature: 1500–1900.
Turner, C. (1992), *Living by the Pen: Women Writers in the Eighteenth Century*. London: Routledge.
Wain, J. (1974), *Samuel Johnson*. London: Macmillan.
Warton, J. (1756), *An Essay on the Genius and Writings of Pope*. London.
Watt, I. P. (1957), *The Rise of the Novel: Studies in Defoe, Richardson and Fielding*. London: Chatto & Windus.
Webster, J. W. (2005), *Performing Libertinism in Charles II's Court: Politics, Drama, Sexuality*. Basingstoke: Palgrave Macmillan.
Wellek, R. (1955–92), 8 vols. *History of Modern Criticism: 1750–1950*. London: Jonathan Cape.
Williams, A. (2005), *Poetry and the Creation of a Whig Literary Culture 1681–1714*. Oxford: Oxford University Press.
Winn, J. A. (1987), *John Dryden and his World*. New Haven, CT and London: Yale University Press.
Winterson, J. (1990), *Sexing the Cherry*. London: Vintage.
Womersley, D. (ed.) (1997), *Augustan Critical Writing*. Harmondsworth: Penguin Books.
Year's Work in English Studies (1919–)
Zwicker, S. (ed.) (1998), *Cambridge Companion to English Literature 1650–1740*. Cambridge: Cambridge University Press.

Chapter 8: Questioning Canonicity

Bloom, H. (1995), *The Western Canon: The Books and School of the Ages*. New York: Riverhead Trade.
Bonnell, T. F. (1989), 'Bookselling and Canon-Making: The Trade Rivalry over the English Poets, 1776–1783'. *Studies in Eighteenth-Century Culture*, 19, 53–69.
—— (1997), 'Speaking of Institutions and Canonicity, Don't Forget the Publishers'. *Eighteenth-Century Life*, 21, 3, 97–9.
Brody, K. J. (1999), *Making the English Canon: Print Capitalism and the Cultural Past, 1700–1770*. Cambridge: Cambridge University Press.
Edmundson, M. (2004), *Why Read?* New York: Bloomsbury.
Engell, J. and Dangerfield, A. (2005), *Saving Higher Education in the Age of Money*. Charlottesville: University of Virginia Press.
Fowler, A. (1979), 'Genre and Literary Canon', *New Literary History*, 11, 1, 97–199.

Guillory, J. (1993), *Cultural Capital: The Problem of Literary Canon Formation.* Baltimore, MD: Johns Hopkins University Press.
Keegan, B. (2005), 'Mysticisms and Mystifications: The Demands of Laboring-Class Religious Poetry'. *Criticism*, 47, 4, 471–91.
Patey, D. L. (1988), 'The Eighteenth-Century Invents the Canon'. *Modern Language Studies*, 18, 17–37.
Ribeiro, A., SJ and Basker, J. G. (eds) (1996), *Tradition in Transition: Women Writers, Marginal Texts, and the Eighteenth-Century Canon.* Oxford: Clarendon.
Richter, D. H. (2000), *Falling into Theory: Conflicting Views on Reading Literature.* New York: Bedford/St. Martin's.
Ross, T. (2000), *The Making of the English Literary Canon from the Middle Ages to the Late Eighteenth Century*. Montreal: McGill-Queen's University Press.
St Clair, W. (2004), *The Reading Nation in the Romantic Period.* Cambridge: Cambridge University Press.
Suarez, M.F., SJ (1996), 'Trafficking in the Muse: Dodsley's *Collection of Poems* and the Question of Canon' in *Tradition in Transition: Women Writers, Marginal Texts and the Eighteenth-Century Canon*, A. Ribeiro, SJ and J. G. Basker (eds). Oxford: Clarendon, 297–313.

Chapter 9: Gender, Sexuality and Ethnicity

Primary Texts

Astell, M. (1694), *A Serious Proposal to the Ladies*. London: R. Wilkes.
Aubin, P. (1996), *The Adventures of Count de Vinevil and his Family*. Oxford: Clarendon.
—— (1723), *The Life of Charlotta du Pont, An English Lady*, London: A. Bettesworth.
Benedict, B. M., Cope, K. L., Mounsey, C., Norton, R. and Spedding, P. (eds) (2002), *Eighteenth-Century British Erotica: Volume 1*. London: Pickering and Chatto.
Brown, J. (1757), *An Estimate of the Manners and Principles of the Times*. Dublin: Exshaw.
Cheyne, G. (1733), *The English Malady*. London: George Strahan.
Cleland, J. (2001), *Memoirs of a Woman of Pleasure*. Harmondsworth: Penguin Books.
Cooper, A. A., Lord Shaftesbury (1999), *Characteristicks of Men, Manners, Opinions, Times* L. Klein (ed.). Cambridge: Cambridge University Press.
Dunton, J. (1703), *The Shortest Way with Whores and Rogues*. London: no publisher.
Egerton, S. F. (1703), *Poems on Several Occasions*. London: John Nutt.
Knight, R. P. (1786), *An Account of the remains of the Worship of Priapus*. London: T. Spilsbury.
Leapor, M. (1751), *Poems on Several Occasions*. London: J. Roberts.
Linnaeus, C. (1802), *Systema Naturae*, translated by W. Turton. (Orginally published in 1735.) London: Lackington, Allen and Co.
Mandeville, B. (1724), *A Modest Defence of Publick Stews: Or an Essay upon Whoring*. London: A. Moore.
Newton, I. (1968), *The Mathematical Principles of Natural Philosophy*, trans. Andrew Motte. London: Dawsons.
Pope, A. (1993), *'Epistle to Cobham' in The Oxford Authors: Alexander Pope*. P. Rogers (ed.). Oxford: Oxford University Press.

—— (1993), *'An Epistle to a Lady: On the Characters of Women' in The Oxford Authors: Alexander Pope*. P. Rogers (ed.). Oxford: Oxford University Press.

Rowe, N. (1714), *Jane Shore, a tragedy, written in imitation of Shakspear's (sic) style 1714*. London: Bernard Lintott.

Swift, J. (1711), *The Battle of the Books*. London: John Nutt.

Wilkes, J. (1763), *An Essay on Woman*. London: J. Freeman.

Wollstonecraft, M. (1792), *A Vindication of the Rights of Woman with strictures on political and moral subjects*. London: Joseph Johnson.

Secondary Texts

Bhabha, H. K. (1990), *Nation and Narration*. London: Routledge.

Carey, B. (2005), *British Abolitionism and the Rhetoric of Sensibility*. Basingstoke: Palgrave.

Castle, T. (1986), *Masquerade and Civilization*. Palo Alto, CA: Stanford University Press.

Foucault, F. (1979), *History of Sexuality*, Trans. R. Hurley. London: Allen Lane.

Goldsmith, N. M. (1998), *The Worst of Crimes: Homosexuality and the Law in Eighteenth-Century London*. Aldershot: Ashgate.

Henrey, B. (1975), *British Botanical and Horticultural Literature before 1800*. Oxford: Clarendon.

Laqueur, T. (1990), *Making Sex*. Cambridge, MA: Harvard University Press.

Nussbaum, F. (2003), *The Limits of the Human*. Cambridge: Cambridge University Press.

Peakman, J. (2003), *Mighty Lewd Books: The Development of Pornography in Eighteenth-Century England*. Basingstoke: Palgrave.

Stone, L. (1977), *The Family, Sex and Marriage*. London: Weidenfeld & Nicolson.

Chapter 10: Maping the Critical Landscape

Primary Texts

Austen, J. (1816), *Mansfield Park*. C. Johnson (ed.). New York: W. W. Norton, 1998.

Smith, A. (1976), *An Inquiry into the Nature and Causes of the Wealth of Nations*. R. H. Campbell and A. S. Skinner (gen. eds), W. B. Todd (textual ed.), 2 vols. Oxford: Clarendon.

Secondary Texts

Aravamudan, S. (1999), *Tropicopolitans: Colonialism and Agency 1688–1804*, Durham, NC: Duke University Press.

Ballaster, R. (2005), *Fabulous Orients: Fictions of the East of England, 1662–1785*. Oxford and New York: Oxford University Press.

Brown, L. (2001), *Fables of Modernity: Literature and Culture in the English Eighteenth Century*. Ithaca, NY and London: Cornell University Press.

Carretta, V. (1995), *Olaudah Equiano, The Interesting Narrative and Other Writings*. London and New York: Penguin Books.

—— (2005), *Equiano the African: Biography of a Self-made Man*. Athens, GA: University of Georgia Press.

Duckworth, A. M. (1971; 1994), *The Improvement of the Estate: A Study of Jane Austen's Novels*, Baltimore, MD and London: Johns Hopkins University Press.

Fraiman, S. (1995), 'Jane Austen and Edward Said: Gender, Culture, and Imperialism', *Critical Inquiry*, 21, 804–21.

Ferguson, M. (1993), *Colonialism and Gender Relations from Mary Wollstonecraft to Jamaica Kincaid: East Caribbean Connections*. New York: Columbia University Press.

Gilroy, P. (1992), 'Cultural Studies and Ethnic Absolutism', in L. Grossberg, C. Nelson, and P. A. Treichler, (eds), *Cultural Studies*. New York and London: Routledge, 187–98.

—— (1993), *The Black Atlantic: Modernity and Double Consciousness*. Cambridge, MA: Harvard University Press.

Kaul, S. (2000), *Poems of Nation, Anthems of Empire: English Verse in the Long Eighteenth Century*. Charlottesville, VA and London: University Press of Virginia.

Lamb, J. (2001), *Preserving the Self in the South Seas, 1680–1840*, Chicago, IL and London: University of Chicago Press.

Landry, D. (2004), 'Slavery and Sensibility: Phillis Wheatley within the Fracture', in *Early Black British Writing: Olaudah Equiano, Mary Prince, and Others*, A. Richardson and D. Lee (eds). Boston, MA and New York: Houghton Mifflin, 377–95.

—— (2008), *Noble Brutes: How Eastern Horses Transformed English Culture*. Baltimore, MD and London: Johns Hopkins University Press.

MacLean, G. (2004), *The Rise of Oriental Travel: English Visitors to the Ottoman Empire, 1580–1720*. Basingstoke and New York: Palgrave Macmillan.

—— (2007), *Looking East: English Writing and the Ottoman Empire before 1800*. Basingstoke and New York: Palgrave Macmillan.

Markley, R. (2006), *The Far East and the English Imagination, 1600–1730*. Cambridge and New York: Cambridge University Press.

Matar, N. (1998), *Islam in Britain, 1558–1685*. Cambridge and New York: Cambridge University Press.

Nussbaum, F. A. (ed.) (2003), *The Global Eighteenth Century*. Baltimore, MD and London: Johns Hopkins University Press.

—— (2003), *The Limits of the Human: Fictions of Anomaly, Race, and Gender in the Long Eighteenth Century*. Cambridge and New York: Cambridge University Press.

Ormrod, D. (2003), *The Rise of Commercial Empires: England and the Netherlands in the Age of Mercantilism, 1650–1770*. Cambridge: Cambridge University Press.

Park, Y. M. (ed.) (2000), *The Postcolonial Jane Austen*. London and New York: Routledge.

Said, E. W. (1978; 1995), *Orientalism*. London and New York: Penguin Books.

Sussman, C. (2000), *Consuming Anxieties: Consumer Protest, Gender, and British Slavery, 1713–1833*. Palo Alto, CA: Stanford University Press.

Williams, R. (1961, 2nd ed. 1963), *The Long Revolution*. New York: Columbia University Press.

—— (1973), *The Country and the City*. New York: Oxford University Press.

Wood, M. (2002), *Slavery, Empathy, and Pornography*. Oxford and New York: Oxford University Press.

Yadav, A. (2004), *Before the Empire of English: Literature, Provinciality, and Nationalism in Eighteenth-Century Britain*. Basingstoke and New York: Palgrave Macmillan.

Index